Ascent

Bruce McGhie

8.07

Ascent

How one quadriplegic fought for a full life and soared

Bruce McGhie

RUDER FINN PRESS

Editorial Director: Susan Slack
Creative Director: Lisa Gabbay
Art Director: Sal Catania
Design Director: Emily Korsmo, Ruder Finn Design
Production Director: Valerie Thompson
Pre-Press: Steve Moss

ISBN 10: 1-932646-28-0
ISBN 13: 978-1-932646-28-3

PRINTED IN THE UNITED STATES OF AMERICA
by Ruder Finn Print, New York
Bryan D'Orazio, Senior Vice President

Cover: Photomontage © Bruce McGhie

For Barbara, whose steadfast love, courage, and humor have empowered me through every trial and triumph.

Preface

As a quadriplegic, I volunteered in the mid-1990s at a well-known center for rehabilitation of spinal cord injuries, leading informal counseling sessions with groups of newly injured patients. From my own experience, I knew that they were mentally and physically traumatized. Some would simply be in denial, others in deep despair. I knew very well what they faced.

Sadly, I only was able to see the patients once or twice because the rehabilitation cycle is so short in today's insurance climate. My problem: How could I leave them with a useful and lasting message in just a couple of hours?

So I used to start by saying that the most important thing for them to do was to consider me. "I am still alive 40-plus years after my accident. I am very healthy, married with two children, and fully independent. I drive my own van, am a licensed pilot, travel a lot, and have retired after 35 years in business." Some would simply shrug and shake their heads; others would perk up and really get interested. The meetings went on to cover many of the very tough things they were facing—no holds barred. I knew that this direct approach gave some of them hope. I could see it in their eyes.

Separately, one of my close friends, Nathan Garland, started me thinking about writing about my life in a wheelchair. Nothing was further from my mind, and my response was, "Who could possibly be interested in my life?" But he persisted, saying, "It might inspire others as well as the spinal-cord injured. Your life has amazed, humbled, and inspired me." I countered that such "dealing with adversity" stories were an overdone literary genre. I did not tell him that I had no desire to revisit many of my life experiences, particularly the injury itself and the several years thereafter.

A few years ago, I began to have more time due to shoulder problems, which sharply restricted my activities. I also knew that most people knew very little about spinal cord disabilities and needed to know more. There are some 250,000 people with such disabilities now in the U.S. and about 11,000 newly injured every year—plus at least 24,000 wounded veterans from Iraq and Afghanistan. Better-informed people would be more accepting of those who are spinal-cord injured and more supportive of research, employment, and accessibility. I began to see the motivational power of my own quest for a full life.

But the reader can in no way understand the uniquely difficult experience of quadriplegia and paraplegia without knowing the realities, unpleasant or not. So writing this book has required me to reveal highly personal details of my physical, emotional, and family life—topics that I rarely talk about even with my closest friends. I had a hard time getting used to the idea of "going public" with these things. But to tell the real story, I knew I had to put down the facts, painful parts and all, and that is what I have set out to do.

Bruce McGhie

Part I

The Wall

Sometimes you come abruptly to a point in life when you know that nothing will ever be the same, when it's clear that your "new" life will never match what it might have been, when you don't have any clue how you're going to cope with the day at hand—much less the rest of your life. This moment is popularly called "hitting a wall." Often you are looking over the precipice at death itself. If the event is a catastrophic disability such as blindness, quadriplegia, paraplegia, stroke, or the like, only time will allow the plot and the drama to unfold, the actors to act, and the consequences to occur, for better or for worse. The odds favor some sort of tragedy. Yet there are surprises. One thing is certain: the souls of the actors will be tested.

The Accident

Late in 1954, I embarked enthusiastically on a new chapter in my life. A recent graduate of Harvard, I said goodbye to my fiancée, Barbara Bruning, and to my family, and I entered active duty in the Air Force as an ROTC second lieutenant. In January 1955, I was in my second week of preflight training at Lackland Air Force Base near San Antonio, Texas. My unit was comprised of a hundred or so other freshly-minted officers from colleges and universities around the country. Although the Korean War had wound down to an uneasy truce, the Cold War was ominously intense, and our military was still on a wartime basis with the draft in effect. Rather than being drafted, I had decided to meet my military obligation as an officer, preferably as a pilot officer since aviation had been a passion of mine since childhood. So, here we were at pilot "boot camp" about to grasp the nettle of the real military (as opposed to the toy-soldier regime in college).

I was actually getting to like it. I'd made some friends, class work was not too demanding, and I was within a few weeks of actually starting to learn how to fly. We marched everywhere as a unit–like basic trainees except with brass bars on our collars.

One part was not good. Although I was healthy, I was not in strong physical shape. This was before the days when "fitness" was popular, and I had been working at a desk job for the previous six months. My last steady exercise had been playing a lot of golf during the past summer—merely walking at that. I could see that I was below average in the number and crispness of my pushups, sit-ups, and other exercises that were part of our daily workouts. In fact, I had never had good upper body strength due to my slim physique and to having been quite asthmatic into my late teens. But I didn't give the out-of-shape problem much thought. "I'll catch up" was my feeling.

Obstacle courses are part of all basic training programs, and there were several at Lackland's preflight school, including one that had a psychological objective. It was called a "confidence course." The idea was that candidates would be run through a series of physically scary obstacles and that successful completion would enhance physical confidence and courage, which would eventually enable us to better deal with the hazards of military aviation. Some of the obstacles were indeed intimidating, involving heights, jumps over empty spaces, balancing maneuvers on high narrow beams, and the like.

Before our first attempt at the course, our training officer told us that we were not required to try every obstacle and that completion of the full course was optional. But, given that any pilot-training program is highly competitive with only a small minority making it all the way through to getting their wings, our performance was always being watched and noted. So as we started through this course early on a cool drizzly morning, the desire to do well was palpable. To say that I was highly motivated would have been an understatement; "Gung Ho" would have been more accurate. Furthermore, I had always been physically adventuresome.

Consequently, I was among those who were leading the group and passing up few obstacles. We came to a tower about 40 feet high. There, four telephone poles, sunk into the ground and angled out slightly, were held together by three platforms, each about ten feet higher than the other. We were to climb up the back of one of the poles, using linesmen's ladder spikes sunk into the wood, and could stop at any of the three platforms. The poles went slightly outward. The top platform was about nine-feet square.

To get down, one had to push over the edge in a kind of giant swing, holding onto a one-inch bar flush with the edge of the platform, then releasing at just the right moment to swing into the platform below, which was smaller due to the spreading aspect of the corner poles. I lay on my stomach, grabbed the bar and inched out over the 40-foot drop. Scary indeed. But there was no going back. To make it even dicier, the drizzle made the bar wet and slippery. Eventually, as intended, my torso weight pulled me over the edge into the giant swing. As I was coming around to vertical, I lost my grip due to the moisture and possibly also to a lack of hand or arm strength. So, instead of swinging in toward the smaller platform below, I just caught its edge with one foot, tipping myself into a head-first fall of 25 to 30 feet.

As I fell, I knew that I was in serious trouble. My descent seemed to happen extremely slowly, even though it was really only a matter of two or three seconds. I can remember thinking very deliberately something like, "Bruce, you've really blown it now." That was true indeed. But of course I had no idea in those few seconds how profoundly it would affect my life—every thought, every action, every minute of my entire existence thereafter—as well as the lives of Barbara and my family.

I landed on my head and shoulders with a stunning, cracking thud and crumpled over limply on the wet sawdust. Still conscious, remarkably, I knew I was badly hurt. I tried to get up, but strong hands held me immobile until the medics arrived. They gave me an injection. The ambulance ride is only a vague memory.

Looking back at this devastating event has never been easy. I have always had this sense of having been injured because of something so stupid, so unnecessary. For most of the time since then, I simply have not wanted to delve back into this painful experience, preferring to get on with a constructive life rather than dwell on something that could never be changed.

Still, accidents have causes, and this one was no exception. Now, as I write this so many years later, I can examine it somewhat at arm's length. Undoubtedly, one of the key factors was my go-for-broke attitude. Both Barbara and my mother later told me that they had sensed a certain bravado in me in the weeks before I went to flight school, and that it had been a real worry to them when I left. Another factor was my physical situation. I was not in top shape, and I did not have a strong upper body. Adding to this was the high degree of difficulty and the condition of the obstacle course. Surfaces were dripping wet and slippery in the light rain. Some weeks after the incident, I was told that the course procedures barred its use in wet conditions. There was no question that it would have been much less hazardous had it been a dry day. Clearly, the training officer was at fault for not following the procedures and made a serious misjudgment to run the course in the rain. It was also true that in my zeal I was stretching my physical capacity. So, as with all accidents, there was a chain of random, but potent actions and circumstances that culminated in the final regrettable event.

One of my children once said, "Dad, it isn't fair that you fell and have to be in a wheelchair." I remember responding that you can't expect life to be "fair." Sometimes bad things just happen, and you have to live with them.

I was never unconscious, as far as I know, right after my fall and during the ambulance ride to the emergency room at Lackland Air Force Base Hospital. But because I had been given an injection, I felt no pain and was only vaguely aware of what was going on. Although such shots dulled my senses and were part of my life for weeks to come, I have vivid recollections of certain experiences. They do not represent the whole story, only what my mind chooses to remember. They form a reconstructed journal of sorts—mostly pretty unpleasant reading. Spinal cord injuries like mine are catastrophic events for the body and mind.

In the emergency room, I was soon lying face down on a raised litter, staring at the small tile squares of the floor two feet below. My chin was suspended in a sling, and the doctors were working on my head. I heard an electric motor, and then a drilling sound, accompanied by a sense of correlating vibrations in my skull. Fluid was running over my temples, around my eye sockets, and off my nose. The tiles were being covered with a widening pool of rich, red blood—mine, I foggily noted. I asked what was going on. "We have to secure your head in traction, so we're drilling small holes for the tongs. They won't hurt once they're in," said the voice, I assumed, of the doctor. OK, I thought, but why let the blood drip and pool that way while I watch? Why not use a bucket? I never got a chance to voice these questions because they then knocked me out totally with another shot.

I was in traction all right. My head was held absolutely still by the tongs, which were attached with a line and pulley to a bag of lead shot. I felt no pain, as promised, but a steady tension pulling at the top of my skull. I awoke to find myself lying absolutely flat on my back on a Stryker Frame, a special device, I learned later, for keeping a patient's neck vertebrae stable for extended periods. I was in Lackland AFB Hospital's ward for neurological injuries, mainly head traumas.

Two neurosurgeons appeared in my limited field of view. I learned some sobering things from them in an extended dialogue that took place in pieces over the next day or two. I had had a very serious injury. My fall had damaged my spinal cord at the seventh cervical level. I was presently paralyzed from the chest down, with major impairment of my hands as well. Sensation was also limited and spotty but not totally lost. I was not able to control my bladder or bowels, and I was catheterized. All this could be temporary or permanent; I could get partial recovery, but it was too early to tell. The Red Cross had notified my family. None of this fully sank in at the time, given my sedated mind and the enormity of the problems described.

I recall staring at the ceiling, smoking a cigarette, trying unsuccessfully through the drugs to get my mind around the implications of all this. Amazingly, in those days, smoking was permitted in hospital wards even by gravely injured patients. I smelled something unpleasant and called over the nurse. She told me that I had just put my cigarette out on the bare skin of my stomach, having missed the ashtray she had put there. I had never felt a thing. This was the new reality. "Great!" I thought.

Within a few days, my mother was able to get things in order at home so that she could come to Texas to be at my side. She told me years later that the several weeks of her stay there were the worst days of her life. As a parent now, I can surely understand how excruciating it must have been to bear witness to her son's situation—near-term, in critical condition; long-term, paralyzed perhaps for life at age 22.

My mother had always been a woman of character. The youngest of four children, she grew up in a lively and supportive atmosphere. But she was adventuresome, and lived with family friends in Italy during the 1920s. After her marriage to my father in 1929, she had a miscarriage, followed by the births of my brother and me and then a serious back operation. Things then began to go well as my father, an independent-minded graduate engineer from MIT, started an innovative construction business and a dairy farm. His ideas were just beginning to pay off in the late 1930s, near the end of the Great Depression, when the Second World War came along, stifling all private construction activity and folding his business. Although we lived pleasantly enough in a beautiful antique Connecticut saltbox house on our farm, financially, we scraped by day-to-day. Somehow, my mother dealt with all of this using a dependable mix of inner strength, steady-eyed toughness, and near-faultless intuition about people, seasoned with warmth and a lively wit. She was popular and respected. As a mother, she was firm with a light touch. My brother, Alex, and I were devoted to her, but never forgot that she had mysterious insights into the nefarious minds of boys.

So it was great to have her there at my bedside for whatever I needed—concern, conversation, a cold washcloth, advocacy, a good laugh, or a prayer (for there were touch-and-go times of just staying alive, as well as times of unrelenting pain). Although I couldn't get to a phone (hospitals were different then) to talk with my fiancée, Barbara, my mother updated her every night, passed on her messages to me, and worked out a plan with Barbara that would bring her down in a few weeks time. Barbara wrote often and warmly, although it must have been an excruciatingly hard time for her what with concern for me, and now, her whole future up in the air. And all this coupled with the harsh negative reaction of her family to my injury and their clear wish that she break off our engagement, which was put to her daily. As for my father, he did not come down to Texas, something I never felt badly about because I knew that he couldn't bear to see me in such shape. But he talked with my mother daily and wrote frequent and wonderfully supportive letters.

I didn't hear from my brother, Alex, for several weeks. He was a lieutenant in the Navy serving on a destroyer in the Mediterranean and had been notified. When I did get a letter, which he acknowledged was tardy, there was some of the older-brother kidding I was used to hearing, but also some puzzling statements such as, "You've managed to shake up quite a large group of people, least of all me. I cannot seem to get as disturbed as everybody else because I know that things will return to normal shortly. Don't ask me why, but I'm so certain of this that I see no reason for worry. Bruce, you would be amazed at the number of people who are very much more concerned than your loving brother…" I couldn't quite figure out that reaction. I knew he was trying to cheer me up, meant well, and that it was partly banter. I was extremely glad to hear from him and to have his support as we had been close since childhood, but I was mystified that, despite what I assume he had been told, he didn't seem to know about the seriousness of my problem. Perhaps my mother hadn't told him everything.

There were many very supportive visits from my friends in the squadron, who told me, among other things, that on the anonymous mutual rating sheets we'd filled out the week before my accident, I had been voted No.1 in leadership potential. This was nice, but obviously something that was not going to be put to the test any-time soon. And there were letters from dozens of friends, parents of friends, classmates, former girlfriends, teachers, golf buddies, and also people I never thought I was close to. I was moved by their concern and encouragement, and I was deeply grateful for the lift the letters gave me at the time. I still have them.

The five or six week period I spent in traction on the Stryker Frame was as tough a time as I ever went through. To start with, the neurological ward in this big military hospital had the searing sounds of tragedy—not unlike those of a medieval torture chamber or madhouse. It was a large open room, dimly lit, with the beds placed closely side by side down the walls.

I couldn't see much except alternately the ceiling or the floor. On the frame, my head held firm with the tongs, I lay on my back on a stretcher-like litter for two hours. Then the orderlies would place a similar litter over me, secure it to the frame, put straps around the whole assembly, and assure that the tubes coming out of me were properly arranged (more than once, this was mishandled with agonizing effect). When all was ready, the whole contraption was turned 180 degrees like pig on a spit so that I was laying on my stomach, my face held in a foam rubber ring. The top litter was then removed and I stared at the floor until the process was reversed two hours later. This constant changing of position was necessary to avoid skin ulcers—always a potential problem for the long-term bedridden.

As for the sounds, the head-injured patients would often randomly scream, moan, and make guttural noises, sometimes in chorus, at any hour. Then there were the families, all trying to deal with terrible problems—loved ones in a coma, brain-impaired, or paralyzed like me. Some were dying. Very few were going to recover to normalcy. Hushed, sad conversations, sobbing, and other sounds of grief were frequent. I couldn't see any of this. But such noises were the backdrop for my own private world of anxiety, pain, guilt, and loneliness—feelings I couldn't escape despite my "support system."

The nights were particularly long, especially during the periods when I was face down. Then I was in serious pain, not from my injury but from my forehead being pressed by the tight traction into the foam rubber ring. It was like root canal work without anesthesia. Call it nerve pain or whatever, no drug they were willing to give me would even touch it. I can remember counting whole hours in seconds: one through sixty, one minute; one through sixty, two minutes; one through sixty, three minutes, etc., etc. Added to this, of course, my mind was filled with the grim knowledge that my life had been knocked terribly off-track, and I had no sense of how it could be made right. When I was turned upright after two hours, the pain would give way to relief and immediate sleep. Two hours later, it was "back to the rack." I had the same pain during the day, but it was more bearable with the distractions of visitors and the life of the ward around me.

About two weeks after my injury, my neurologists and I began to talk about the chances for my recovery. It wasn't encouraging. As yet, there were no signs of return of motor response or sensation. If I were to improve, it should have begun by then. Clearly, my spinal cord had been damaged, but the x-rays showed no signs of a serious fracture. They proposed doing a laminectomy, which would involve cutting through my cervical vertebrae and exposing the spinal cord to see if any bone fragment was pressing on it or had punctured it—something they might repair.

But the prospects were grim. It was an invasive, major operation, which was risky in my condition. According to them, it was the only way that held any hope for improving my state. I pressed them on the odds. Not good. My chance of not surviving the procedure was about one in four and the chance of any improvement was less than one in ten. After a long sleepless night of thinking and then discussion with my mother in the morning, I decided to go ahead, whatever the odds. My reasoning was that if I didn't, I would always wonder whether I had passed up my only chance for recovery.

The night before the operation, I had a long talk with my mother, my main message being something like, "If I don't survive, it's OK. I've had a good life with many advantages—family and all. I made it through Harvard, where I overcame difficult problems. I have a fiancée who still cares, etc., etc. Not to worry." I'm sure this was not very comforting to her at all, but I really was at peace with the decision despite the bad odds.

When I found myself alive 18 hours later after surgery, I was relieved, but I was now experiencing a whole new dimension of misery: There was pain in the cervical area, where bones had been cut and things pulled apart, and the grandfather of all sore throats due to the abrasion of the tubes that had kept me breathing. (Later the surgeon told me he would never again do a laminectomy without a tracheotomy, where they create a separate opening below the Adams Apple for breathing tubes.) I was in such difficulty that it caused my mother to cry—highly unusual for her because she knew it made it harder for me to see her in distress. I remember saying, "God help me" out loud, over and over.

Painkillers and sedatives blur the bad memories of the next week or so. I do recall, however, the first coherent talk I had with the neurosurgeons. They said, "You have a great constitution to survive that operation, but we found no way to improve your situation. The spinal cord, when we inspected it, seemed perfectly normal with no sign of exterior damage. There is probably some internal contusion or latent blood clot from the impact of the fall that is causing the spinal cord dysfunction." They were totally frank, as I had request-ed, and the message was clear: I was paralyzed from the chest down for life and that was that. Period.

This news, which I somewhat expected, was head numbing, so much so that I really didn't know how to process it at that point. So, I just tried to focus on getting through the physical miseries of post-op recovery and the Stryker Frame, day-by-day. Since there was nothing that they could do in terms of repair, I was moved out of the neurological trauma ward to the Officers' Ward as soon as I was stabilized.

End of the Beginning

The words above were used in of one of Winston Churchill's speeches during the Second World War. It's an apt description of the time when I was moved from the trauma ward to standard care on the Officers' Ward. But I was still in serious pain and due for several more weeks of torture on the frame. I had a long journey ahead with no known destination.

About this time, I had insisted on reducing my pain medication. I just didn't like the woolly headed, dazed feeling and was concerned about potential addiction. But clear-headedness brought a better sense of reality, and it was then that the irrevocable truth of my situation bored into my soul.

It happened one day when I was lying on my back on the frame. I was holding on to the small trapeze bar above me when I became aware of the muscle atrophy in my hands and wrists—deep gaps where firm strong flesh used to be. I could only imagine the situation with my legs. In my mind, of course, I knew I was paralyzed.

For weeks, I had tried many times to move my feet and legs, even a single toe, applying the full straining force of my mind—total concentration on getting the nerve signal through. But now this visual revelation of atrophy brought the message home with brutal impact. It was then that I fully grasped that my body was irrevocably reduced to a fraction of its normal functional state—a devastating moment. I fell into a sense of deep despair that lasted several weeks. There were a few times when I could not hold back brief periods of bitter tears, especially during sleepless nights in the darkened ward when I was in pain. I doubt that anyone who has not experienced serious disability can know the intensity of lonely anguish that wells up when all hope for full recovery finally falls away and the dawn breaks on a future where there are simply no acceptable outcomes.

You begin to think about all the things you enjoyed and that will no longer be possible. First to mind is standing and walking. Then you think of all the other things, like playing golf, skiing, and riding a motorcycle that you'll never do again. Then there is your sexuality. You know that you probably won't be able to father children and that sex will never be the same, but you don't know how it will be different. This is a crushing loss, given how central these things are to your sense of manhood and psychological well-being. The mind wanders to other questions: "What about Barbara and me? What will I look like? I used to be a decent looking guy. Now I'll be a 'cripple' and get pitying looks. Will I be deformed? How will I deal with the bathroom problem? How will I make a living? How will I get around? Where will I live? How will I get up and down steps? What will people think of me? Will I be totally dependent on others for everything? What is there to look forward to? What is there left to life?" Sadly, there was no counseling at the hospital. I was totally alone with my demons.

Somehow, this dark period gradually began to fade as the cold realities seeped into my consciousness and denial was pushed aside by the clear and forbidding facts of my situation. I began to think along the lines of, "There it is, Bruce. It's really bad, but it isn't going away. You're deep into this mess and you have no way to deal with it unless you start to face up to it—all of it—no matter how long it takes." To maintain sanity, I continued to live only in units of one day. I would say to myself, "Just get through today with minimum pain. And for God's sake, don't think too much." I'd relish the simple escape of talking to the staff and other patients, particularly the banter. I would enjoy TV even though I could hardly see the one tiny screen at the end of the ward. But I'd watch anything for distraction—even the soaps. So, in this way despair gradually gave way to sober resignation.

One of the many problems with spending the long night hours kept awake by the pain was that I had to deal with certain very real fears, all having to do with my inability to do anything for myself. Primary was the fear of fire. Lackland Air Force Hospital was a large and excellent facility. But it was made up entirely of GI barrack-type buildings all lined up in rows and connected by covered walkways. Made of softwood, they were highly combustible and would have burned to the ground in minutes. Would there to be time for me to be rescued, cumbersome frame and all? I feared not. So concerned was I that one night I worked out an escape scenario by which I would tear out the tubes, roll myself off the frame onto the floor and crawl with my elbows to the nearest door. It wouldn't have worked, but at least I had an action plan.

Another fear was the very uneven way the orderlies did my 180-degree turns on the Stryker Frame (12 times a day). It was a scary procedure at best. If carelessly done, the tubes could be pulled out or you could somehow slip out of the litter "sandwich" to the floor in mid-turn. The best orderlies I had were two young African-American men—real characters from urban backgrounds (one had knife-fight scars on his arms). I liked them. They were upbeat, loose and funny. But they were serious about caregiving. They sensed my concerns and would do everything deliberately, telling me what they were doing before each step. When they got to the turn itself, they would say, "You ready sir? We're goin' to go clockwise to your right. Got that sir? One, two, three—turn. You are OK Lieutenant Levi!" (This was a nickname they dreamed up for me. When Barbara arrived, they called her Mrs. Levi.) About that time, I had a serious problem with one of the night orderlies, a white Texas boy with lip who seemed to take pleasure in doing the turns too fast and in different sequences that I wasn't prepared for, despite my objections. He had a sadistic streak. I once told my day orderlies, and they didn't like it at all. "Don't worry Lieutenant Levi, we take care of him good." One day, they came early to overlap shifts with the Texas kid, grabbed him, and after a scuffle, strapped him tightly into an extra frame that was out on the porch. They spun him around at high speed for a full ten minutes until he was dizzy and sick, pleading to be released and almost crying. "You like that, boy? That what it feels like if you don't do it right. You do it right or we'll give you more lessons. You take good care of 'the man.' You got that boy?" He ceased to be a problem, and at least one of my fears was taken care of.

About this time, a major turning point was reached. Barbara had broken with her parents and defied their adamant objections to come to Texas to be with me. When she arrived, my mother was able to head home after her courageous stint at my bedside. It had been a grueling period that, while testing her inner strength to the fullest, had given me great comfort and support.

The moment Barbara arrived was electric, given how our situation had changed since I had last seen her. On the one hand, I knew that we would have to reconsider together the whole idea of getting married since I was now vastly different physically than before—paralyzed, with severely affected bodily functions and sexuality. On the other hand, we were in love and had a deep bond after three-and-a-half years of dating and a year of being engaged.

She came into the ward, spotted me, came directly over, and gave me a warm and wonderfully familiar kiss. If it was a shock to see me as I was, she didn't show it. In a few seconds, her trademark broad smile and unique laugh were there as always. To say the least, it had been a rough six weeks for each of us, and we had a lot of serious catching up to do. But somehow, in those first few minutes, I had the overwhelming sense that we were going to get through this. We telegraphed strength to each other. It was powerful.

Barbara was a remarkable young woman. The first thing I'd known was her record as a top woman golfer, which was written up extensively in the New York newspaper sports pages the summer after our freshman year at college. That year, she won the NCAA Golf Championship, known then as the National Intercollegiate, as well as the New York State Championship and several other New York metropolitan area tournaments. Several years earlier, she had been runner-up in the USGA National Junior Championship. I followed her career that summer with interest, being an avid low-handicap golfer myself, and particularly took note that she was a student at Wellesley College near Boston (and from her pictures couldn't miss noticing that she was attractive as well). When I returned to Harvard that fall, I thought to myself, "Bruce, you've never played golf with a good woman golfer. Why don't you call her up and ask for a golf date?" When I put this idea to my roommate, he scoffed, "First, you don't have the nerve to call cold, and second, why would she want to play golf with you anyway? She doesn't know you from Adam." That was just the nudge I needed, and I called her on the chance that I could talk her into it. Well, it took several calls and a lot of reassurances that I was not some sort of creep or fast character before she agreed to a date. Even then, she told me later, she would have backed out in an instant if she didn't like the look of me when I showed up at her dormitory.

For my part, I was immediately taken with her. She was the epitome of wholesome good looks—an open, clean-featured face with a dazzling, warm smile surrounded by clear, suntanned skin with a dash of freckles and wavy auburn hair. About five-foot-seven, she was slim and athletic, but in no way heavy-limbed. Apparently, what she first saw of me didn't put her off either, and we headed out for our golf game accompanied by my roommate, who had gotten us onto a local private golf course. We played poorly. Later, she got him a date with her roommate, and we went out for the evening and had a lively good time. As my roommate and I drove back to Harvard after dropping off the girls, the first thing I said to him was, "That's the most natural, unaffected girl I've ever met. She shows no sense that she's any kind of celebrity despite her attractiveness and all the attention she's gotten from people and the press. Amazing." And to myself I thought, "Also, here is the rarest of people—a genuine straight arrow. You say something to her, and you get a pure, open, and intelligent response. Good sense of humor. Laughs easily." It was very refreshing then and still is. She is, with no exaggeration, the best liked and most respected person I know, by peers, golf competitors, store clerks, cab drivers, neighbors, everyone. All this is not to say she is mere sweet naiveté. On the contrary, she is quick and smart—and can be tough. When things are not right, her response is equally open and direct.

But shortly after our reunion at the hospital in Texas, our resolve was put to the test. The next day when she came to my bedside, she burst into tears, terribly upset. Before she had gotten to my ward, she had been pulled aside by a Red Cross social worker who took it upon herself to warn Barbara in explicit terms that she should not consider her engagement to me to be binding and that marriage would be ill advised. Putting my disability and potential rehabilitation in brutally pessimistic terms, she cautioned her not to recommit to our relationship in any firm way. Barbara should hold back and not get involved in what would be a completely different life with me than had been expected. Already under great stress from her parents' disapproval and having made this difficult and courageous trip to Texas, she was badly unstrung by the harshness of the message and the blunt way it was delivered.

I was extremely angry that this person had inserted herself gratuitously into our lives in such a negative way. I told Barbara that this person had never even met me and had no idea of our attitude. We had no intention of rushing into anything and needed time to absorb the full implications of my injury. We needed time to talk, time to think, time to make rational decisions about our future. Barbara never talked with the woman again. And the first day I was up in a wheelchair after two months of recovery, several weeks later, I had the orderly push me directly to her office unannounced. I rolled in and gave her a blistering dressing down for having caused us this additional pain, telling her among other things, "Never, never, never intrude in our case again. You were unprofessional and wrong to do it the way you did. " Later, I had a twinge of guilt for having unloaded such hostility on her because no doubt she had meant well. But Barbara and I often looked back on the experience, at moments such as our fortieth wedding anniversary, saying, "Wouldn't it be interesting if that Texas social worker could see us now."

Although I have since learned that various forms of physical pain and discomfort are a permanent part of the life of a spinal cord-injured person, nothing was ever as bad as what I experienced on that Stryker Frame for about six weeks. That part abruptly came to an end when one spike of the two tongs implanted in my head began to dig into the skull. This was excruciating, especially on top of the pain I had been enduring all along. Barbara got the nurse and very shortly one of my doctors appeared. He checked it out, reviewed my chart, and announced that traction was no longer necessary—just like that! (I wondered then why it took this episode to make the decision when obviously, it seems, the frame had no longer been necessary.) Instead of trying to readjust or reinstall the tongs, he decided to take them out altogether, and I could get off the frame and be moved to a normal hospital bed. As the tongs came out, relieving both the digging pain and the long-term agony, I felt as though I had been paroled from Hell, despite the ongoing serious nature of my situation. What a moment! Even today, I can reach up with my fingers and feel the indentations in my scalp. That night was my first restful sleep since the accident six weeks before.

The next six or eight weeks were a kind of holding pattern in that we were stuck at the military hospital until my retirement was finalized. By this time it was April, and every day became a little hotter and drier and less comfortable. Patients came and went, and I seemed to be a permanent fixture. I became more knowledge-able, although no more encouraged, about my limitations. I was still totally dependent on the staff for my every physical need. I remained catheterized. I needed help to eat, to turn over, to sit up, and so on. Barbara was wonderful in the hundreds of hours she spent with me day after day in that dreary military barracks ward—keeping me comfortable, dealing with issues of my impending disability retirement as we talked endlessly about our future and what it held. We were bored and frustrated. The problem was that while the wheels of the military retirement process were grinding very slowly, I was undergoing no rehabilitation. This was strictly a military hospital, a very good one, but with no facilities or program to deal with long-term recovery from catastrophic injuries such as mine. With Barbara taking the lead on the research, we made progress in learning that that there were several Veterans Administration hospitals specializing in spinal-cord injuries, there being so many wounded in this way in WWII and the Korean War. One of the best regarded was at West Roxbury,

Massachusetts, a part of the world we both knew well, having gone to college in the Boston area. I applied to be sent to this institution. Meanwhile, although I was very well cared for over these many weeks, I was making no progress physically and was anxious to get on with my future, grim as it was. Finally, in early May, my disability retirement came through, and I was ordered to travel by air ambulance to Massachusetts and to the VA facility. I would be glad to leave this bleak and depressing part of the world, where I had suffered much and nearly died.

Something began to happen to me about this time. I'll call it the Douglas Bader factor. It's an eerie thing, but I had fortuitously read a book about Bader, a WWII hero and double amputee, six months before I was injured. It had a profound effect on how I dealt with my own injury—not only in the early crises, but also in my whole life later as a disabled person in the real world.

The book was *Reach for the Sky* by Paul Brickhill (W.W. Norton & Co., 1954). The subject is the story of Douglas Bader, the RAF's famous legless air ace in the Battle of Britain. Bader was quite a character. As a junior career officer in the early 1930s, he was an intensely competitive and aggressive pilot, and a great athlete (a starter on the national rugby team). In 1931, on a dare, he attempted a low altitude stunt that ended in a serious crash, crushing both legs and leaving him a double amputee.

What was remarkable about Bader was that he adamantly refused to accept that he was finished. In the 1930s his kind of disability put one with all the other poor old blokes of WWI, who spent their pensioned days in veterans' homes or on crutches watching the world go by from a park bench. From day one, he fought against the system that would relegate him to this kind of future.

He was an impossible, uncooperative patient, a trial to those who were trying to help him. He was angry, bitter, and alone in his misery. I never wanted to emulate his "son-of-a-bitch" side and the way he mercilessly took it out on those around him, but what caught my attention was his will to prevail. For example, after months of healing, when his stumps could take the pressure, the therapists fitted him with artificial legs. As he went through the awkward and painful early attempts to relearn to walk, he refused to use crutches or canes. He was constantly falling down and struggling to get back on his feet, refusing any offer of help even though it might take 20 minutes to do it alone. They told him he would "never walk again without a stick." Angrily he replied: "Damn that! I'll never, never walk with a stick." Well, he prevailed in never using a cane, and was the first double amputee who ever did so. In fact, he eventually took up golf and played to a seven handicap—excellent golf for anyone, unthinkable for a double amputee.

Subsequently retired from the RAF for eight years, Bader was frustrated to be left out as the ominous clouds of WWII gathered in the late 1930s. He fought to be reinstated as a pilot—something that had never been done even for a single amputee. He badgered the authorities relentlessly and used every bit of influence he could muster as a former rugby star to get an exception. Finally, after many delays, he was given a flight test, which he passed with a bravura display of aerobatics. The rest of the story has become legend. He was an ace in the Battle of Britain and eventually became a Wing Commander and an innovator of new fighter formations and tactics. He was shot down over Europe, escaped from a POW camp, and rejoined his unit. He was shot down again and then put into the Germans' maximum-security prison (they had to take away his artificial legs at night). Ultimately, he led the victory fly-over of London in 1945 as a much-decorated national hero.

What Bader had was an implacable sense that he could overcome any tough obstacle. He was going to be equal to or better than the next man, disability or not. He defied conventional wisdom and got away with it by sheer force of will and perseverance. I had been deeply moved by Bader's attitude and acts. When I found myself, unbelievably, in similar and in many ways more difficult circumstances after my accident, I had the vicarious benefit of his secret of success: You have to be tough and extremely hard-minded; you have to have a never-give-in attitude. Time and time again, this approach made the difference when I was dealing with my own struggles.

Although this kind of attitude was a big factor in what I was able to accomplish, it made me a more steely person than I had been. "He's a tough rooster—has to be," one doctor told Barbara after I had embarrassed her by making a scene in some restaurant over being seated in the back because of the wheelchair. She understood this, but I surely was no longer the happy-go-lucky guy she fell in love with. It has never been easy for her, having to live with my harder side, which shows itself from time to time. But she endures this hard edge as a consequence of my battle for survival and a decent life.

I don't advocate making scenes, although sometimes it can't be avoided. Mostly, it was Bader's diamond-hard determination that I liked. As for dealing with other people, I found out that what usually works best is just to expect people to treat you with respect, and when necessary, be firm and civil about what you may need that is different. Disabled people who have chips on their shoulders cause resentment, hurting themselves and also the next disabled person who comes along.

Rehab Reality

The air ambulance trip to Massachusetts was a mixture of excitement, anxiety, loneliness, and discomfort. My traveling companions were perhaps a dozen men in various severe medical situations strapped into litters set in racks on the sides of a 1940s twin-engine, Air Force Convair, a converted passenger airliner, which was noisy, drafty, and bumpy (non-pressurized in those days, so it was flown through the weather rather than above it). Since it was staffed by elite flight nurses and doctors, we were well attended to. But clearly, many of the other patients were in dire if not critical condition. Judging from what I heard and saw, I'm sure that a number were close to death. In those days, the Korean War fighting was over, but we had many badly wounded and disabled who were still in the military and Veterans Administration medical system.

We stayed overnight near Birmingham, Alabama, and I recall a dingy, dark, echoing ward. I didn't sleep very well. There I was on some no-name Air Force base a long way from home, being looked after in my helpless state by people I had never seen before and never would again. Talk about "being in limbo." It was a long and lonely night. As dawn broke, I began to feel better about things. We were given breakfast and then loaded back into the Convair for the last leg to Boston. As the engines droned on, my state of mind was a mixture of concern for the unknown that lay ahead and a kind of eagerness to come to grips with the future—at least the beginning of the future.

After a long and very carefully managed unloading process in Boston, each patient was taken on his way to his assigned hospital. I was surprised to find myself alone (for the first time in five months) in a VA-hired private ambulance on my way to the West Roxbury VA Hospital. The EMTs stayed in the front seats once I was secure. As we began to get into the venerable and gracious parkways in Brookline, I was suddenly stunned by the sight of lush green grass and trees and shrubs in bloom this spring day in May. So rich and fertile was the ground I had always taken for granted! I laughed out loud for joy to be back in familiar New England and gone from the harsh, flat, and dry scrub desert-like landscape around Lackland Air Force Base in Texas. When we stopped for lights, pedestrians would steal a look in the ambulance window to see what poor soul was suffering inside only to be greeted by a guy on a stretcher grinning ear-to-ear and waving at them. They must have thought I was a mental patient.

West Roxbury was a "spinal-cord injury center," one of four or five such VA facilities in the country. A "VA boot camp" would have been a better way to describe it. Chief of the center was a Dr. William Talbot, who I soon learned from staff and patients alike was a "real son-of-a-bitch but knows what he's doing." A brilliant urologist and graduate of Dartmouth and Harvard Medical School, he had foregone a lucrative private career to become one of the world's foremost experts in spinal-cord injury treatment and rehabilitation.

He had taken over this hospital some five years before when it was just a rundown VA backwater filled with sloppy staff and dispirited wheelchair-bound veterans, many of whom were both drug addicts (on pain medication prescribed by the doctors) and alcohol abusers as well. He took Draconian measures, firing staff and cold-turkeying the patients who were on drugs. He instituted rigorous rehabilitation programs with regular attendance required by all—even the old-timers who had long since decided to live at the hospital at night and play the horses and hang out at taverns during the day. Cool of manner, he was not popular—even hated by some—but he was respected. His hospital was a kind of institutional version of "tough love."

Because of its excellence, the West Roxbury VA was made part of the prestigious teaching-hospital community in the Boston area, and Dr. Talbot was always conducting research, lecturing, and writing papers for medical journals. During Grand Rounds on Monday mornings, ten to fifteen doctors and other medical luminaries would accompany him. He was familiar with every patient's case. He gave special training to his doctors, nurses, and orderlies so that they would follow his rigorous methods of rehabilitation. He got results.

Life on the spinal-cord injury wards at West Roxbury was an eye-opening experience. Each ward had about fifteen patients, the beds six or seven feet apart, the heads against the wall all around the room. One could pretty much see anything that went on except when the curtains were pulled loosely around a bed for some nursing or medical activity. Privacy was not an option. The room was spotlessly clean and bright, and the staff was on the whole sharp and professional —all in keeping with Dr. Talbot's high standards.

There was inevitably a real mix of ages, races, and backgrounds. Equally differentiating was the degree of disability—from total quadriplegics paralyzed from the neck down, who could do nothing for themselves, to almost fully independent paraplegics, whose injuries were in the lower spine. Everyone was in a different state of rehabilitation—from the newly injured like me, who had a long way to go, to the men who had reached the highest level of independence that was possible for them. Sadly, there were also many who were to live out their lives there because of their inability to live at home or because they had serious, chronic medical problems related to their injuries. Given all these differences, we collectively lived out an ever-changing drama of pain and relief, sadness and triumph, boredom and keen interest, comedy and tragedy.

The atmosphere was a lot like a military barracks, which in a veterans' hospital was not surprising. There was much kidding and banter—mostly good-natured and supportive, but occasionally piercing and hurtful. Every crowd has its good guys, clowns, bullies, blowhards, and bitter souls.

As a new patient in this small world of Ward 2-South, I knew that it would take a while to be accepted. The other patients were pleasant enough but not openly welcoming. I gathered by an over-heard comment or two that they knew I had been an officer, albeit a very junior one, and I think this put some of the patients off. Most of them were former enlisted men, and some still bore resentment for the military hierarchy. I shuddered at the thought that they might also learn that I had gone to Harvard—not an image that I wanted to project. But I knew from past experience that the best way to gain respect was to keep my mouth shut, tend to my own business, and to accomplish whatever I could. Actions, not words, were important in this down-to-earth environment. Being accepted was a process that would take time.

It was a struggle to get used to a totally different physical and psychological regime—and I felt somewhat daunted by what lay ahead. It was clear that the other patients, who were curious to see how I would cope with my own particular corner of the Hell we all shared, were observing me. And I, in turn, was taking in everything around me and trying to learn the ropes. At first, I felt self-conscious to be undertaking my very personal journey of rehabilitation, whatever it might turn out to be, in this goldfish-bowl environment. Later, I came to see that the atmosphere and dynamics of the ward, though intrusive, were major factors in my being able to get back into the mainstream of life. Being exposed to how others were dealing with similar problems hastened my learning process.

The man in the next bed was a big help. He and I became friends quite quickly. Frank was his name, and he was an amazing person. Totally paralyzed from the neck down, he was similar in condition to Christopher Reeve, including the severe breathing difficulty. I remember the hiss and pump sound of the respirator he had to have on at night to rest his lungs. He could do nothing for himself and relied totally on the staff. But, the unique thing about Frank was his attitude. He never complained or lost his cool when things weren't done right, which happened fairly often; he was invariably cheerful and was liked by the staff. They were with him a lot and, in time, he got to know them well and was genuinely interested in their lives and families and even remembered their children's names and ages.

Frank was highly intelligent and observant, which helped me because he knew the ways of the hospital and the personal dynamics of the ward, and I had a lot to learn. On top of that, he was interesting to talk to on most subjects because he was smart, had a curious mind, and was articulate. He took an interest in my progress and cheered me on. His wife had divorced him, and I don't recall his ever having visitors. I used to wonder how could he endure his bleak and helpless life? Frank gave me two priceless gifts. The knowledge that despite what I thought were my very serious problems, I was looking at a person who was so much worse off, but who had retained his dignity, self-respect, and the respect of others. Somehow, he was still his own man. The second gift was his patience with life. He accepted his misfortune without self-pity, and lived out his fate day after day—despite his dependence on others—on his own terms. He was in his own way a true hero whom I have never forgotten and who provided an important example for me in those difficult early weeks at the VA.

Days came and went pretty quickly in this setting, but one day stands out as a kind of epiphany for me.

Something I had learned was that I was not like typical quadriplegics, who had limited or no use of their hands and arms. According to the neurosurgeons in Texas, the damage to my spinal cord was probably somewhere between the seventh cervical and the first thoracic vertebrae—an unusual point of injury. Although one of the two main nerves (ulnar and radial) running to my hands and arms was not functioning, the other was. So my hands were substantially weakened by the lack of many of the muscles—a functional loss of perhaps 80 percent. But some remained, holding out the possibility of gaining strength and getting back partial hand use through therapy and devising new ways to do the thousands of things hands do that are taken for granted. But I had a very, very long road ahead of me.

Another important result of my injury level was that I had retained the full use of my triceps—very rare for a "quad." These muscles on the backs of the upper arms are used to straighten out or extend the forearms. It doesn't seem like much, but it has great significance because the triceps can be used to lift the body from one place to another. In other words, I might be able to transfer from wheelchair to bed to car seat to anywhere without assistance. This could be the "magic door" in my rehabilitation. I was very fortunate although I didn't know then just how fortunate. It made me kind of a hybrid—essentially a paraplegic with serious hand limitations. Sometimes people with my level of ability were referred to tongue-in-cheek as "half-ass quads" by the other patients.

Several weeks into initial rehab, after observing and talking with other veterans, and soaking up whatever I could from the staff, I had an experience that caused me to come to a radical conclusion: maybe, just maybe, I could achieve full physical independence—unheard of for my high level of injury. But it was such a long shot that I told no one then, not even Barbara.

In the early weeks, a therapist came to my bed every day to help me build up whatever shoulder, chest, arm, and hand strength remained, through the use of mild weights, stretching, and the like. I also had to learn how to handle my body in bed—to get to a sitting position and then maintain balance, none of which is easy when you have no thoracic, hip, or leg muscles to help. The sensation is like being up on stilts—very wobbly. Falling over in bed and struggling back up was something I did dozens of times. Then there was the wheelchair—how to sit in it, move it around, and not fall out of it. One of the things no one ever thinks about, say, is how to open a drawer. You just reach out and pull, right? Wrong. You have to lock the brakes first, hold on to the chair with one hand, and then pull the drawer with the other. Otherwise the drawer stays put and it's the wheelchair that goes to the drawer, or you pull yourself out of the chair. Next was getting in and out of bed. This was frustrating, a little scary because of the balance problem, and exhausting—a milestone if you could do it solo.

I was making good progress in all this bedside work, but it was slow and I yearned to get down to the therapy department for more serious workouts. I kept bugging the therapist. Finally, one morning at end of the session she said, "Well as soon as you can learn how to get dressed yourself and you can solo transfer into the wheelchair, you can come down to the gym." There goes another couple of weeks, I thought disgustedly, as she walked out of the ward.

Sitting there feeling frustrated produced in me a kind of defiant attitude. This is too slow, dammit! I asked the orderly to get some sweats and some shoes and socks out of my locker and put them on my bed. After he moved out of range, I started out on my own to learn how to get dressed.

Socks first. OK, sit up, balance yourself. Now reach down and slip a sock over the toes. Oops. Fell over. Try again. Same thing. This went on for a while, and I finally got a sock over the toes, one-handed. But how to get it over the heel and pull it up? After quite a struggle, I managed to do so. This episode took about forty-five minutes—one sock! Jesus! I was sweating. Now number two. Got that on in twenty to thirty minutes maybe. Pants—another problem, over the feet the hardest part. Then under the butt while you're sitting on it? Seems impossible. Wait, I have an idea: roll to one side, pull them up over a hip, roll to the other side and pull them over the other hip. It worked. Hour-and-a-half so far. I'll worry about the shirt later.

Next, getting into the wheelchair. This was the first time I had tried it without anyone standing next to me. I moved with the utmost deliberation because if I lost my balance and fell, it was to the floor and possible injury. Inch by inch, I crept to the edge of the bed and then pulled my butt backwards ever so slowly into the chair. Aha! I put my feet on the pedals. Now the shirt. It was tricky and awkward, but it got done. I had started this whole performance well over two hours ago. I was totally beat. I just sat there in a sort of stupor. After a while, I realized that I hadn't eaten my lunch, which had languished there cold for some time. I ate that ravenously and began to feel pretty good about getting this far. Now to the Physical Therapy Department.

It was a long, exhaustingly slow push. I rolled in and asked for my therapist. She came over and I said, "Well, here I am. When can I start?"

"I can't believe this. You mean you got totally dressed and into your chair completely solo—today? I just left you mid-morning."

"Yup."

She looked at me in a funny way. Was it respect? Skepticism? Disbelief? It was hard to tell if she was pleased or not. Maybe she thought I was nuts. I didn't know. Then there was a slow smile and a knowing look.

"You can start next week. I'll get you on the schedule. Now get out of here and go to bed. You look beat."

I didn't go back right away. I went down to the canteen, ordered a large vanilla Coke and some Oreos, and sat there feeling really great. Now I knew a lot more about Douglas Bader and his goddammit approach to rehabilitation. You have to push against the system, which is based on a kind of statistical average of patient response. It wasn't only the Coke that tasted good. This was my first real progress toward regained independence, and nothing was the same from then on. Full independence? Maybe, just maybe...

When I got back to the ward, one of the WWII guys stopped me as I passed his bed. "Saw you got dressed. First time, right?"

"Yes."

"It's a lot easier to put on your socks and shoes if you pull your foot up and rest it on your opposite knee when you're sitting up in bed. No reaching. No falling over. You're more stable."

"Thanks," I said, "But why in hell didn't you tell me when I was doing it?"

"Everybody has to learn this game the hard way."

Most people think that not being able to walk is what makes paraplegia and quadriplegia such serious disabilities. Sadly, this is only partially true. What I call the hidden handicaps are far more difficult. Not to be able to walk is hard—brutally hard—no question. But the mobility that has come with the technology of modern wheelchairs, vans, and lifts, together with the increasing accessibility of public places, does make this a factor less difficult than it was in the past. People don't realize that the unseen problems of incontinence, vulnerability to skin ulceration, chronic pain, impotency, and more are the issues that can cause the most difficulties and anguish for the disabled, their families, and their caregivers. And although they are physical in nature, these aspects have deep psychological implications for the minds and relationships of all concerned.

Good rehabilitation programs include learning how to cope with and manage these multiple handicaps. One never overcomes them. It's a matter of finding ways to deal with them the best you can.

For me, injured at 22, it was hard to grasp that I was permanently stuck with incontinency of the bladder and bowels, a demeaning problem long associated with the elderly or mentally disabled. In the long hours that I stewed over it, I gradually concluded that feeling sorry for myself wasn't going to help. There was no other way but to accept the reality and focus on learning to handle it on my own. I did not want to depend on Barbara or anyone else. It was a major hurdle in the quest for total independence because unless I solved it, I was never going to be able to function alone in the outside world, period.

I'll try to avoid the "grizzly details" on this aspect of rehab, but there is no avoiding the blunt truth at least in general terms. So bear with me for a few pages.

At the hospital, Dr. Talbot had decreed that everyone would participate in "bowel training." This meant that the newly injured such as myself were required to sit in the bathroom every day for as long as it took to achieve some sort of success. The idea was that if the bowels got into a daily routine, the process of elimination could be more predictable, more "regular." We were taught various techniques, all very unpleasant, to get around the problem of lack of control. At best, they were only inconsistently effective in the beginning.

In a VA Hospital, privacy doesn't exist—on the wards, in the halls, and also in the bathroom. This was one of the toughest things to take. An open bathroom scene (no booths) like the one I endured for months was shown in the movie "Born on the Fourth of July" starring Tom Cruise as a Vietnam vet paraplegic. I couldn't bear to go to see it. I had had enough of the real thing.

This activity was orchestrated by a team of orderlies, and I can't praise them enough. Most were African-Americans from the tough Roxbury section of Boston. They were highly trained in Dr. Talbot's rigorous fashion and had to be the best on the ward to be assigned to this bathroom duty, for which I believe they were upped a pay grade. It was gross in the extreme, and the patients were understandably unhappy, embarrassed, sickened, depressed, angry, sometimes tearful, you name it. With only the rare exception, the orderlies were gentle, firm, patient, and compassionate. There was a lot of crude, mostly humorous banter by both patients and orderlies, but I never once saw an abusive situation.

For me this everyday ritual went on for about three months until I was discharged. However, about a month into it, I discovered that one of the night-shift orderlies was taking in a few early risers to ease the day shift overcrowding in the bathroom. I volunteered for this program, which got under way at a bleary-eyed 5:00 a.m. It was much better because the bathroom was often empty, and the whole process was quicker.

Did "bowel training" work? For me, yes. For many patients, no. The key was persistence. I was determined to give it my best shot and kept at it. Patience ultimately paid off. There was no dramatic breakthrough, but after a year or two of not missing one day of this routine, the process began to take less time. Gradually, things became more regular and predictable—hardly "normal," but successful day after day. Although not directly involved, Barbara was a great help in all this primarily because of her encouragement and patience. I am still using these highly unpleasant but reliable methods today; and there are probably not many normal people, particularly of my age, who have healthier or more regular digestive systems. It has indeed worked. Thanks, Dr. Talbot.

I recently discovered that many people have the misconception that people like me have to have colonoscopies to function. I have never heard of one, although there may be isolated cases among the spinal-cord injured.

The bladder problem was similar in that one did not have control. When we were newly injured, this was dealt with by use of an indwelling catheter. In some cases, the catheter had to be permanent due to spasticity or other problems. This solution was not healthy in the long-term for it almost always led to frequent infections and contributed to other problems such as kidney dysfunction. In my case, it was possible after a month or two to remove the indwelling catheter and rely on other methods of dealing with the issue.

The alternate approach favored then was the use of a so-called "Texas catheter" system involving an exterior collection device strapped to the leg.

This method, said to have been devised by WWII fighter pilots for long missions, is now used by astronauts, U2 pilots, and other long-duration flyers, who know it as a UCD (urinary collection device). Once perfected, it is a very practical solution. But it takes a great deal of diligence to make it work. One must pay unremitting attention to taking care of the gear and to personal hygiene. Today, however, the favored method for those with spinal cord injuries is "intermittent catheterization," by which the bladder is emptied a number of times during the day by temporarily inserting a disposable catheter. This wouldn't have worked for me because there were virtually no accessible booths in public bathrooms until well into the 1970s. This method also requires close attention to sterile techniques. Otherwise, for both methods, there is a high risk of chronic urinary tract infections, one of the most persistent ailments faced by the spinal cord-injured individual.

The great advantage of the system I use is that one can go anywhere and circulate in normal society. In an extreme example, I once took a flight from Johannesburg to Paris that, because of delays, lasted more than twenty hours from boarding to de-boarding—occupying my seat the whole time. I had devised a special UCD system to deal with it. I've used the Texas catheter method successfully now for more than 50 years. But not surprisingly, there have been several dozen mishaps. A number of these incidents were in public and embarrassing, some extremely so. During these episodes I have to admit that I felt totally alone and found myself thinking thoughts like, "How could anyone ever, ever know how hard it is to be a quadriplegic?" Then I would get a grip and move on with whatever was needed to sort things out. Barbara endured a number of the scenes with me, and it was just as tough for her in a different way. But she never made me feel more upset than I already was. It seems that the occasional mishap simply was part of the price one paid to be out in the real world as a seriously disabled person. It was worth it.

When my son John was young, he once asked me, "Dad, what's the first thing you're going to do when you get to heaven?" My immediate reply was, "I am going to go into a bathroom and relieve myself the way God intended me to."

Chronic pain becomes part of daily life for virtually every spinal cord-injured person, varying greatly from one to another. For some, it is so severe as to be totally debilitating. For others like me it's always there but bearable. And for still others, it's quite minor, hardly noticeable. The problem in non-technical terms is that the central nervous system, having been severely damaged, is sending erroneous messages to the brain—like the well-known "ghost" feeling that an amputee may have that his leg is still there. Mine occurs in two ways. My feet always feel ice cold, as if I had put my feet in ice water and they were transitioning from sharp pain to numbness. Another is that my midsection always feels as if it was belted too tightly—a constant constricted feeling, not exactly pain, but permanently uncomfortable. The intensity of these feelings varies. Sometimes they are really distracting. Then there are days when they are mild. Painkillers have no effect. Often people have their nerves surgically cut in order to eliminate unbearable pain, but even that doesn't always work. And there are special drugs, something I never wanted to get into. I can't remember what it is like to be free of pain.

As for vulnerability to skin ulceration, again it varies tremendously with the individual and his or her physiology. The two main causes are that muscular atrophy takes away muscle mass, removing the cushion between the skin and natural bony protrusions. In addition, immobility gradually impairs blood circulation and skin health. So when pressure is exerted from weight on the bony areas when sitting in a wheelchair or lying in bed, the blood (already inhibited by poor circulation) can't deliver enough oxygen to the affected skin tissue. This causes skin cells to die. If caught immediately, healing can take place relatively quickly. But if it gets out of hand and several layers of skin and even tissue underneath are affected, the problem becomes serious, often taking many months or even longer to heal. If a spinal cord-injured person is healthy, has a good diet, uses proper cushioning, and takes care to change position constantly to relieve pressure and maintain circulation, ulcers can usually be minimized or avoided. For some reason, some people are more susceptible than others. I have worked hard to avoid this problem, designing and fabricating my own cushions and being extremely careful. I have had only a half dozen or so problems in my many years of quadriplegia, contracting mostly superficial but slow-to-heal ulcers, and those only very recently. For the more susceptible, skin ulcers can mean very restricted lives.

As a postscript to the description of hidden handicaps, I should add one more—not a health issue and less serious, but an everyday source of frustration. Because I am always sitting down, I am in effect four feet tall (I used to be 5' 10."). I am in a way a "dwarf." Obviously, it is never a problem when others are seated. But there are so many situations every day that require me to look up as I speak while others are looking down—as if I were always talking to a pro basketball player. It's a subtle thing, but I can't help wishing we were eye to eye. The rare person who senses this either sits down or squats next to me to talk. In social situations, such as parties where most people are standing and the conversation is lively, it's extremely difficult to hear the people I'm talking to and for them to hear me. Typically, I find a space next to a couch or table where I can talk with people who are sitting down. Other problems also arise, such as needing a book on a high shelf or trying to deal with a bank teller or room clerk over counters above my eye level. The dwarf factor is nobody's fault, just another fact of life in a wheelchair. Technology is coming to the rescue through a new wheelchair on the market that can stand up and balance on its rear wheels (controlled by gyroscopes), raising a person to his or her full former height. The trouble is, though, it is more than twice the cost of a regular power wheelchair.

The general view of "rehabilitation" is greatly oversimplified when applied to spinal cord injuries. Most people think rehab is just physical therapy, rebuilding of strength, and learning how to use prosthetic devices in the hospital. But the complex reality when dealing with quadriplegia and paraplegia includes those basic things but goes much deeper. It involves a practical learning curve that is entwined with profound psychological adjustments—particularly in terms of those hidden handicaps. You have to come to grips with a harsh new life, relearn how to handle functions long taken for granted, face the fact of your forever being "different," try to regain your self-esteem and confidence, adjust to radically changed personal relationships, and finally, figure out what to make of the rest of your life—all according to a whole new set of parameters. This is the reality of rehabilitation. It is a life-long, uphill, and lonely journey that has its rewards but requires deep reserves of patience and set-in-concrete determination.

Long Hot Summer

In June and July, as the warmer days occurred more frequently, I became acutely aware that I was affected by the heat. I am one of the many spinal cord-injured who don't perspire below the level of their injuries—in my case, from the chest down. I never realized how important it was to perspire. Since there is no moisture on the skin, there is no evaporation, hence no natural body cooling. A fever results as the body temperature rapidly rises, sapping energy and causing severe discomfort. None of the wards, save one, at West Roxbury were air-conditioned and by late morning they became hot and muggy. I took to scheduling my physical therapy and other commitments for the cooler early hours. Then I would lie on top of the bed with very few clothes on and continuously wipe down my body with a wet washrag to keep my skin moist, which provided only partial relief. These were miserable days that would drag until Barbara came for her evening visit and we could at least sit outside in the cooler evening air.

I didn't realize it in the early summer, but we were fast approaching a period that can only be described as "crunch time."

When I had left Texas for Massachusetts, Barbara came to Boston at the same time. She stayed for the first weeks with my uncle, Jack Platt, and his wife, Vee, who lived ten or fifteen miles from the VA Hospital in Hingham. Uncle Jack, then a retired Army colonel, had always been a favorite of mine. Also, I was close to his two college-age children, Jack III and Polly.

Before my injury, Barbara had been working for AT&T designing long-distance circuits for the Long Lines Division headquartered in White Plains, New York, where she lived with her parents. For her Texas sojourn, AT&T had given her a leave of absence, and she had stayed comfortably with a Wellesley classmate in San Antonio. However, the best that AT&T could do for her in the Boston area was a job as a business representative in the Roxbury section—a low-income neighborhood in Boston. This was hard and made worse by the dreary single room in Brookline that she had found to live in. Fortunately, we were able to locate a better room for her in the house of the woman who was head of the VA hospital's physical therapy department, a fine and supportive person living less than a mile away. For transportation, I financed the purchase of a used Ford two-door sedan.

Barbara was the single most important external factor in my rehabilitation. If anything, our relationship had deepened since my accident. She had shown great courage in defying her parents to join me. She was bearing up at working at a less-than-satisfactory job, living in a single room, and getting around with minimal transportation. Yet she visited me nine days out of ten, spending hours at my bedside or sitting next to my wheelchair in the dingy lounge or outside on one the benches on the park-like grounds. Not only did she always provide support and encouragement, but also the very existence of her loyalty spurred me on to try to rebuild my seriously damaged life to the point where we might see a viable future together. It was tough in a lot of ways for both of us—just as much for her, but for different reasons, as it was for me. There was a lot of stress, and there were crises, setbacks, and tears at times. But there were triumphs, too. She had a lively sense of humor, and it helped us both to laugh about some of the bizarre things we experienced. We had always enjoyed each other's company, and that never changed. What sustained us were our essentially optimistic natures and a kind of unspoken determination that we would prevail—how, we didn't know.

The painful problem Barbara had had with her parents over joining me in Texas persisted through the summer. Ever since my injury, they had vehemently opposed her continuing her engagement to me—so much so that when she had departed for San Antonio in February, they refused even to drive her to the airport. Her father's doctor had told him that, given my C7 level of injury, I would always be a helpless cripple confined to a wheelchair—sickly and unable to make a living. He undoubtedly told him also about the incontinency and impotency problems. What the doctor did not say, and had not bothered to find out, was that WWII had produced thousands of spinal cord-injured men and that, as a result, rehabilitation medicine had made quantum leaps in dealing with their health and other issues.

My injury aside, I had sensed that her parents had never been enthusiastic about me or our engagement in the first place. I was a fresh-faced 22-year-old heading for at least four years in the Air Force, career direction unknown. Barbara was an outstanding golfer—probably the best in the Northeast and among the top half-dozen in the country. I think they wanted her to pursue her fame and, were she to marry, would have much preferred an older, more settled man who could support her golfing career. It seemed to me that my injury must have just made things unacceptably worse in their eyes.

One of the lowest points for me in this whole saga was a letter I received from her father at the hospital one hot summer's day in July. It was my first contact with him since my injury. It was a long hand-written letter. There were a few words of sympathy for my accident. Then he set forth his objections to our continued engagement in direct and accusative language. He said, among many other things, that I was exploiting Barbara by leading her into a marriage that would consign her to being a lifelong nurse and caregiver. Furthermore, there was something to the effect of: "If you really care for her, you should have the courage to let her go."

The reality was that Barbara and I had not yet decided to marry. We were talking about it all the time, all the angles, but had agreed that we should not go forward until I had a better feel for how independent I could be physically and how I would end up financially—namely, what my VA compensation might be. This was all new territory for us. We simply didn't yet know whether we could put together a lifetime commitment that would work.

His letter was understandable, I suppose, given what his doctor had told him, but I was angry and hurt by the substance and the tone of his approach. That he would attribute such motives to me went down hard. It was a brutal thing to do. After my temper cooled several days later, I decided the best way to deal with her parents was to keep my composure and not respond in kind—just state my case and ultimately let my actions speak for themselves. For one thing, I did not want to give them the satisfaction of seeing me hurt. For another, I had by that time come to realize that I might just succeed in gaining virtually full physical independence so that Barbara would not have to be a caregiver. Also, I realized that for him to want to protect his daughter, whom he doted on, was a natural and instinctive reaction. Finally, it was clear that a lot of the bitterness that was coming our way was because this was the first time that Barbara had ever defied her parents—a particularly galling thing for her mother, who had always kept Barbara firmly under her thumb.

I wrote him back in an even tone. I told him that he was totally misinformed on the potential for my rehabilitation and that, furthermore, I was making good progress. I also said unequivocally that I had no intention of marrying Barbara unless and until I was physically independent and able to support us both financially. After I mailed it, I destroyed his letter, never wanting to read it again. It is destructive to wallow around in bitterness, anger, and ill will. Whether they wanted to do so was their problem. I wanted to move on and to get a life. I didn't show his letter to Barbara because I knew it would upset her terribly; but of course, I told her the essence of it and what my response was. All this just hardened my resolve. I intended to "get even," if you want to call it that, simply by proving them totally wrong.

By August, I was making gains on a lot of fronts with only occasional temporary setbacks. The catheter had been removed, and I was dealing with the issue. The bathroom program, onerous as it was, was coming along. My upper body was getting a lot stronger, which was a big help in making transfers. I was dressing and undressing solo. And after some prodding of the staff, I had been cleared to take driving instructions for hand controls in preparation for getting a new driver's license. By this time, they knew that I was keen to move forward and were cutting corners to push up my scheduling. Everyone liked Barbara, and I could sense they respected what we were trying to do. An important milestone was when I was graduated to a self-care ward—unusual for a quadriplegic. The advanced patients and hard-bitten old-timers were now more friendly—partially I think out of respect for my dogged perseverance and success—and I had made some good friends among the men my age.

We began to widen our horizon a little as I practiced my wheel-chair-to-car transfers into Barbara's Ford. We would drive around, possibly have a meal out, visit my uncle, or even go to a drive-in movie with a little restrained sex thrown in (we needed a lot more time explore this side of things given the new realities). It was a tremendous relief to get away from the hospital and actually have a good time.

The financial situation was also progressing. The problem was that to recognize a serious lifetime disability, the VA required the veteran to go through a laborious administrative maze—forms, reports, medical evaluation boards, and on and on. The basic requirement was understandable because they would be committing the government to a substantial lifetime entitlement. It's just that at the VA, bureaucracy has been raised to an art form. Very soon after I arrived in May, I had received excellent advice from a seasoned WWII vet who was well known in advocacy circles. He suggested that I join the Disabled American Veterans and then give them power of attorney to handle my case. He was right. They went all-out, and one of their agents hand-carried my papers step by step through the whole sequence, compressing a six-month process into two. By late August, I was designated 100 percent disabled, plus an added factor for loss of use of my hands, even though I was getting them to work pretty well. My VA pension, known as "compensation," was established, and it was just enough to give us financial viability. In addition, an allowance was granted for half the purchase price of a car with hand controls. Within a week, I had placed an order for a new Buick 2-door hardtop—a sharp-looking car with a big engine.

Although many challenges loomed ahead, the long summer was winding down, and I headed into September with a lot more bounce and confidence.

Given all this progress, we began to think seriously about marriage. No question, we were still in love, perhaps even more so. Barbara seemed to have no doubts about going ahead, and I was certainly as enthusiastic as ever about marrying her. But I was concerned that before we made the final decision she should be made fully aware by a third party of all the implications of being wedded to a quadriplegic. In those days, counseling as we know it today didn't exist in VA rehab hospitals. People like us were facing daunting emotional and physical challenges as well as such life-shaping questions as "shall we get married?" totally on their own.

However, I felt we must get some professional input and struck on the idea of talking to the formidable Dr. Talbot. The question was would he give us the time? If so, I was sure that he would give us his straight-from-the-shoulder opinion. I got up my nerve and stopped him in the hall one day and asked him point blank. To my surprise he agreed immediately. So I made an appointment with his secretary for the next week.

He listened attentively to our story—our backgrounds, how I came to be injured, and what our hopes and plans were. He knew the state of my health and my rapid progress in rehabilitation. He asked a few questions then talked at length about what the future might hold for me physically. At best, it would never be "normal," and there were serious health vulnerabilities. The life expectancy for quadriplegics then was only around 25 years after injury. But he said that he knew of many men who had gotten out into the real world and led fulfilling lives and had marriages that worked—and also of many that didn't. We would be childless in all probability and have a lot of other things to overcome. He was specific on all the tough topics and minced no words. However, he thought I had done well so far and that we seemed to have the right attitude in going about the decision with our eyes wide open. He was optimistic it would work out provided that we were realistic about the limitations and were prepared to face the inevitable challenges, known and unknown. It would not be easy. He wished us luck and said he would see us any time if we had questions or wanted to talk further. He even smiled!

One thing he said was very interesting. "Disability, even one as serious as yours, is a relative thing. You are nowhere near as disabled as a man who, for example, has to drink a pint of alcohol a day."

Dr. Talbot hadn't told us anything we didn't already know, but he put things in perspective, and it was encouraging that he was upbeat about our prospects. So marriage became final in our minds, and we were relieved to have it set. Predictably, her parents became even more upset and continued to try to dissuade us. Barbara took the brunt of all this with her mother leading the charge. Mrs. Bruning could be an unpleasant woman and was used to ordering her daughter around, for Barbara to defy her was unheard of, and her mother said some very hurtful things. It wasn't long before they were hardly on speaking terms.

Barbara's older brother, Ted, was deputized to come to the hospital to talk with me, and we sat in a corner of the lobby for a "man-to-man." What he had come to say was essentially the same argument put forth by her father in his letter. Although he did not put it so bluntly, the clear implication again was that I was taking advantage of Barbara. It was obvious that these people had no clue how much we had been going through and the exceptional progress I had actually made despite the "fires of hell" that were part of my daily life. I was fed up with this destructive attitude and the hurt it was causing us, particularly Barbara. They saw me as "a cripple," stigmatized for life, unable to work, and dependent on Barbara as a caregiver. Also, they apparently did not believe how seriously I had taken my commitment to be independent both physically and financially before undertaking marriage to Barbara. It was also obvious that they hadn't gauged the full measure of our resolve and our mutual commitment to make this new life work.

Patiently, but sort of through clenched teeth, I led him step by step through the rehabilitation process I was going through so that he could understand something of the difficulty, the progress made, and what it might lead to. I restated what I had written to his father and made it crystal clear that Barbara and I intended to go ahead on the basis of my having met the independence benchmark. Then I expressed the hope that we could have a conventional wedding with all sides participating in the normal way. He left without making much of a response, and we parted with a handshake and a smile—but little else. Ted was and is a very good-hearted person. Yet I was sorry that he remained the dutiful advocate for his parents and didn't see our side.

About this time, I passed my driver's test and got my special license marked "restricted to drive with hand controls." A week or so later, I took delivery of my new car. I hadn't told Barbara of the exact day of delivery wanting first to assure myself that I was able to handle the car and get in and out of it independently. On the day the car came, I picked it up in the morning and spent most of the rest of the day driving it in different kinds of traffic, practicing getting in and out, and working on the difficult process of loading and unloading the wheelchair. There were no real problems, and after Barbara got home from work, I called her to tell her the good news and that I would be by to pick her up within the hour.

What is it about a man and his car? It meant so much to me when I was 16 and received my driver's license. But this was an entirely different experience. It is impossible for me to describe the intense pleasure it gave me to actually be driving myself around independently. In fact, getting into and riding around completely alone in this big shiny set of wheels was for me the ultimate symbol of my achievements so far in this extended process of rehabilitation. When Barbara came out of the house and jumped in the passenger's seat, we both were beaming ear to ear and would have done a high five if that triumphant gesture had been in use back then. We went out to dinner to celebrate, sat around enjoying the car and the evening, and finally drove back to her place. Wow! An actual date! I could hardly believe it.

As the unsatisfactory back-and-forth between Barbara and her parents intensified, it became obvious that they had no intention of sponsoring a wedding that they were so opposed to. Even the Presbyterian minister that Barbara had known for many years sided with her parents, on the basis, I assume, of the same misleading prognosis her father had received from his doctor. So it became our choice as to what to do. When my Uncle Jack and Aunt Vee heard of this setback, they offered immediately to have a wedding reception at their house and approached the Episcopal parish in Hingham to see if the wedding could be held there. After we had met with the priest and discussed our situation and plans, he agreed to officiate at a ceremony in his church. Now we had a church and a reception venue and were able to set a date for three or four weeks later.

My family was highly supportive. Not surprisingly, they liked Barbara, had a great deal respect for her accomplishments, and admired her for her tenacity and courage. They wanted to help us in any way they could. Everyone in my family had visited the hospital over the past several months, including my brother Alex. But he surprised me again with an enigmatic comment as he visited at the hospital and saw me for the first time as a quadriplegic. As he got up to leave, he declared, "I see you've got an excellent attitude. All this will just be an inconvenience." Inconvenience? I thought: If only that were true.

The wedding plans rapidly took shape. It was agreed by all that it would be a small wedding, only family and several friends, one of whom was to be Barbara's maid-of-honor. Alex was able to get off from the Navy to be my best man.

Meanwhile, Barbara set out to find us an apartment in Boston. Not only did we both love that city, having gone to college nearby, but I also needed to be near the hospital for a period of time to continue physical therapy and in case I ran into any problems. Within a week, she had found a one-bedroom apartment with a terrace in a modern building overlooking the Charles River Boat Basin. It had a garage in the basement with a level entry to the elevator, which was ideal for me. Furthermore, it was on Pinckney Street at the base of Beacon Hill, a pleasant neighborhood and a great find.

We advised her parents of the wedding plans as soon as they were made and invited them to come. True to form, they equivocated and would not indicate a commitment, leaving us to wonder. Finally, in one sad and memorable telephone conversation, Barbara's mother brought her to tears in a dispute over the wedding date. She handed me the phone, and I simply told her parents that the date and arrangements were firm and that they could come or not as they wished, period.

There followed an intense few weeks of preparation. All the usual things: wedding dress, ring, flowers, presents for wedding party, altering one of my suits, getting the apartment set up (kitchen stuff, linen, furniture, food, etc.). Most of this was done by Barbara with help here and there from my family. It was intense, and I really don't know how she managed it. Meanwhile, I was trying to finish up at the hospital so that I could be discharged and then return as an outpatient.

Finally, the day was upon us. First, I finalized my discharge and left the hospital. Departure was with mixed emotions: on the one hand, it meant independence, privacy, peace, and a major step toward a more normal life; on the other, it meant that I didn't have a nurse, aide, or doctor close at hand in the event of a problem. I had restarted life after an injury leaving me unable to do anything for myself and then ten months later was leaving the protective cocoon of total care for a life where I had to do everything. And I was getting married—all on the same day. I admit to being pretty nervous as I drove out of the parking lot.

We gathered at the church, some 35 of us, right on time and ready to go. No one had heard from Barbara's parents so we assumed they weren't coming. Then five minutes before the wedding, they showed up, looking grim, and were greeted by my cousin Jack, who was acting as usher. Barbara's brother, Ted, accompanying them, said to Jack something like, "This wedding is just a tragedy." Jack had just returned from Marine officer candidate boot camp—one tough guy—and he very nearly flattened him, thick glasses and all. Luckily for Ted, Jack held back. When Barbara asked her father to give her away, he refused, saying he would only walk with her down the aisle. She then had to delay everything and come back into the sacristy for a hasty conference with the priest, who calmly reassured her that he would simply leave out that part of the service—not to worry.

Finally, the music got under way, and Barbara and her father started down the aisle. He looked very stern, but she was radiant with a broad, warm smile, very calm and deliberate, looking directly at me. Gone was the anxious anticipation. I, too, felt serene in the sure knowledge that after this long, tough time we were doing the right thing in the right way. These unspoken feelings were instantly exchanged with our eyes, and we knew we were aglow in the moment. This carried into the service, which went off smoothly with our vows firmly given, her family notwithstanding. It seemed also that everyone else recognized that there was something special about this wedding, which was undertaken joyfully against all odds. There weren't many dry eyes.

The reception at my Uncle Jack's house was a whirl of smiles, champagne, hugs, slaps on the back, congratulations, and general celebratory buzz. Fortunately, my new mother- and father-in-law did not come. We cut the cake with my uncle's Army saber, followed by a few brief toasts. Soon two hours had gone by just like that and Barbara went to get changed. We said our goodbyes, climbed into my car, and drove away to the loud cheers of all.

I drove until we were out of sight of the house and pulled into a side street. We fell into each other's arms for a long emotional moment. We had this profound and triumphant sense of pride and relief that I was out of the hospital, that the wedding was successfully over, and that Barbara was released from the oppressive dependence on her parents. Some years later, Martin Luther King, Jr. was to proclaim, "Free at last. Thank God Almighty, I am free at last." That was how we felt.

There was a bizarre postscript to this event. It was pitiful really. We went immediately to our new apartment, marveled at our new surroundings, and fell exhausted into bed. The next morning at about nine o'clock, we were awakened by a knock on the door. Must be the "Welcome Wagon" or a vacuum cleaner salesman, we thought. Barbara put on her robe and went to the door. She was stunned to see her parents standing there. They wanted to see the apartment and had the gall to show up the morning after our wedding night without even asking or calling ahead. Her mother gruffly asked, "Why aren't you dressed yet?" Barbara, furious, let them see the living room and kitchen and ushered them out the door. Good riddance! We were dumfounded. It was more than a year before she talked to them again.

But within the hour, she had whipped up a hearty breakfast— our first meal in our own place—and we were just plain happy to be completely alone and at peace. I had "hit a wall," we had scaled it together, and now we had just reentered the real world.

There is a passage in the Bible that I came across a few years ago in St. Paul's Letter to the Romans. I think it captures the essence of the extraordinary ten-month period we had just been through: "...we also boast in our sufferings, knowing that suffering produces endurance, and endurance produces character, and character produces hope, and hope does not disappoint us, because God's love has been poured into our hearts..."

Part II

The Climb

Fast-forward to May of 1972, some 17 years after our wedding. I was in a Boeing 747 somewhere high over the Atlantic, returning from my second—and very successful—business trip to South Africa in six months. My destination was New York, where we then lived. Barbara had joined me on this trip but was returning on a later flight. Lunch had been served in the First Class cabin, and I was finishing a glass of wine while listening to music on the stereo headset and gazing contentedly out the window at the glistening ocean some 40,000 feet below. Just then, I had a surreal sense of this moment being juxtaposed with my situation in 1955, when my accident had nearly ended my life at age 22, leaving me with a severe and permanent disability and the beginnings of a very tentative reentry in the real world. Now at age 40, after many years of "toiling in the vineyards," I felt that with these trips I had broken through to a new level of achievement. Meanwhile, Barbara and I were headed home to our children aged 12 and 10, and to our recently purchased apartment overlooking the East River. Although we were dealing with many challenges—health problems for Barbara, parenting issues, a tight budget, and the predictable stresses that most marriages go through—she too had been doing well. She had recently become head of all volunteer work and fundraising activities at one of New York's major hospitals.

On this trip, we had felt like two determined hikers who stop for a rest while ascending a demanding mountain trail. They turn around and look with wonder at the expansive view—amazed at how far they had wound their way up from the dark valley below.

Starting Somewhere

Such things as travel to Africa, any kind of travel—or even working—were unthinkable right after we were married in 1955, ten months after my injury. To be sure, we had accomplished a lot in that first year that had appeared to be impossible. I had gone through hospital rehabilitation and had reached an unusual level of independence for a quadriplegic. Barbara's day-by-day support had been a major factor. She had made the break from her embittered family, and we were living in a comfortable small apartment in a good neighborhood in Boston. My VA compensation was enough for us to have an independent, though modest, lifestyle. Above all, we were elated to be free of the restrictions of hospital and family and truly on our own. We continued to enjoy our independence and began to form some new friendships and rebuild a social life.

But the reality of the overall situation was far from reassuring. Physically, I was very vulnerable this early in my disability to all kinds of problems—urinary tract infections and other elimination

71

troubles, the potential of skin problems, and fatigue. In fact, once in those early months I did have to return to the hospital for a few days to deal with an infection. Furthermore, I was still an outpatient at the hospital, continuing to build up my upper body strength in physical therapy sessions. In truth, it was an anxious time for me. Now that I was on my own, I was separated from the protective atmosphere of the hospital. And it was also difficult for Barbara. She too was concerned about my physical well-being and our future. How long would she have to work? Would I ever be able to handle a full-time job? Would she be able to realize her outstanding potential as a golfer? Meanwhile, she continued her job at the telephone business office in a scary neighborhood. We had no idea what the future held and were simply feeling our way forward day by day, thankful to have come this far.

I had noticed at the hospital that a large number of the veterans —even the ones who had moved into their own homes—didn't do much except hang out. Some came back to the hospital and talked with friends or played cards or cribbage. There was a group that dropped into the coffee shop every morning. Many would head for the tavern or racetrack in the afternoon. Others stayed around home mostly, watching TV and puttering around the house. I'm sure though that there were a lot that found something useful to do— work, hobbies, or the like—but I didn't get to know them because they were busy and simply weren't around. A number of the brighter guys ended up working in veterans' advocacy groups such as the Paralyzed Veterans of America. (That particular group became highly effective and brought about profound changes in accessibility, employer acceptance, travel barriers, and social equality—benefiting all disabled). It is hard to imagine how hard it was then to find work and be able to sustain a career, much less rise to a good paying job. Also, attitudes toward disability were very different than today— more pitying and patronizing—and the physical obstacles (steps everywhere, no curb cuts, virtually no accessible bathrooms) were daunting. The very idea of an Americans with Disabilities Act would have provoked laughter.

But just "hanging out" wasn't for me. Perhaps it was the Puritan work ethic. I wanted to do something useful, something worthwhile, make a difference. Furthermore, it was just too boring to sit around all day talking about baseball scores, the physical attributes of the new nurse on Ward 2-North, or the weather. Also, I wanted to learn how to cope in the normal world without feeling inferior. Finally, I wanted to earn a living beyond my pension to provide us with a better lifestyle.

By the end of the year, some two months after our wedding, I had gained enough strength and energy to begin thinking very tentatively about what I might do. I knew that my pre-injury plan to go into corporate management after my military commitment was impossible. The hard-driving nature of that career path—travel, long hours, and intense competition, not to mention getting to manufacturing operations that were totally inaccessible to the wheelchair-bound, was simply out of the question at that time. Barbara thought I could be a cartoonist, using a talent that I had dabbled with for years. I could work at home and have great flexibility. I even went so far as to introduce myself to Al Capp, the legendary creator of Li'l Abner, who had a studio in our building. He looked at my slim portfolio and wasn't too encouraging. So much for that.

Then I thought of being an English teacher. I liked young people, I had majored in English in college, I had never been uncomfortable speaking to groups of people and, more importantly, at that stage in my recovery, a teaching job could be part-time if necessary. We talked a lot about various options, and while teaching had never been a goal of mine, we felt that the main thing was to start somewhere. It could always be changed.

The first step then was going back to school for a master's degree. Having graduated less than two years earlier from Harvard,

I knew that the historic buildings where English courses were given were completely inaccessible; so I looked into Boston University, where it turned out that most such courses were given in a building I could get into by a basement entrance that had an elevator. I applied, was accepted, and began the spring term taking two classes. I got decent grades that first term and by the summer, I was stronger and much less anxious about living away from the hospital.

Meanwhile, my parents had modified a bedroom and bath on the ground floor of their house in Connecticut for us to use, and we started visiting them. It was bittersweet to return home in such a transformed state—nice to be in the familiar place where I had grown up and to see old friends and well-wishers, but I winced when, for example, I found myself at the bottom of the stairs looking up suddenly to realize that I would never see the bedroom of my childhood again.

On one of these visits, my father suggested we go out for a drive and have a talk. He was interested in how I managed my car's hand controls, and we drove around what was then mostly picturesque farm and estate country in Fairfield County. Eventually, we stopped for some iced tea at an old country inn and found ourselves at a quiet shady table at the edge of a pond, where swans were serenely drifting around under the willow trees.

My father had a reserved, somewhat formal manner and was not easy to know. We had never been close in the sense of his taking much interest in my personal life, whether it was school, sports, friends, or anything. As children, my brother and I hardly knew him. I don't think he knew what to make of children in general, much less Alex and me—how to talk with them, play with them, or interact. I knew he was fond of us, "the boys," but never knew how to express it. And he was nice enough, even when he was correcting our table manners, but distant and self-absorbed. We knew he worked very hard and that my parents were not having an easy time of it financially in the Depression and then WWII. So, except for meals, Alex and I were mostly "seen and not heard." My mother handled all the day-to-day side of parenting. As I got into my teens, I got to know him a little better. I had developed great respect for the hard work and long hours he put into trying to build a career that would give us more financial stability. He borrowed heavily against his life insurance to give us the best possible education. And I learned that he had a sense of humor, which occasionally surfaced, and we developed a pleasant, if not relaxed, relationship.

One of the few times he ever directly became involved in my life was when I was having academic difficulties at Harvard, which I later found out was due to a learning disability. He came for a weekend visit to see what the problem was. He had graduated with honors from MIT and he was making sacrifices to send me to college. So I didn't know what to expect. To my great surprise, instead of making me feel as though I was messing up, he said, "I have absolute confidence you can pull yourself out of your slump." He was right. I did, eventually. It helped a lot to have his unqualified support.

When I was injured, my mother told me later, he was so upset that he couldn't bear to visit me in Texas. She said that, "It's the only time I've ever seen your father cry." Some people thought that it was strange that he didn't come immediately to the hospital. But I didn't think so and have never held it against him, knowing that he was introspective, private, serious, and unable to deal face-to-face with emotional situations. I think he was painfully shy. I knew, however, that he cared deeply by his frequent supportive letters. It was clear from their content that he agonized with my mother every day about my travails in those first few weeks.

Now, over iced tea, we were having our first real one-on-one conversation since before I was injured. He was interested in the specifics of how I was managing my daily life, and we talked about that for a time. Then he asked what I thought about the future—

what I might be able to do. I told him of my concept of teaching English and how things were going at Boston University. He heard me out and praised me for the initiative. "But," he said, "I have a proposal: I want you to think about joining my business."

His consultancy business, which he had started some seven years earlier, was making gradual progress and he wondered if I wanted to join him as an assistant. He was frank to say that there really wasn't enough work to warrant it, but he wanted to offer the job as an experiment for me to see if I could go back to business, as it had been my ambition before my injury. I would have flexible hours and I could quit at any time. He would pay a modest salary (which would be out of his pocket because the business hadn't yet broken even), and I could determine among other things whether I could deal physically with working—first part-time then full-time if I thought it possible. All this assumed of course that the business would eventually grow enough to support my salary in full. This offer was put forward without any pressure from him, and we talked at length about his business—its problems and prospects.

He had created a unique consulting service for the executives of large companies, assisting them with their financial communications to their shareholders—annual and quarterly reports, press releases, and presentations to investors and to the professional financial and investment community. It was a highly important function because they relied on these constituencies to finance their growth. Yet very few companies had departments that specialized in such communications, and, as a result they were cobbled together by ad hoc in-house committees and individuals who may have known their manufacturing business but did not have the skills or time from their regular work to be effective communicators—to produce meaningful, readable, and informative reports under the demanding disclosure requirements of the SEC. Most of their reports were dull, dense, uninviting tomes that shareholders and other recipients simply threw out when they came in the mail. And since these were poorly managed crash projects, there were inevitable cost overruns and missed deadlines. Plus, they were expensive and onerous chores dreaded by all who were involved.

What my father offered was a consulting service so revolutionary that most executives didn't believe it could be done. He proposed to come in, study their business in great detail and get to know its policies, strategies, operations, products, and the thinking of senior management. Then he would research the year's operating results— the new developments, problems, successes, surprises, and important changes. Finally, he would analyze the financial results so that they could be credibly reported to a readership that included everyone from the sophisticated financial analyst to the untutored layperson. After the research was complete, he would write the report, working closely with management. He likened it to "putting a grand piano through a keyhole." At the same time, he worked with qualified vendors of his choice for photography, graphic design, typesetting, proofreading, and printing—all of which he was managing within a budget and on schedule in parallel streams of incredibly intense activity as the publishing deadline approached.

He said, "My idea is to do this work to high professional standards —of the kind one might expect from first-rate law or accounting firms—and get well paid for it." Such professional firms did exist and still do despite the many publicized excesses of the 1990s. "I want to avoid the hucksterism of advertising and the hyperbole of the typical public relations firm. I want to increase the credibility of corporate financial reporting and at the same time make it more user-friendly. I want to bring more integrity to the process."

What prospective clients found hard to believe was that someone from the outside could, in a short time, become so conversant with large, complicated businesses that he could prepare credible reports speaking for management—actually writing the reports, in fact. It seemed to them as though someone else was proposing to walk around in their shoes and think their thoughts. The fact was that my father was a trained consultant—a highly intelligent MIT graduate engineer, a "quick study," who knew how to dig deeply into the workings of a business and its finances, and he had the ability to write understandably about complex, technical subjects. But it was difficult to convince executives that he could deliver, and since no one else had ever offered this service, they were reluctant to be "guinea pig" clients.

It was a hard sell indeed, which accounted for his practice's very slow development. It took a year and a half to get his first client—pounding the pavement, writing sales letters, making presentations, networking, etc. But he was so good at what he had undertaken that the first client's report was chosen by the Harvard Business School to use in "Accounting 101" as "an example of the best practices in modern financial disclosure and reporting." Once he got a client and prepared their report, that company was almost invariably hooked, and their report became a repetitive project. He had chosen a demanding, high-stress business.

I felt that my father's offer had real possibilities—especially the fact that I wouldn't be plunging into the deep end of the pool in the business world. I could test the water in terms of my stamina, my concentration (the constant physical discomfort of quadriplegia was a distraction), my ability to navigate around the city in a wheelchair, and whether I would be viable in an office job. Most important, I could see whether I really wanted a career in the corporate world. Then, if things did not work out, I could back out gracefully without any damage being done.

There were, however, several things that made the decision difficult. We would have to move to New York, and since commuting would be impossible, live in the city where we had no friends or contacts. I would be five hours away from Boston and any familiar medical help in connection with my quadriplegia. The cost of living would be more than in Boston. Finally, there was the uncomfortable question of whether I really wanted to work for my father. He was a perfectionist and a controlling type of person, well-meaning but difficult. There simply was no arguing with a man who always knew he was right, and he was not easygoing. Also, I realized that because he had struggled financially in the Depression and WWII, he had a distorted idea of what was fair compensation in an economy that had moved on to better times. I knew he was never going to pay well.

I thought long and hard about his proposal and its pros and cons, and Barbara and I discussed all the angles at length. In the end, we decided that I should give it a try even though it took some courage to leave the secure status quo in Boston. We knew that the only way to regain some degree of a normal lifestyle was to get back, however tentatively, into the real world of work and social interaction —not easy because there was so much to overcome: the physical obstacles to wheelchairs, the self-consciousness and loneliness of being "different," the patronizing or superior attitudes of many who look down on the handicapped, and lots more. But I knew that I owed it to myself and to Barbara to fight the temptation to stay in the shelter of the all-disabled scene.

An important consideration was that, for Barbara, returning to the New York area would be something of a homecoming, despite the falling out with her parents. She could reconnect with her many friends in Westchester County and conceivably resume her competitive golf in familiar territory where she was a top player.

People have often said, "I don't know how you faced the outside world. I don't think I could have done it." I never let that comment go by without an argument and would say, "Listen, if you had such a stark situation, there really wouldn't be a choice. Either you take the hard road or just quit and face a meaningless and possibly self-destructive life. No choice there."

So we got busy with the move, spending a lot of time at my parents' place an hour's drive from New York. There was apartment hunting, and like our Boston experience, Barbara came up with an excellent small apartment on Second Avenue and 39th Street. It was only ten blocks from the office and had a good garage setup, which was hard to find in New York. I bought some new suits and checked out the office arrangement. It was far from ideal except for its central location across the street from Grand Central Station in midtown. My father's two-room office was small and the outer room had to accommodate his secretary/accountant and myself, as well as an occasional part-time typist. The building was in no way easy for a wheelchair. The revolving door at the entrance meant that every time I wanted to come and go, the elevator starter had to unhook the door leaves and fold them back to let me pass—a chore that was often resented. In addition, the bathroom was awkward to get into and had no means for me to have *any* privacy. I had to go home if I wanted to sit on the toilet. This was 1956, and there were no public bathrooms anywhere that were suitable for the disabled. Accessible bathrooms didn't appear until the 1970s and then only sparsely.

By the end of September, we had moved to New York and I had started work. Barbara had done a heroic job getting the apartment organized, unpacked, and very pleasantly usable. At first, I worked only half the day, with Barbara chauffeuring me to and from the office. I'd come home for lunch and then rest in the afternoons—sometimes sleeping as long as two hours. It wasn't long before I was able to increase my hours gradually, and within a year, I was working full-time. Also, in an important breakthrough, I obtained a coveted Special Parking Permit so that I could park in "No Parking" zones. These were only given out to severely disabled full-time workers and students and were closely monitored by the NYPD to avoid abuse. Due to traffic density, there never has been "Handicapped Parking" in New York like that in other cities. With the Permit, it was possible for me to go around town alone, and I began to commute to work solo, a great relief for Barbara. Meanwhile, she had found a part-time job as a physical education teacher at The Brearley School, one of the city's top private schools.

Working for my father proved to be a test of patience, as expected. I started out doing clerical tasks, handling the phone, proofreading, making travel reservations, and doing the odd research assignment. Often without any specific assignment to do, I would undertake extensive menial projects such as reorganizing key client files, which would take days of detailed drudgery. Even in those projects, I did not have a free hand, as my dad needed to be in on exactly how things were set up, including the label system and individual folder wording. I certainly became well grounded in the back-office operation and was learning the consultancy business from the ground up. I was also building up stamina and discovering that I could handle full-time work, as well as learning how to get around the city in a wheelchair and a hand-controlled car. But I yearned for work that was more demanding and interesting. After several years of this and some serious nudging, he began to give me small client projects, including at last some minor research, writing, and editing assignments. It was around that time that I began to feel that I was capable of growing into the business and making a real contribution. Gradually, my father realized this as well. When he gave me an assignment, minor or not, I did it fully and to the same high standards he held himself to. Although he was never one for much praise, I could see that he was satisfied with my performance. Unfortunately, he wasn't paying me even close to the level my peers were getting in advertising or public relations firms. Being of the old school, he was never even open to discussion on pay levels. So there was a mix of frustration and satisfaction on my part. But the main thing was that I was working, I was measuring up, and I was dealing with the physical challenges.

Getting There

When you really stop and think about the specific physical obstacles of meeting the simple day-to-day commitments of a job and personal life out in the normal world alone in a wheelchair, it almost seems impossible. You want to turn over and go back to sleep. Fortunately, I never did think about them in any overall, systematic way. I just started doing things, trying to tackle the obstacles one by one as they came up. First, I had to be able to "get there"—to commute to my office, to get to where I had to be. And second, if I was to work with our clients, I needed to get around the city during the day and sooner or later face the question of traveling to other locations.

Getting around New York for anyone is a challenge—especially so in rush hour or bad weather. The crowds, the noise, the distractions, and the general edginess of all those around you are factors. Virtually everyone is a stranger you'll never see again. Each person has his or her own destination or agenda, and being in a hurry is universal.

After all, this is The Big Apple, where "hustle" is the way it is. And there is the diversity factor with a capital "D." There is a complex mix of races, colors, religions, and languages—rich, poor, and all in between—hustler to haute couture, beggar to billionaire, dishwasher to doyen.

Now when you mix the limitations imposed by getting around in a wheelchair into this equation, it can get really challenging. My offices were within a block of Grand Central Station. This neighborhood was right there in the "mid" of midtown. I often went to clients' offices in other parts of town, though, and personal activities, such as social events, entertainment, parenting, and church, took me to many different destinations as well.

Although my Special Parking Permit let me park in "No Parking" zones, I was still always competing with delivery trucks, idling limos, or the ubiquitous parking violators. After I was parked, there were other hurdles. Curb cuts simply didn't exist and were not mandated until the last few years of my time in the city, and even then installing them was a gradual process. This meant that whenever I had to cross a street, I needed help off the curb on one side and up the curb on the other. If the curb was three-to-four inches in height or less, I could "pop a wheelie" (balance the chair on the two large rear wheels) and jump it. Otherwise, I needed help.

Another problem was getting the wheelchair in and out of the car while sitting in it—not easy, but doable with a three-or-four minute routine I had learned in rehab. On a day of several appointments or meetings, this process would be repeated eight or ten times. Often, instead of the sidewalk, I would be getting out onto the street and into the traffic—sometimes even stopping it if I didn't have enough room. Not all drivers were happy with the wait and blew their horns. I waved to them anyway to shame them into a better attitude. Finally, the doors into building lobbies could get difficult, particularly when they were the revolving type. In that case, I would have to get a volunteer to go inside and get the security guard in the lobby to come and fold back the door panels. Getting from the car seat into the wheelchair, up onto the curb, and then into the building could take as long as ten or fifteen minutes, depending on my parking location. If it was raining or snowing, the difficulty/frustration factor would be intensified. In these scenarios, asking for and receiving a lot of help was simply part of everyday life, so I came in direct contact with a real cross-section of the population, each person with their own attributes and attitudes. Eventually, I sorted them out in my mind into several categories in descending order of their usefulness:

- *Smart, willing, and strong.*
  Waits for instructions. Makes deliberate moves.
- *Dumb, willing, and strong.*
  Needs lots of instructions and close direction.
- *Reluctant, nervous, and in a hurry.*
  Needs coaxing, close watching, and many "just take it easy"s
- *Willing but weak or uncoordinated.*
  Keep an eye out for a quick substitute if things get risky.
- *Too willing, officious, or over-eager.*
  Can be hazardous.
  Many "Wait! Wait! Let me tell you what to do"s
- *Too willing and totally incompetent.*
  Must send away quickly and politely.
- *Avoids eye contact or wants no part.*
  Let him go ("the bastard," I would think).

Of the many thousands of times I was helped over those years, one interesting fact stood out. The people who offered help most frequently and smilingly were people of color or on the lower economic rungs—dishwashers, busboys, squeegee men, shoeshine people, hospital orderlies, messengers, and the like. Keep in mind that I'm visibly more prosperous than they, dressed in a good suit, polished shoes, necktie, with a leather briefcase in my lap. It didn't seem to matter. In a typical experience, I would be at a curbside during a busy lunch hour, trying to catch someone's attention. An African-American bicycle messenger screeches to a stop. "You want some help man?" Hops off his racing bike, locks it to a lamp post, pops me up in a clean "wheelie" onto the curb, unlocks his bike, asks, "You okay now?" And when I gratefully say, "Yes, and thanks a lot!" he replies with a smile, "No problem man"—all this being done with quick, smooth moves. As I would watch him hop on his bike and accelerate into the fractious torrent of midtown traffic, I would try to figure out why this group would be the most helpful. The best I could come up with was this: These people were working poor and probably had difficult lives. They were empathetic with my plight and also could see that I needed help—and probably figured that I didn't live an easy life either whatever clothes I was wearing. I don't think my appearance made the slightest difference to them. I call it the "You're a brother" factor. The same theory could probably be attributed to the many homeless men who also seemed eager to help. They were down and out, but here was someone that even they could help.

The most bizarre experience I ever had involved a very hard-of-hearing man. Sitting in my front seat getting ready to leave a curbside, I was about to tip my folded wheelchair back on its rear wheels on the sidewalk to balance the front wheels on the outer edge of the floor behind the front seat. Then I was going to slide across the seat, fold down the back of the driver's seat, and pull the chair into the well in front of the rear seat. To the observer, this looks awkward and difficult. It isn't easy, true, but I had done it thousands of times. When people offered to help, typically I would say, "Thanks, I really appreciate it, but I'm all set. Thanks again." (I wouldn't want this person put off by being rudely turned down because the next disabled

Bruce McGhie

86

person might desperately need his help.) The reason I turned down help for this tricky maneuver is that it was very hard to instruct anyone else in getting it right, and too many folks would just barge ahead and get it wrong.

In this particular episode, I was approached by a sixty-ish man who didn't heed my wish to do it myself. He said "That's OK," and proceeded to grab the handles of the chair and try to jam it into the back. It wouldn't fit that way, and seeing that he was determined to keep going at it, I pleaded, "No! Stop! Let me tell you how to do it if you insist on doing it." He kept at it, seemingly oblivious, pulled the stuck chair out, turned it around, and forced it in backwards, as I gave up resistance. Then I saw the problem. He had a big hearing aid in his breast pocket, and the wires leading to the earpieces had got tangled in the chair handles and had pulled them out of his ears. No amount of shouting would work. He proudly exclaimed, "There you are." I had given up totally, but realizing his good intentions mouthed, "Thank you." He smiled, waved cheerfully, and headed down the sidewalk. Passersby had stared at this comic Keystone Cops "adventure-in-disability" and walked on. As soon as he rounded the corner, I wrestled the chair out of the car, turned it around, and put it in the right way. I closed the door, chuckled at the absurdity of the scene, started the car, and drove off.

Proving that even friends can sometimes be less than helpful, one of my regular lunch buddies and a long-time friend was pushing me back to my office one day. The sidewalk on our block was slightly downhill, and he was behind holding the handles of the chair. Suddenly, I began to pick up speed rapidly. He had let go with the idea that as I steered myself down the incline, he could come up next to me to make talking easier. The trouble was, he hadn't told me that he was letting go; so I wasn't holding the handrails on the wheels to control the speed and to steer. I picked up speed rapidly, still oblivious, and within a few seconds veered over to the edge of the curb going quite fast and struck a glancing blow along the side of a parked limo, nearly frightening the half-asleep driver to death. No damage was done because I hit the car's protective side strip. I stopped the chair as my friend came running up. We apologized to the driver for this seeming DUI wheelchair incident and laughed about it ever after. My friend claims he just assumed I would know that he let go. It was lucky the limo was there because I could have been seriously hurt had I tipped off an open curb onto the street.

Weather is always a much bigger problem in a wheelchair than if you are ambulatory. You can't hurry. You can't use an umbrella. Raincoats are a bitch to get on and off. Your hands slip on the wet wheel rims. Other people (your potential helpers) are in a hurry and are more reluctant to stop. Occasionally, you just had to accept that you were going to get soaking wet regardless, and I kept a bath towel in the car to dry off as best I could. Snow is practically impossible because your wheels spin. I don't know how many times some wise guy would pass me as I was having trouble negotiating snow and say, "What you need is snow tires, Buddy." Ha. Ha. But I was determined to get to my work whatever the weather—even if it was extreme. To be sure, the pressure of our consulting practice was always there, and I wanted the office to be covered even if others couldn't make it in. Another thing was the challenge I would put to myself: "I am not going to let the wheelchair keep me from being competitive, period." But it took planning and extra effort.

The following scenario happened several times with slight variations. A heavy snowstorm would be forecast, and it would be accumulating rapidly in the evening. My problem would be that when I got to work in the morning, the snow would be piled so high on the sidewalk where I parked that I wouldn't be able to open the door tight to the curb, much less put out the wheelchair, get in it, and push into the office building.

So at 9:00 or 10:00 that evening, *i.e., the night before*, I would get my son John, then a teenager, to "ride shotgun" with me to my office location—deserted at that hour. He would then shovel off the sidewalk and the edge of the street at the corner where I would hope to park the next day. Then I would head back home for the night. Leaving very early in the morning, perhaps at 6:00, I aimed to get to that spot before delivery trucks could usurp the place. Snow would have fallen during the night, but I could open the door, and using a shovel or a brush, make a clear place to hike out the chair. The corner spot had an added advantage. No one could box me in from behind, and I would have a clear shot at getting out into traffic going home without getting stuck. The other trick in a snowstorm was to avoid any narrow streets that could get tied up by one immobile vehicle. The wider streets were always better plowed. The system worked. I missed very few snow days, and I never got stuck. But I certainly was vulnerable to being stranded (there were no cell phones in those days).

Early in the disability game, I learned something about getting help. Trying to prove something by doggedly insisting on doing everything by myself was counterproductive. Asking for help and accepting help when needed got me to places and made possible experiences and achievements that would never have been possible had I tried them alone. I've had an interesting and experiential life due in large part to the extraordinary amount of help I've received along the way.

Much of it was on the streets of New York City.

There was, however, one incident in the city that put a brief kink in my normally jovial relationship with Barbara. It was a cold wintry Sunday afternoon in New York, and we decided to go to the movies at the Beekman Theater, where they featured good first run foreign films and classic reruns. As we drove out of the garage, Barbara pointed out, "You're very low on gas." True, the meter was down, but not quite all the way. I replied, a little annoyed, "Not to worry, I take care of these things, and trust me, we have plenty for a 20 or 30 block round trip." So we headed for the show and found a spot right in front of the theater where I could park with my handicap permit. The movie was great (something by Woody Allen, I recall), and we emerged into the bitter wind at twilight and got into the car— Barbara putting the chair in (one of the few people I allowed to do it because she did it so fast and well). I started the car to warm it up to get the heater going. It died. I tried again. It died. We were out of gas, sure enough, and sitting in the cold. She had been absolutely right, and I had been dumb to ignore her advice.

There was a period of silence before Barbara, furious, said, "I knew it! I knew it! Now what are we going to do?" Well, there aren't a lot of gas stations on New York's Upper East Side and most are closed on Sundays, particularly late in the afternoon. But I knew of a station maybe five blocks south on Second Avenue that might be open. Of course, since I couldn't possibly go for gas, she got out of the car, very quiet and angry, and headed off to see if she could buy a couple of gallons to get us going. Meanwhile I was kicking myself for getting us in this mess and feeling helpless because I couldn't personally extricate us from the situation. It was cold in the lifeless car as the time slowly ticked by. She returned in about 25 minutes, shivering, with a two-gallon gas can. We were lucky the place was open. Now, the next scene was played out under the bright lights of a theater marquee with people coming in and out as the show changed. So, we had an audience. There I was sitting in the driver's seat looking perfectly normal, as my wheelchair was not visible, and here was my attractive wife struggling to gas up the car in the cold wind. They must have wondered: "What kind of a hopeless jerk is that in the car?"

Things got worse. The gas cap was set into the vertical side of the fender, four-plus inches back from the outer surface. So when she tried to pour gas out of the can, which had no spout, only a screw top, it wasn't making it into the tank. It was spilling on her feet and ruining her nice shoes. This was getting really bad. I saw a drug store across the avenue and, thinking they might have a glass funnel for medical purposes, suggested she try that option. Reluctantly, she did so, in desperation. But I knew we were running out of options and probably were going to have to abandon the car for me to deal with in the morning—when I should be focusing on the backlog of work that I knew would be at the office. As I was stewing, I had another drugstore idea, which I thought was just too crazy. Then my eye fell on an old theater Playbill program stuck above the visor and had a bright idea. Barbara returned with a small funnel, which only resulted in more gas on her shoes. While waiting, I had rolled up the program to make a crude funnel-spillway device.

I got out of the car into my chair, realizing it would be impossible for her to pour and hold the "funnel" at the same time. So, I held it while she poured. The gas was still spilling—now on both of our shoes—but a lot was getting into the tank. Finally, we emptied the can after perhaps a gallon-plus had made it. I climbed in, and we drove to the gas station to fill up. So all was OK—except of course for Barbara's steely silence, the stained shoes, the acrid smell of spilled gas, and the spoiling of a nice afternoon. To break the mood, I told her about the crazy idea I'd had: "Listen," I said, "You could have gone back to the drugstore and bought an enema bag. We could have filled it with gas, attached it to that little sidewalk tree next to the fender, inserted the tube into the gas pipe, undone the clamp, and let it go right into the tank." (All the while with the theatergoers watching!) The silence continued for a while. Then came her hearty trademark laugh, and she said, "Very funny." I apologized for all the hassle, stupidity, etc., etc., which she readily and smilingly acknowledged, nodding her head. By the time we got to the end of the block, the whole episode was history and we were back to normal. But, it has since survived in the family lore.

The fact was that she had been great to see it through as she did, doing the things I couldn't do, keeping her cool in an embarrassing situation, and ultimately being a good sport about it. It was vintage Barbara. Since then though, I have seen to it that we have never even come close to running out of gas in the several decades of our marriage. By the way, that enema bag idea actually would have worked. I know it.

About three years into my job, something unexpected came up in the business, and I found myself facing that inevitable need to travel to another city—for the first time since my injury. My father had gotten an important new client, Kimberly-Clark Corporation, whose headquarters were in Neenah, Wisconsin. He was out there trying to get out their annual report under extreme deadline pressure while still meeting other clients' needs on work that was in progress before the K-C business came along. He called saying, "Bruce, I'm having real difficulties trying to do all this alone. Is there any way you can get here to pitch in? I really need some help." He gave me the name of the best motel in town. I said I'd get back to him promptly, but that I needed to figure if and how I could do it.

I called Barbara at home because I knew I couldn't do it alone. There were barriers where I'd need help from her (like getting up the step into the motel room, which was a standard obstacle everywhere then) or for her to get help from someone else (like finding the handyman to remove the bathroom door because all such doors were too narrow for wheelchairs in those days). We'd have to drive in order to have a car when we got there. We worked out the mileage from the office atlas at about a thousand miles—at least two days of driving one way, given that the Interstate System we all take for granted today was nowhere near complete then. The longest we had driven before was the 500-plus miles to my parents' cottage in Maine. True to form, she was game, even though she'd be at loose ends out there while I was working. This was on a Thursday. We could leave sometime Friday and be there comfortably for me to start working on Monday, barring any major problems on the trip. I called my father and told him to his great relief to expect me Sunday at the motel. We set out the next day on what was a pretty adventurous trip for a quadriplegic and his wife in the days when you rarely saw anyone in public in a wheelchair (unless you were near a VA hospital), much less traveling 1,000 miles on business.

Due to a late start, we only covered about 300 miles the first day, getting as far as central Pennsylvania. The motel wasn't easy for the usual reasons, but we got through the night. The next day we decided to try to make it all the way to Neenah to avoid another challenging night like that. We made it to Neenah in the early evening, quite pleased with ourselves and collapsed into bed exhausted.

We rested Sunday, and I plunged into the work at K-C's head-quarters Monday. I was able to take over a lot of the detail work that was getting my father bogged down, and after a few days he began to be confident that he would meet his deadlines both for K-C and the other clients. We worked fast and effectively as a team. Once I had learned the basics of his work in the first year or two, I had picked up the important skills quickly. We had the same standards and communicated well as boss and assistant, so we didn't need to waste a lot of time on discussion. Later, when I was to take up major research and writing assignments for him, it was much more demanding.

The hard part of this first trip was the physical side. Everything then was just so much tougher in a wheelchair. Two examples: The carpeting in Kimberly-Clark's executive offices where we worked was deep and I'm sure quite comfortable to people's feet. But to me, it was sheer hell. It made pushing three times harder and because of the varied directions of the fiber, it was impossible to push in a straight line. After a few yards, I would simply have to stop and rest. Then there was the bathroom in the motel. I couldn't get my knees under the sink; so I was basically trying to shave at arms length, sidesaddle, with no mirror to look at because it was placed for standing up folks. And try washing or combing your hair in these circumstances. Showers or baths were impossible. Likewise, getting to the toilet was often a tricky (and dangerous) transfer because I couldn't get the wheelchair close enough. Over the years, I learned or devised methods to get around most of these issues, and I never gave up a trip because I knew the bathroom was going to be difficult. Somehow you find a way. But even today, when handicapped accessible bathrooms are available, many are poorly designed and are only good for certain disabilities.

Barbara had a tough time with not much to do in Neenah, a pleasant but very quiet small Wisconsin city. Fortunately, her cousin Gertrude lived there and they spent some time together, which she enjoyed. But she most remembers the scare she had one afternoon as a severe tornado watch was issued (it was that time of year) when she was alone at the motel. It touched down in a nearby county to everyone's relief. I was hard at work in K-C's contemporary climate controlled-headquarters and oblivious to the whole episode. She had been a great help as my support system, and we had had a fun time in many ways. My work for my father was finished by the weekend, and we headed back to New York with his gratitude, some travel lessons learned, and another notch up on the confidence scale. In fact, I had gained enough experience so that from that time forward, virtually all of my business trips were done solo.

My first taste of air travel came a year or two later when a similar situation arose with my dad again needing help coping alone with a new client while trying to meet prior commitments as well. This time, though, he was in Lewiston, Idaho, which would have taken five driving days to get there. Flying was the only way to go. It was the early 1960s then, and it's hard to imagine today how difficult airline travel was then for the disabled. Today, most commercial flights include at least one or two people who need wheelchairs, often many more. It's taken for granted. Some are like me and use a chair all the time in their daily lives. Others just use them for boarding and getting around the airport. Airlines must now provide this service by law.

When I started out this first trip, there was no such law, and hard as it may be to believe today, United Airlines was the only major airline that would accept wheelchair users. This made things very difficult. Nothing less than extreme bullheadedness, imagination, patience, charm, and guile were needed if you wanted to get somewhere by air, as will become obvious as I describe this trip.

My father's new client was Potlatch Forests, a large lumber and paper manufacturer headquartered in Lewiston, Idaho, very near the eastern border of the state of Washington, about 125 miles south of Spokane. In a major breakthrough that year, Avis was inaugurating the rental of hand-controlled cars, which meant that once at my destination airport, I would be able to get around independently. Their supplier of hand controls was the same as mine, so I assumed I would have no difficulty in driving the car.

The idea was to fly from New York to Spokane, rent the car and drive to Lewiston. Northwest Airlines had a direct jet flight from New York with only one stop in St. Paul. Perfect, I thought (I hadn't known yet that United was the only option). But reservations said they don't take people in wheelchairs. "Why not?" I asked. "Well our insurance doesn't cover us for that." I protested, and the agent put me on hold to talk with the supervisor. After a long wait, she came back on the line and said that they would book me only if I hired an ambulance and two aides to board me in New York and I'd have to have the same setup in Spokane for the de-boarding. "No way. No thanks," was my response. God, I was mad.

My only chance was United, but they had no direct service to Spokane, except for a commuter-type flight from Portland, Oregon, with many stops. Plus, they had no direct jet flights from New York to Portland. But they did have a non-stop jet to Seattle and suggested going from there to Portland and then taking the commuter flight to Spokane. This would take two days and would involve a lot of boarding, de-boarding, and extra hassle. But I was glad that there was at least a way, convoluted as it was, and bought a ticket. I also reserved a hand-controlled Avis car in Spokane. No guts, no glory.

One of the complicating factors then was that all the airlines were gradually transitioning to pure jets from propeller-powered airliners. Most airports didn't have jetways, so getting on and off could be awkward. But United, to their great credit, had a consistent system at every airport they served. If there was no jetway, you were wheeled out onto the tarmac next to the boarding stairs. There, a forklift truck equipped with a special platform for chairs raised you up to the plane entrance and in you went—always windblown, and also soaking wet if it was raining.

Once, I talked with one of the managers to thank him for letting us wheelchair guys fly and handling us with safety and consideration. "Listen," he said, "it's company policy to take anyone who wants to fly, within reason. You're one type of unusual passenger, but we also take orchestras and their instruments in the cabin—think of five bass fiddles or, say, tubas. We take sports teams and their equipment, you name it. Your money is as good as anyone else's, we fill empty seats, and we don't have to put on extra staff." It was good business, and the policy earned United an intensely loyal group of customers among the few handicapped who were flying in those days.

My leg from New York to Seattle on the regular jet was not without incident. It is standard procedure to take the wheelchair passengers off after the other passengers have left. On this trip, after we arrived at Seattle and my time came, the chair was brought up from the baggage compartment with damage. One of the foot pedals was in three pieces. Something in the hold must have jammed it hard. The agent responsible for getting me off was upset. "I'm so sorry sir. I don't know how we can help you. Can you get another part?" His other problem was that he had to get the flight emptied so that the plane could be prepared for its next trip.

I saw that a bolt had been sheared, which accounted for the separation, but also that one of the shafts had been bent as well. Sizing things up, I suggested that the best thing was to get me and the busted chair up to the waiting area, where we could assess the damage away from the cramped space of the cabin. This was managed awkwardly but safely. Closer examination showed that it might be temporarily fixed without getting a new part, which would have been impossible to obtain on short notice anyway.

I asked the worried agent if there was a mechanic down on the flight line who could be spared for a few minutes. He had one up shortly. The man was instantly recognizable as a leathery, experienced "grease monkey" of the old school, who probably learned his trade in the military, WWII or Korea. Just as I had hoped, he was used to "bailing wire" solutions. He disappeared and was back with a new bolt of about the right size, duct tape, and some tools. He had everything unbent and usable in about ten minutes. "Now young fella, I think that'll hold and it don't look too ugly. Agent tells me you're going to Portland tomorrow morning. If anything goes wrong with this, just gimme a holler because I'll be on duty. Good luck now." He handed me a piece of paper with his name written out on it and was gone. In those days, "flying the friendly skies of United" wasn't just an advertising slogan.

Very early the next day, I was at the airport for the first leg of my nomadic—you could say quixotic—journey to Spokane. Up on the truck lift and into my seat for an hour or two flight south to Portland. No jets on this route. It was a Douglas DC-4, a reliable four-engine transport plane that was made famous by its use as the main freighter in the historic Berlin Airlift. After landing in Portland, out came the forklift for the de-boarding and then back up into another DC-4 for a three-stop trip to Spokane. This was going to be a long, long day.

I have always loved to fly—in anything. Although this was a difficult journey, the sounds, smells, and sights of traveling in this wonderful big old workhorse of a plane were unforgettable. When the four Pratt & Whitney R-2800 engines were started, a total of five times on the trip, first the huge propeller blades of the outboard left engine began turning slowly around against the complaining whine of the starter motor. Then the engine would catch, cough once or twice in a cloud of noxious smoke, then fire up in a roar—rough at first but quickly settling down—all 18 cylinders. At that exact moment, the next engine would take the stage for the same gruff reawakening—followed in turn by the last two. By that time, conversation was impossible because of the noise and vibration. This was no cream puff jet engine startup. Rather, the big muscular bird had noisily brought itself to life, shaken its feathers, and was ready to claw its way into the sky. On to Berlin!

Since there was no pressurization, we flew at 12,000 feet or less. The bad news was I was in for a turbulent ride in the rising thermal air. The good news was that in the old DC-4s the windows were about three times the size of today's jets. So I was treated to a slow moving carpet of the fascinating topography and rural scenes along the picturesque Columbia and Snake River valleys—farms, vineyards, forests, sawmills, barges, grazing cattle and sheep, and much else.

Finally, after sitting in the same seat for three legs of the trip, through three sets of landings, de-boardings, aircraft-servicings, boardings, and takeoffs—the last one from Walla Walla—I was relieved when the engines were shut down for good in front of the small terminal at Spokane Airport. As the pilots came down the aisle, I recall them saying something like, "You still here? You don't give up easy, do you?" Out came the forklift, and in minutes I was in the terminal. It had been roughly eight hours of stop-and-go, up-and-down flying since that morning. Had I been able to fly direct on one of the many flights from Seattle, it would have been two hours or so and no hassle. All those flights were Northwest, which of course didn't accept wheelchair passengers.

But there was a problem at the Avis counter. The anxious agent said, "I'm sorry, sir, the hand controls didn't come until an hour ago, and the mechanic is installing them. They're new to him, and he is not sure about some things. Could you go and have a look?" This I did. He was concerned about the adjustments and the general safety of his installation. This was my first exposure also to rental controls. So, after a very careful examination, a few tweaks, and a test run around the parking lot, I signed off on them.

Now for the last lap—120 miles south to Lewiston, Idaho. When I got out on the open road, a well-maintained two-lane highway, I became more and more interested in the country I was passing through. It was late afternoon, and a retreating line of thunderstorms had just been through, setting up a dark sky as background to beautiful farm country just washed in heavy rains and now glistening in the bright glow of late sunlight. Every hilltop I crested revealed a new vista of rolling fields of golden winter wheat stalks after harvest. Large John Deere tractors in their trademark bright green were plowing the stalks under to make ready for the next planting. Revealed under the plows was the richest deep brown earth I had ever seen. What a palate of color. And to complete the bucolic scene, small clusters of neat farm buildings set in poplar stands were tucked into the washes between the hills. I learned later that this area was called the Palouse Section and was known to be among the richest farmlands in America. It certainly was one of the most beautiful.

Traveling south, the Palouse comes to an abrupt and eye-filling end. After an hour and a half, I crested yet another hilltop, this time to a view of the broad Snake River valley, whose floor was 3,000 feet below me. You could see for 100 miles in every direction ahead. At the end of the steep, switchback road in front of me was Lewiston, Idaho, my destination. An hour later, I checked wearily into my hotel.

I was in the West all right. I had made it solo. But I didn't expect to feel as though I had ridden on a stagecoach for two days.

Air travel gradually got easier as jets became the predominant equipment and jetways at airports were standard. No more forklifts in the rain. Although for a guy in a wheelchair, there always seemed to be some challenge to deal with.

In the mid-1970s, a very busy time for our consulting firm, I took on as a client a well-known construction equipment company with headquarters in Milwaukee. My work for them required me to be there every six weeks or so for several days, sometimes as long as a week. I would fly from New York's La Guardia Airport on a Northwest Airlines direct flight (this was 12 or 15 years later than those early days when Northwest wouldn't accept wheelchair passengers). It was a 6:30 p.m. flight, which worked well for me because I could get in a full day's work in New York, have dinner on the plane, and be ready for an early start the following day after a good night's sleep in Milwaukee.

These trips were never easy, particularly in the winter, because Milwaukee is famous for its abundant snow and bitingly cold and damp winds coming in off Lake Michigan. Pushing a wheelchair in snow and wind can be difficult, sometimes impossible.

On one of these trips during January, I ran into a problem. All went well until our arrival in Milwaukee. Since wheelchair people are always the last to be de-boarded, I waited in my seat. But after 10 or 15 minutes without my chair being brought up from the baggage compartment, I began to be concerned. The flight attendant didn't know what the delay was and queried the gate agent. Finally, a tall man in a red blazer carrying a hand-held radio appeared.

"Sir, I am the gate agent supervisor for this airline in Milwaukee, and it seems we have a problem: Your wheelchair was not on board your flight. We have done a total search of our baggage system here. It's not in Milwaukee and we're sure it was not transferred to another flight."

I was dumbstruck at first, which quickly turned to anger. "This is very serious for me. I'm here on business, and I can't go anywhere without my chair." He was all apologies and quickly said, "But you'll be all right sir. We have our own chairs here on the ramp. You can take one of them. Then when we find your chair, we will bring it to your location in the city."

"No, that won't work," I said. "I must have my own chair, which is custom-fitted for my needs. For me to use one of your chairs would be like you spending the day walking around in someone else's shoes. You have to locate my own wheelchair, period."

"But sir, that will take time. We don't know how long. They're making calls now. You can wait in one of our chairs."

"I'm not moving until you tell me where my chair is."

He left looking resigned, and I sat there in my first-class seat in the now empty airplane, which was through for the night. A rather unhappy but understanding flight attendant was required to stay with me. After a long half hour, the agent returned. They had found my chair. It was still at La Guardia Airport in New York! Apparently, after they had boarded me, the chair had been taken down the ramp stairs and left for the baggage crew to load into the hold. The chair's wheel brake must not have been engaged because the wind caught it and blew it along the tarmac until it came to rest at some other airline's ramp 50 or 60 feet away. No one noticed, and our plane took off without it.

"The problem is, sir, that there are no more direct flights from New York to Milwaukee until tomorrow. We can have your chair for you then."

"But there must be some way," I insisted, not yet ready to give in." What about some other airline? What about some other route? Look, I'll get into your chair and wait in the lounge out of the way while you keep trying. There has to be a way. Try anything. It's important. I'll wait."

He arranged for me to de-board to the lounge area and then disappeared again. The airline chair was a terrible fit, and I was all slumped over. But at least I had my own custom cushion to sit on, so I wasn't too uncomfortable.

About 20 minutes later, he returned, looking more cheerful. "We've got your chair on a Northwest flight to Chicago. It should get there in time for the last commuter flight to Milwaukee." At last, a ray of hope!

"Great," I said." But how can we be sure the chair will make the switch in Chicago? Do me a favor. It's an unusual case, and there could be a screw-up. Can you call a Northwest agent at Chicago and get him to take personal responsibility for meeting the incoming flight and making the wheelchair switch?" I knew I was asking a lot, but he seemed resolved to see things through. He went back to his office and returned in a few minutes saying that an agent had been assigned to personally make the switch.

I told him I would sit tight there at the Milwaukee airport until the chair arrived. He looked at me disbelieving. "But," he said, looking at his watch, "it will be at least three hours before your chair will get here. That would be midnight, earliest. Don't you want to go to your hotel?"

"No. I have to have my chair first. I'll be all right. Don't worry about it." He seemed relieved, but was reluctant to leave me on this remote empty concourse alone. Wouldn't I like to go to the main concourse where there are people around if I needed anything? I agreed, and he pushed me there. On leaving, he said he would soon be going off duty but would have the senior agent check in with me every hour. It was then about 9:00 p.m. local time. Before he left, I asked for his card and thanked him for following through on the chair. I assured him that my anger and stubborn attitude were nothing personal. "Sometimes, I just dig in my heels out of frustration and the need to get where I'm going." He said he understood.

My meetings the next day were to start at 9:00 a.m., but I had been too busy with other commitments in New York to prepare for them. So my plan had been to get to bed early in Milwaukee and get up at 5:00 a.m. to do the preparation. Now I had three hours to kill while stuck in the airport, so I went to work on preparing for the next day. Time went quickly.

At around 11:00 p.m., the duty agent let me know that the chair had arrived OK in Chicago and had made it to the commuter plane. At 12:15 a.m. or so, it finally arrived. I transferred into it to my great relief—fully viable again. I thanked all hands profusely and headed for the cab stand.

A few days later I wrote the Northwest Airlines CEO to praise the Milwaukee agent supervisor's response to the foul-up, giving his name. I hope he got due credit because he had been very patient with my irate and demanding attitude and had gone way out of his way to get a difficult situation resolved. Quite a contrast to Northwest's 'no-wheelchair' policy of the 1960s. Progress!

It's a fair statement to say that travel got easier over the years. But it was never "easy" in a wheelchair. Consider these adventures during one of my many trips to Los Angeles.

As one who lived for 25 years in New York—which is not everyone's favorite city—I'm in no position to find fault with Los Angeles. You just had to get used to the monotonous sprawl, the smog, the slower pace, and being a slave to the culture of the car and the freeway. What I did like though were those beautiful days in the winter when it was warm, dry, and clear with the Santa Ana winds blowing the air pollution offshore. And I liked the quirky people, the variety of types and attitudes that one just didn't come across on the streets of New York and certainly not in New England, where I grew up. Maybe it was the movie business, maybe it was the climate, maybe just the more laid-back nature of people in California. Whatever it was, L.A. was an enjoyable place for me.

In the 1970s and early 1980s, I was there two or three times a year on business, where I worked with a good team of graphic designers, typographers, and printers to produce one of our corporate annual reports. Surprisingly, I found that I could get higher quality results for less than in New York, which more than made up for the extra cost of being 3,000 miles away. I would fly out and spend two or three days in meetings on creative and production matters.

On one trip, I had a dinner engagement scheduled for the day I arrived. There was plenty of time because my flight got into LAX at 3:30 or so. But when my chair was brought up from the hold, it had a flat tire—one of the large wheels. When I got up to the concourse, there was no agent free to push me and, being in a perverse mood, I decided that I would push to baggage claim on my own. Bad idea. It was a manual chair and it was really hard as it took a lot more effort and pulled to one side with the flat tire. My arms were aching by the time I got halfway down the long corridor, perhaps 200 yards, to the main concourse. But dammit, I had decided to do it solo, and I was going to do it. It didn't help my mood that people kept going by saying things like, "Hey, buddy, do you know you have a flat tire?" Duh!

I finally got my luggage and went outside. But what to do? It was Friday afternoon about 4:15—not much time left in the working day. The weekend was coming up. I had to get the tire fixed. There was a phone booth nearby, but as usual, the phone book was not reachable.

So I got a volunteer to hold it for me as I searched for some medical equipment store that dealt with wheelchairs. My helper also had to feed coins into the phone and dial for me (this was long before there were accessible public phones or cell phones). I finally found a store that was open. But it was in the Lakewood section, 15 plus miles southeast in the opposite direction from where I was eventually headed, which was Century City, to the north. But the technician at the store was sympathetic to my plight and promised to wait for me past closing time.

I hailed a cab, and we were on our way, except that at that hour, the San Diego Freeway was jammed solid. So we plunged into the vast flat sea of strip malls, small stucco houses with chain link fences and a palm or two, stoplights by the dozen, fast food emporiums, gas stations, and used car lots. But he knew his way, and 45 minutes later we were there. I stayed in the cab while the technician, a smiling Hispanic, took my chair into the store. He was out in ten minutes with my tire as good as new and showed me the carpet tack that had been the culprit. The bill was something like $20, and I gave him an extra $20 for waiting the 45 minutes. He wouldn't accept it, though, and was adamant despite my entreaties. So he got my profuse thanks and God's blessing for his trouble, and we drove off with me marveling at how often bad things can turn into good things.

Now, on to Century City. At 5:30, the traffic was even worse, and a twenty to twenty-five mile ride took a solid hour or more. Although I was late for my dinner date, it all worked out.

The Century Plaza Hotel in Century City was where I stayed when in Los Angeles. It is a complex of office buildings, upscale stores, restaurants, and a hotel built on what had been the main lot and studios of 20th Century Fox, which were just south of Beverly Hills. Excellent for wheelchairs, the complex made it easy for me to stay in a good hotel and have some freedom to shop, eat out, and even go to movies without taking a cab.

I believe the hotel was one of the first to make a sizable open cocktail lounge the centerpiece of the main lobby. In this case, it was a large sunken space furnished with couches, coffee tables, and roll-around armchairs so that parties could be flexibly grouped or just one or two people could set a space to have a quiet drink. Large potted palms were the main decor, and there was always a pianist playing show tunes or other favorites on the piano. Very pleasant, indeed. I routinely enjoyed a drink there before dinner. But since I couldn't get down into the sunken area, I would sit at one of the half-dozen tables for two that were located above, overlooking the lounge on the back side. Behind these was a 100-foot glass wall facing west, consisting of numerous tall windows at least thirty feet high. When the sun streamed in, vertically hanging curtains were let down; but when it set, the curtains were raised to reveal the fading twilight and lighted fountains in a garden.

The main attraction wasn't the Hollywood-like setting. It was the people who gathered there for cocktails. To be sure, a lot were traveling business-people like myself, but there was also an abundance of movie and show-business types who came and went. Over here would be half-a-dozen people hunched over a table with drinks and cigars appearing to be going over a script or contract. Over there would be some slick looking dude talking intimately with a gorgeous blond. Occasionally, some person alone would sip a drink watching the lobby door, looking often at his or her watch—and sometimes, disappointed when no one came, pay the check resignedly, and leave. Now and then, you would see a celebrity or someone that looked so familiar that you must have seen them in some film. Then you would see a wide variety of international types: Asians in saris and turbans, many Japanese business people, and well-to-do Africans in native garb. The attractive waitresses all looked to be either movie hopefuls or ones who hadn't made it. Beyond this was the main lobby with all the comings and goings. All in all, having a quiet drink and a dish of peanuts while watching this ever-changing, quintessential Hollywood scene was very entertaining.

Once, however, it was I who provided the entertainment, if you could call it that. While sitting there reading the newspaper and watching the passing scene, I suddenly felt the wheelchair levitating. Yes, the chair and I were slowly rising! "What the hell is going on?" I thought. The problem quickly became serious because the chair was tilting forward and was still going up—now maybe a foot off the floor. I dropped my newspaper and drink and was holding on to the chair's arms for all I was worth. I think I yelled "Hey!" or maybe it was "Help!" The angle became steeper as the chair continued to rise, and I simply slid out and fell on the carpet, falling on my side. By this time, people had noticed. Somebody screamed, and I was shortly looking up into a circle of worried faces with my chair hanging on the curtain behind their heads. "Are you all right?" "What can I do?" "Here comes security." All this took place in less than two minutes.

Then I understood what had happened. My chair had been against the curtain, and when they started to raise it at sunset (probably with a switch at a remote location), one of the back handles of the chair got hooked in the fabric. Up I had gone in quiet dignity, nicely silhouetted against the sunset. Luckily, I had fallen in such a way so as not to be injured, as far I could tell. They got the chair down, replaced the cushion that had fallen out, picked me up gently, and set me in my chair. At this point, I was laughing. The whole thing was so utterly ludicrous. Security wasn't laughing though. I think they were seeing a big lawsuit coming their way. Actually, it had been a little frightening, and I was no doubt somewhat wound up. I told everyone I was all right. Not to worry. I *really was* OK, and what I needed was a fresh vodka Martini and a new dish of peanuts.

That seemed to ease the atmosphere, and everyone drifted back to their previous places "on the set." In five minutes, all was as before: the buzz of conversation, the rattle of ice in cocktail shakers, and the piano playing a familiar theme from some movie. My second drink was on the house.

By far the most daunting challenges I ever faced in my business travel were overseas during in the 1970s when I made many trips. The U.S was difficult enough, though getting better; but the rest of the world was in no way prepared for the handicapped, especially a quadriplegic traveling alone in a wheelchair.

One business trip was particularly testing. The 28-day plan called for me to fly from New York to Johannesburg with a weekend stopover in Rio de Janeiro. In South Africa, I worked for a week with a partner organization on a continuing investor relations joint venture that we were pursuing. Then, I flew to Paris, taking a break for two or three days to see the Paris Air Show. Next was a visit north of Frankfurt, Germany, to a subsidiary of a client, who manufactured large construction equipment. From there, it was on to Stockholm, Sweden, and then north to Umea near the Arctic Circle, where a paper industry client had just built a large pulp and paperboard mill with a Swedish partner. Finally, I was to return to New York after an overnight stay in Stockholm.

I made seven stops at hotels, and with two exceptions, every bathroom presented some problem to be overcome. Door openings were too narrow, so doors had to be removed. Toilets were often enclosed in small closets—totally inaccessible—each situation requiring an imaginative alternative set-up to be worked out by myself or with the staff (often at the end of a long, busy day). To get to hotel dining rooms, I was occasionally carried up staircases; and I frequently found myself traveling through bustling kitchens and dingy back hallways, as well as being required to use freight elevators to get around. These were good hotels, three of them with "five star" ratings. Imagine if I had been on a more modest expense account and was using the hotels a notch or so lower in facilities and service. On this, as well as most other trips, I rarely saw another wheelchair traveler. It was not surprising.

However, the real crunch on this trip came when I showed up at Frankfurt Airport for my Lufthansa flight to Stockholm. I checked in early at the counter and discussed my special boarding needs and how to deal with the wheelchair. All seemed in order, and I headed for the gate 45 minutes before departure time. On my way, I was met by two female senior agents in Lufthansa uniforms. They said, "Good morning Herr McGhie. We are sorry to inform you that you will not be able to board this flight to Stockholm because your papers are not in order. Due to your situation, you need a medical order from your doctor certifying that your condition is satisfactory for flight and that you will present no difficulty for your fellow passengers. This is a Lufthansa requirement, and we do not find it in your records."

I was stunned. I had to get to Stockholm that day to meet my business commitments. "This is impossible," I replied, "I must board that flight. I have flown Lufthansa before with no such requirement. I have made four flights before to Europe without this problem on any airline. It is imperative that I be on that flight. Please talk to your superiors, and get this straightened out immediately. We don't have much time—now only about 35 minutes," glancing at my watch. They left quickly and got back about five minutes later to say, "It may be possible for you to fly, but our doctor must examine you first in the dispensary. We have arranged it and will take you there now." I was steaming mad but couldn't refuse, and they hustled me down an elevator and through a rabbit warren of corridors and locked doors to the dispensary, where I was immediately ushered in to see the doctor, a competent looking middle-aged woman.

I told her that my reservations, including this flight with Lufthansa, had been made and confirmed well in advance with full notice of my condition and that since they had not objected, I insisted that they had no right to delay me now on this technicality. Then, I gave her a capsule medical history along with information about my previous extensive air travel. She asked a few questions, took my vital signs (probably indicating highly elevated blood pressure due to my frustration), and promptly signed a medical release with an apology for the inconvenience.

My escorts showed up with the news that time had run out, the flight had completed boarding, shut the door, and had been pushed back from the ramp. Again, I demanded to be on the flight since the delay was entirely their fault. After an intercom talk with their supervisor, they said the flight had been stopped on the taxiway and that I would be boarded from the tarmac.

I then went through a bizarre 15 minutes as I was rushed through the highly secured lower floor of the airport (keypads on every door) to a VW minibus waiting in an underpass near the flight line. Heavily armed, unsmiling guards with automatic weapons and flack jackets took over, gave me a full hand frisking, including my seat cushion. (Though this kind of thing has been common practice since 9/11, such measures were rare then. Germany, however, was still reeling from the terror attacks on the Israeli Olympic team at the 1972 Games in Munich.)

Then the ground personnel drove the bus about a quarter mile down the taxiway, where my plane, a Boeing 737, was waiting, engines idling. The door was opened, and I was hand-carried from the vehicle up the stairs by these men without a word and placed in an empty seat being held in the first row of First Class under the watchful eye of a very pretty flight attendant. I checked out the window to see that my chair was being loaded below. Meanwhile, the rest of the passengers—probably confused about the delay, wondering who I could be, and mystified by the whole exercise, including the men in the flack jackets—looked at me as if I had just landed from Mars.

As soon as we were airborne, the flight attendant came by with a warm smile and apologies. Would I like a nice drink, a Bloody Mary perhaps? Then bending over, she whispered, "I make it a double, yes?" I nodded and began to wind down after yet another one of my air travel crises. But I made it to Stockholm on time and had a fascinating first visit to Sweden with no further serious incidents.

Needless to say, I was not immune to incidents traveling in home territory either. Just taking the elevator in my own building could turn out to be adventurous in a wheelchair.

However, this would never have happened if I hadn't gotten into a routine method of taking the elevator. We all get into regular routines. How we get dressed, how we make breakfast, how we get the kids off to school, how we read the newspaper, and on and on through the day culminating in how we get into bed. Since it is a lot more complicated to get through the day if you are disabled, the tendency toward establishing routines seems even more pronounced; at least for me it was. I found myself looking for the simplest methods to handle the smallest repetitive actions.

Take boarding the elevator in my office building in New York. I was on the top floor, the eighteenth, and there were rarely any other people in the car when it arrived. So my routine, particularly later in the day, after five, was to press the button, and when the light came on over the arriving car's door, position myself with my back facing the still closed doors. As the doors drew back, I would roll in backwards, already facing the front of the car with no need to negotiate a 180-degree turn. Made sense. But it didn't on one occasion.

It was Thanksgiving eve one year in the late 1970s. This was a very busy time in my business, when overtime was the norm from November through March as we produced year-end annual reports for several major corporations. I left the office around 6:30 and headed for the elevator and pushed the button. Following my routine, when the doors slid open I started to roll back between them, not looking. As I went over the threshold, I tipped off it into empty space. "My God," I thought, "I'm falling down the shaft!" But there was a sudden hard crash as I hit the elevator car's floor, which had stopped some three feet below my floor level.

When it hit, the wheelchair was tilted back about ninety degrees. The main wheels took the first impact, followed by the push handles up near my shoulders. Then the chair bounced back with my head hitting the rear wall and my briefcase flying off my lap. I was stunned for a second but not hurt as far as I could tell—more surprised and shaken up than anything. My body was still in the chair in a sitting position, albeit lying on my back.

I lay there for a minute to assess the situation. Obviously, I needed some help. At that hour, the night before a holiday, all the offices were empty, but there was a watchman at the main lobby desk. Problem was how to get his attention. The button panel including the red alarm switch and the emergency phone were high up on the front wall of the car (no low buttons for the disabled in those days). There was no way I could right my chair and get up into it much less get high enough to reach the panel. And there was also no way that I could climb up the three feet to the 18th floor lobby. The cleaners had already done our floor, so they would not be around. And shouting for help eighteen floors above the lobby wasn't going to do any good either.

First things first: I needed to sit upright. So I rolled out of the tipped-back chair onto the floor, got out my seat cushion and lifted myself up on it in a sitting position. I had to get at that control panel. It took some time to hike the cushion and me to the front of the car in half-inch increments. I was still too low to reach it. Searching around for an idea, I took off one of the detachable arms of the chair and was about to extend my reach with it and hit the emergency switch when I heard the other elevator door open. Someone had come up in the other elevator.

"Hey! I need some help," I yelled. Silence for a moment, and then to my utter amazement, I heard the voice of my teenage son saying, "Dad?" And then as he peered around into my car, "Holy shit, Dad! What happened?" I told him I didn't know and I was OK, but that the best move right now was to get me out of there before something else happened. A powerful seventeen-year-old, he jumped down, and in less than a minute had loaded me, chair, cushion, and briefcase out of the car up to the 18th floor lobby. Finally, he lifted me carefully into the chair. He was the perfect rescuer because he knew how to make these moves without injuring me or even messing up my suit. He was very concerned, and I had to assure him that I was indeed not hurt.

Never was I happier to see him. Grinning, I clapped him on the back and laughed out loud at this great stroke of luck—a total coincidence as it turned out. He was coming home from school for Thanksgiving and had arrived by train at Grand Central Station at about 6:15. Instead of taking the bus uptown, he came over to my office to see if I was still there so that he could hitch a ride home. He had certainly earned it.

We took the other elevator down and reported this accident to the totally amazed watchman. He couldn't believe that I wasn't injured and furthermore that I wasn't hysterical. To put him at ease, I said, "You know, a person could break their back in that kind of accident." John chuckled at my attempt at dark humor, but the watchman was too upset. He never cracked a smile. This building was a very well managed, upscale location, being the head office of Conde Nast, *Vogue* magazine, *The New Yorker*, and the rest of that publishing empire, located next to Brooks Brothers at 46th and Madison Avenue. Needless to say, they were all apologetic the following Monday.

When I got home, I cleaned up and poured a stiff Scotch. I couldn't help thinking just how serious the episode could have been—various scenarios, all bad. Well, it didn't turn out to be serious, thank God. But I will never forget the terror of that half-second of free fall down what I thought was the elevator shaft—indeed it was the stuff of nightmares.

Being willing and able to travel made a big difference in my business career and in our social life as well. Just showing up in a wheelchair as if it was normal behavior—particularly if it was at some remote location—defied the stereotypical expectation people have when they learn you're disabled. Anytime you can distance yourself from the stereotype is good. I had thought long and hard about trying to compete on an even playing field with normal people in business and also about being accepted in everyday social contexts. I had concluded that the best approach was to make the disability my problem (or our problem if Barbara was with me), not a problem for the other people to deal with.

First, I would take care that my personal appearance was as normal as I could make it (not easy because your clothes don't fit or hang properly when you are perpetually sitting down) and that my grooming was good, shoes shined and all. Too often, I noticed that wheelchair folk let their clothes, the chair itself, and sometimes their personal hygiene go to seed. It's a real turn-off. As for the first contact, my number one priority (soon it became a habit I never even thought about) was to put people at their ease over the wheelchair—some joke or lighthearted remark just thrown in that would say, in effect, "Look, I'm OK with the chair and all that goes with it; so you can be at ease as well." If it was business and I was hired, I would simply arrive in my wheelchair without comment and go to work. The only concession I would ask is that I fly first class, which would be reflected on my expense account. Coach travel really heightened the difficulties, and no client ever questioned my first class travel.

It was always my feeling that if I did good work, was a dedicated professional, and didn't make my disability an issue, it wouldn't be a factor. This proved to be the case to the best of my knowledge (although I never really knew whether I lost any new business on account of the disability because, if so, the prospect would never had said so). In fact, I actually believe that if a handicapped person has the demeanor of a normal person and expects to be treated as one, people take their cue from that self-assurance and treat you as normal. Furthermore, an unexpected plus is that you gain respect simply by the way you deal with the issue, and this enhances rather than decreases your competitiveness in that you stand out somewhat from the crowd.

A good example came toward the end of my business career. In a sense, it was my biggest career victory and emblematic of the other areas. I was able, against long odds, to land the annual report account of Bowater Corporation, the nation's largest newsprint manufacturer. I had heard that they were "demerging" from their British parent company and were going public as an American-based independent. That meant they would need to issue financial reports to the public explaining what they were all about and start building credibility in the U.S. financial marketplace through their public communications. Since I had no contacts at Bowater and no one to introduce me, I wrote them cold. I described our unique services in the field, and asked if I could make a presentation. It was a virtually impossible long shot, at best.

To my surprise, they said yes to my making a presentation even though they had received proposals from two other better-known firms. One was the world's largest PR firm, Hill & Knowlton, and the other a sizable printing company that offered writing and design services to augment their print business. Both were already doing work for the company. Bowater sent a long list of topics I should specifically address concerning their special situation as a big new-comer from overseas to the financial marketplace. So this wasn't going to be a typical off-the-shelf presentation. I did a lot of research and creative work on it under severe time pressure and developed what I thought was a comprehensive response—a personal presentation plus six to eight single-space pages in a written version to be handed out during the meeting. My design colleague, Nathan Garland, thought I was giving away too many ideas before getting the work, and my response was, "Bowater doesn't know me. Unless I give them a 'free sample' of my thinking, how can I beat out the others who are known quantities?"

The only advance notice I gave Bowater that I was wheelchair-bound was when I asked about accessibility to their building. When I rolled into their conference room, there were five people waiting. "Here goes nothing," I thought. "At least I have a good presentation." I made my detailed and deliberate presentation. This was followed by a lot of discussion of my proposals, questions, and thoughtful cross-examination. After an hour and a half, the meeting was over, and I was on my way back to my office. Driving along I thought, "That's the end of that, I suppose, but I gave it my best shot."

The next day, the VP called to say that they had chosen us for the work even though ours was the highest fee and overall cost estimate. I was taken totally by surprise. "Why?" I asked as tactfully as I could. He said, "You were the only one to address all our questions in a thoughtful and creative way. The others made superficial, canned presentations only touching here and there on our questions. As one of my college professors said, 'You can make the most brilliant statements on your exams, ladies and gentlemen, but if you don't answer the questions, you flunk.' You addressed the questions. The other firms flunked." What counted was that I had done my homework and had come forward with workable solutions. The wheelchair, as far as I could see, was not a factor, and I had beaten out some heavy hitters. That began a highly successful ten-year business relationship. This was very satisfying proof that the wheelchair problem tends to go away when you know your business, do good work, and act normally even though you may be disabled—and when you are determined to "just do it" in the Nike slogan sense.

The fact that I have always expected to be treated like a normal person, as in the Bowater case, works in social situations as well as business. Many people have told me that they get so used to the chair, they forget it. I find that hard to believe, but it has happened so often that I guess it must be true.

There was a surprising unintended consequence of my gradual but growing effectiveness as a businessman and managing to do it all as a quadriplegic. It was a family thing. I became quite close to my father-in-law—the man who had bitterly fought Barbara's marriage to me and blasted me with a hurtful letter when I was struggling in the early days of hospital rehab. After we had defied him and her mother and gotten married, he apparently accepted the *fait accompli*, decided not to dwell on it, and put it behind him. Likewise, I did not hold the conflict against him, and over time, we took a liking to one another. He was CFO of a mid-size paper company—very professional, tough-minded, and with strong opinions—but a real straight-arrow and a likeable person. At first, he thought I was foolish to even try to make it with my disability in New York, and he frankly told me so. But of course, I did make it and with some success—and it was in the financial communications business, a vocation with which he was intimately familiar. So my guess is that, as he watched the way I dealt with the obstacles, got around independently, and saw my progress in business, his respect grew. I think he also saw that Barbara and I were making a success of our marriage despite the obstacles. He became fond of our children. As the years passed, we became close and had a very pleasant relationship. He never once admitted that he had been wrong on any count, and I never expected him to. It was just an unspoken thing, but the way it all turned out was very satisfying.

You hear the saying, "Getting there is half the battle." For a man in business in a wheelchair, it was most of the battle. The work itself was not a problem. I enjoyed it except for frequent long hours and the heavy stress that came from deadline pressure, not to mention the competitive nature of our field. We were definitely in "an ulcer business," as my father once said.

There is a magic moment in any enterprise (particularly an innovative one) when it moves from the gestation phase, with all the anxious professional striving, and takes a mature form as an accepted, legitimate service—where business begins to come in from referrals and you can charge decent fees. You never really know for sure, but for our consultancy, that moment happened somewhere in the mid-sixties, about ten years after I had joined my father. We went from not having enough business to having a little more than we could comfortably handle. So we were working very hard and struggling to meet commitments—not actually able to really enjoy the fact of our success because of the pressure. Furthermore, my father was still unwilling to expand out of our cramped office quarters and, stuck in a 1930s mindset, was paying me far below what I should have been getting considering the contributions I was then making and the long hours I was putting in. He began talking about "continuity," which was his code word for retirement, and we started a two-year dialogue about how that should come about.

Because we needed more help and because I knew that when my father retired, I could never handle all the work alone, I suggested we hire my brother Alex, assuming he was willing. At that time, his job didn't appear to be showing much opportunity for advancement. Although we had never worked together, we had always had a good relationship—growing up as kids on a farm, walking to and from school, and playing endlessly, just the two of us (there not being many other children in the neighborhood), and double-dating as teenagers. I had introduced him to the girl he married and was his best man. He had a fine mind, could write well, and had the kind of integrity that was an important requisite to the way we approached our work. Even though we had very different personalities and ways of doing things, I thought we could continue to make the business prosper and grow.

He came on board, and we finally got my father to expand the office space so that we were at least not sitting in each other's laps. This was in 1964, but it wasn't until 1968 that my father finally retired. The financial issue had been the sore point, and he wanted far more from the business in terms of residual financial interest than Alex and I thought was fair. Finally, we told him that we simply wouldn't do it under his terms, and proposed a much more modest package, which he eventually accepted. It was the only time in my life that I completely defied my father. Alex and I took over on January 1, 1969, as equal partners, renaming the business McGhie Associates. We incorporated, and it fell upon me to be named president because of seniority.

Finally, I began to earn closer to what I was worth, and it was a great relief. I believe that first year I made twice my previous year's earnings. The business had come into its own. Although Alex and I set out to modernize its procedures and make the office and our identity more contemporary, there was never any talk of changing my father's brilliant original business plan, which generated highly profitable, repeat business with top companies.

Over the years, we substantially increased the firm's revenues and profitability, making good livings, educating our children, and enjoying comfortable life styles. In 1987, I decided to retire when in my fifties. My rationale was something like this: "Bruce, you're a quadriplegic who has already lived beyond the 'normal' life expectancy for such people. You're still very healthy and have a lot of energy. It's time to do the other things you've wanted to do." Within a few months after retirement, for example, I became an art student at Yale. However, I did get drawn back into business on a part-time basis. My former client, Bowater Incorporated, had hired the celebrated PR firm, Hill & Knowlton, to do the work I had been handling and were very unhappy with the results. They pressured me to come back under favorable terms, and I accepted. Thus I began an eight-year stint as a part-time consultant working out of my home office (putting in probably only about 20 percent of the time I had in the firm). I found this approach both mentally stimulating and highly profitable, and I was able to spend most of my time pursuing many other interests.

TOP | I receive my commision in August 1954.

WOMAN GOLFER WINS HOOP--ROLL—Barbara Bruning, 21, of White Plains, N. Y., former N. Y. State women's golf champion, shown after winning annual hoop-rolling contest at Wellesley College. (Other photos on page 5.)

(Photo by Charles McCormick, Globe Staff)

Harvard Entrants Dunked
Wellesley Golf Champ Wins Famed Hoop Race

WELLESLEY, May 1 — An auburn-haired Wellesley College senior ran off with the honors of the traditional hoop race this morning.

Barbara Bruning, 21, of White Plains, N. Y., won the bride's bouquet by guiding her hoop over the finish line ahead of her classmates. By tradition, she'll be the first girl married after graduation—though she said she's not even engaged yet.

The hoop race isn't the first contest Barbara has won. In 1951, she won the National Intercollegiate Golf Championship; in 1951 and 1952 she won the New York State Women's Golf Championship. She was the youngest girl ever to carry off that title.

At Wellesley, where she's still an enthusiastic golf player, she majors in economics.

Married Wellesley seniors added their distinctive touch to the hoop race by entering—with baby carriages. The 24 pushed the buggies down the hill together with their hoop-rolling pals.

And two dark horses—Harvard men—entered the race, too.

They didn't raise too much excitement, however, for Harvard entries have become a custom at the race. The boys were grabbed and dunked in Lake Waban after the race, however.

Spectators lined the route of the race—from Tower Court Hill to the Chapel on the Wellesley campus—to watch the fun. Among the crowd were almost 300 fathers of sophomores, at Wellesley for the weekend to take part in the eighth annual sophomore Fathers' Day.

ABOVE | Barbara is a winner and an outstanding golfer.

Malcolm McGhie

Scott Hovey

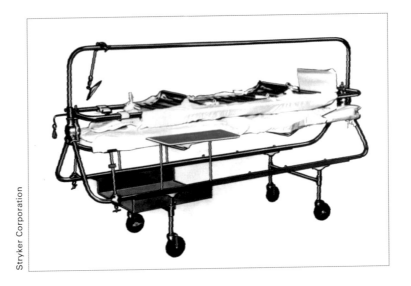

Stryker Corporation

TOP | Tower on the obstacle course, scene of my accident.
BOTTOM | The Stryker Frame—dreaded but life saving.

Alex McGhie

Alex McGhie

TOP | We were married in October 1955.
BOTTOM | With Anne on Thanksgiving 1962.

ABOVE | With Bill Adams, the chairman of St. Regis Corporation, in 1965.

Alex McGhie

Group Editors, Ltd.

TOP | Kite lesson with John in 1971.
BOTTOM | At a meeting in 1972.

Lou Bernstein

Building a Family

The other absorbing challenge that Barbara and I had undertaken in our early years was to see if it was possible for us to have a family. Once I had gotten fairly well established in the business with my father and the prospects seemed favorable for a career in this field, Barbara and I took up the difficult issue of creating a family despite the disability. We knew it would never be an easy process to think about much less implement. But we also knew we had to face it early on while we had the energy and ambition to make it happen if it were possible.

There is an old saying: "The only thing worse than having children is not having children." Unfortunately, one of the consequences of having a spinal cord injury is that having your own children is a long shot. Although sexual performance is greatly diminished, sexuality for many is not entirely eliminated. It's very possible to have enjoyable sexual experiences so long as a positive attitude and sensitivity exist on both sides. However, there is no denying the fact that the full rewards of normal sexual relations are not in the cards. It would have been great to have had today's pharmaceuticals in those days. Conceiving children in a more natural way would have been much more possible.

This aspect of spinal cord injury is not surprisingly one of the toughest challenges faced by the injured person and his or her spouse. Impotency for a man is a deep psychological wound as it goes to the very heart of his maleness, his most basic reason for being, his perception of himself as a man.

Many men with spinal cord injuries have never been able to cope with this loss, which I believe accounts for a lot of the self-destructive behavior I've witnessed in my peers—alcoholism, drug abuse, even suicide.

For their wives, there is not only the absence of normal sexual gratification but also the probability that they will not be able to bear their own children. These, too, are deep psychological hurts because the woman's natural yearning for motherhood and family creation are unfulfilled. Sadly but understandably, these factors account for many divorces and broken relationships among spinal cord injury couples.

Barbara and I were engaged, of course, when I was injured, and facing up to this whole side of our lives then and for the future was one of the hardest issues to confront before we got married. We spent a lot of time talking and thinking about the consequences and got some professional input at that time. Ultimately, we decided to get married with our eyes wide open. We were deeply committed to one another in a loving, solid relationship that was then four years old, and somehow we felt that it was strong enough so that we could deal with the sexuality and family issues as they arose. This in fact proved true, although not without periods of doubt and unhappiness.

The question of having children came alive after about two years of marriage. We had agreed that until we got settled and I got established in some sort of career, we didn't want get serious about children. In the beginning, I had no idea whether I could hold down a job or if in fact I would even have the energy to work a full day. Within two years, my work for my father was going quite well, my health was very good, and I had built up my stamina. I had gotten out into the real world and was discovering that I could get around and be taken seriously in business.

Barbara took the initiative on the idea of children, while I was still dubious about whether we could handle it. Her contemporaries —classmates at college and others—were starting families, and her desire to fulfill the wider promise of marriage by nurturing children was strong. In those days—the mid-fifties—it was the time of the "nuclear family," a far cry from the lifestyles of the succeeding three or four decades. My doubts centered on my long-term viability as a bread-winner and whether, being in a wheelchair, I could adequately fulfill the role of being a father. Then, of course, there was the impotency obstacle. We went back and forth on the whole topic and in time concluded that we should proceed and see where things led—a "go for broke" kind of thing. We didn't want to be looking back 20 years later with regret, thinking that we may have deprived ourselves of having children and a broad and fulfilling family experience.

Since we were unable to conceive children on our own despite drawing on the best expert medical advice available at the time, it even-tually became clear that adoption was our only chance. Adoption in those days, just as it is today, was intensely competitive. There are a lot more options available for would-be adoptive parents now, such as babies from overseas, and the rules are looser. But it's much more expensive, and it seems a permanent condition that there are always many more couples wanting children than babies available.

The fact that I was disabled was, of course, a major competitive disadvantage. In the 1950s and earlier, there was a stigma attached to disabilities that was completely at odds with the attitudes we are used to today. There was no Americans with Disabilities Act. Curb cuts, ramps into buildings, and equal-opportunity employment simply didn't exist—and these things weren't even on the horizon then. Our friends thought it would be impossible for us to adopt because I would be considered unable to fulfill a normal role as a parent. But our approach had always been to try to overcome the wheelchair obstacles, and we'd had considerable success in doing so. We thought, "Let's just ignore the obvious and go ahead as if the problem didn't exist." Sometimes, if you're bold enough, you get taken seriously. Furthermore, we elected to approach one of the two top agencies in the country, where the competition would be toughest. All they could do is turn us away. Our feeling was that if they were as good as their reputation, they might even have a more enlightened view of the disability factor. Then if that failed, we would move down to the next level. No guts, no glory.

The agency we chose had a reputation for making every effort to find a baby whose natural parental background was similar to yours (a luxury that is unheard of today in what is an even more competitive adoption market). Another reason that we picked them was that they sustained an impenetrable wall between the adoptive and natural parents. Both sets of parents could expect total confidentiality. We also liked the fact that they worked just as hard to counsel and help the natural parents, particularly the mother, through the trauma of pregnancy, childbirth, and parting with the baby—remaining on the case as long as needed to assuage the inevitable pain, guilt, or other fallout. But most important was their commitment to the well-being of the child, their primary focus.

We could see immediately by the detail and thoroughness of the application that they were going to want to probe every aspect of our suitability—psychological and physical health, marital stability, lifestyle, financial status, and so on. The first major step was getting the application accepted out of the hundreds that they receive. As I recall, it had to be submitted with multiple reference letters and other supporting documentation. Unfortunately, at this stage, all we could do was to reveal that I was disabled with no opportunity to make a case face-to-face. Getting all this together took a couple of months, and we submitted it without much optimism. Adding to our doubts, Barbara learned that while they had no formal policy on the disability issue, they *had never placed a baby with a disabled adoptive parent*. However, they didn't discourage us from applying—which I took as a good sign.

The wait seemed interminable, but to our great surprise they contacted us in about two months with an acceptance of the application. We had made the all-important "first cut," which took out the majority of couples. But the acceptance was somewhat qualified. Having never taken such a seriously disabled applicant before, they felt they would have to do a more intensive evaluation than usual in the next phase, which consisted of a series of interviews. Nevertheless, this was great news! They were probably only accepting about two in ten applications. So we had at least gotten up to bat in this competitive game, despite the wheelchair.

Within a few weeks, we had been assigned a person who would be our main contact—Miss Breeding, of all names. First, she interviewed us in our apartment. Then we were interviewed together and then separately at the agency by a professional evaluator. This was their standard routine. It was all very courteous, but the questions during the hour-and-a-half sessions left no stones unturned in terms of our backgrounds, lifestyle, health, attitudes, relationships, problems, prospects, hopes, and dreams. All this took place over two or three months. The fact that we had remained in the game that far was encouraging. Finally, with apologies, they asked me to come in for an extra interview that would focus solely on the disability issue. I'm sure they had no doubt about Barbara's qualifications. The same interviewer asked me questions along these lines:

- *How do I feel about having to spend the rest of my life in a wheelchair?*
- *How do I manage my day-to-day life and activities? In detail?*
- *Do I ever get depressed?*
- *How does Barbara cope with my disability?*
- *How can I compete in business with able-bodied people?*
- *Does it bother me when people look down on me as less-than-whole?*
- *How do children react to me?*
- *Does it make me uncomfortable to be unlike everyone else?*
- *Did I have friends who are not disabled?*
- *Do I miss not doing things I could do before?*
- *What is my proudest achievement? Worst disappointment?*

Most of the questions were obviously digging for underlying anger, hurt, bitterness, paranoia, or other baggage that could be destructive in my possible role as an adoptive parent. I tried to answer them factually and openly. I said that it's impossible to face the many difficulties of quadriplegia without feeling "different" or without having some sadness, occasional anger, and frustration. To deny it would be to delude myself and others. The test is how to deal with it, and I talked about my approach and how I coped specifically with the various challenges, the ups and downs, and the successes I had had so far.

She also posed some hypothetical questions dealing with parenthood. This is the one I particularly remember: "Suppose when Barbara was out of the house your son refused to obey you and then hid under the bed where you couldn't possibly reach him? What would you do?" After a little thought, I replied that I would position myself in the doorway, say nothing, and simply wait—for however long it was necessary—for the child to appear. Sooner or later, the child would get curious, hungry, or have to go to the bathroom. I would be there waiting to deal with the issue between us. There was no escape because I had the will to outlast him. She laughed and agreed that it would no doubt work.

This interview concluded the review process, which had taken more than a year from our first approach. We sensed that they had responded well to us as we went along, and their demeanor had been positive. So we were hopeful. Now, all we could do was wait— and wait—for their decision. It was not easy. We knew we had started out as a very long shot for adoption.

Within two weeks we had our answer, and it was yes! We were approved by the agency and placed in the pool of adoptive parents with whom a child would be placed. We were off the wall with joy. What a triumph! We had been chosen by what was thought to be the most selective of all agencies. In itself, that was good; but to have done it as a couple with one seriously disabled partner was to have a third-party endorsement by real professionals of our progress together in trying to build a normal, well-adjusted life.

Four days before Christmas 1959, we were presented at the agency with a beautiful baby girl, five weeks old. As Barbara held her, they told us a few things about her background: Born of college students in the eastern U.S., her natural family was of English origins and on both sides went back to colonial days; the last four generations had had college educations; and there were no health concerns. We asked a few questions. Then, as was their procedure, they left us alone with the baby in a small sitting room so that we could consider whether to take her. We were entranced with this light-complexioned, fine-featured child, whose intense blue eyes, extremely alert, followed our every move. We had settled on a name a day or two before as soon as they had told us it was to be a girl, and after a few minutes, I believe it was I who expressed what was in both our minds, saying, "She looks like an 'Anne' to me. It would be hard to do any better than this baby." Within a half hour, we were on our way with her.

The first several months were considered probationary just to be sure that the new parents were comfortable with the child and to allow for any unforeseen misgivings on either side. The agency kept in regular contact. There were no misgivings. We chose to adopt Anne, and the rest is history.

Within two years, we were back in the same sitting room contemplating a boy about three months old. It was so different to hold a solid little boy, compared with the sylph-like Anne whom we were used to. The face was distinctly male—wide-set large brown eyes and a square jaw—as compared with Anne's delicate features. As for background, his natural parents were also college graduates, the father being over six feet tall and an excellent athlete. His origins were primarily English-German, matching Barbara's and mine. But an intriguing fact was that there was Indian heritage on one side of the family that would make this child one-eighth Native American. In his case also there were no health concerns. Again we had no hesitation with this fine baby, scooped him up after the amenities, and brought him home, giving him the name of John.

In the case of each child, we went through the process of legal adoption two years after they came. So, in 1963, we became a full-fledged family of four.

Adoption is so totally different from the natural process. It is a deliberate, rational decision and it is a highly stressful, competitive undertaking strictly governed by law. The most important point of difference is that we chose to adopt and we chose to adopt these particular babies. We reached out for them with our hearts, and I think they sense it. Because of these factors, I believe that successful adoptive families foster deep and very special relationships.

We have always been amazed at how close a match the agency had succeeded in our physical, intellectual, religious, and genealogical backgrounds—even to the extent of the exceptional athletic prowess of Barbara and John and the pre-Revolutionary War ancestry of

Anne and me. I believe that for some reason they "went the extra mile" for us.

From the first day these children were with us, we felt that they were our own just as if we had been their natural parents, and of course we treated them that way. In fact, we often joked that we would have had a hard time producing such fine specimens on our own. We revealed to them early that they were adopted and tried always to be open with them about the subject. Although each child has no doubt gone through unhappy times over the issue of adoption —dealing with the idea that one's biological parents gave them up can never be easy, to put it mildly—neither ever revealed much to us on the subject. Out of respect for their privacy, we have never probed into the extent of their thinking.

Mostly, our relations with them seem normal, very like what we observe with other kids with their natural parents—a mix of warmth, humor, constructive experiences, and good times interrupted by the usual measure of conflicts, tension, and occasional blowups that simply go with the basic relationship of child and parent. I can only remember a few times that adoption came up in a serious way. Once when John was a preteen and he and I were at loggerheads over some discipline issue, he shouted, "I don't have to obey you; you're not my real dad." I shot back with something like, "I may not be your natural father, but I am your 'real dad' in every other way, including legally—and I love you just like a dad loves a son." He ran into his bedroom and slammed the door. As I recall, an hour or so later, I knocked on his door and went in as if nothing had happened, and we slipped back into our usual convivial relationship with nothing further said. Was this a call for reassurance disguised as an intentionally hurtful challenge? I think so.

As for Anne, she talked occasionally with Barbara about adoption. But the only time that it came up with me was when she learned that New York State had passed a law that permitted a chink in the hitherto impenetrable wall between the natural parents and the child who had been given up for adoption. It was after she became a parent and wanted to know more about her biological parents' health background. She had (after asking us) approached the adoption agency to learn about her natural background, and they told her of this new law. A state office had been created that could be contacted by either side for information on the other. However, before anything could take place, the natural parent or parents, the adoptive parents, and the adopted child all had to agree in writing to opening up contacts. But all three had to come forward of their own volition to sign such documents. No advice would be given to any side as to whether the other parties had done so until all parties had done so, and the law was intentionally not publicized. So it was a long shot at best. Anne asked us if we would sign a release, which we readily did, as did she. Apparently, neither of her natural parents came forward as nothing ever came of the matter. Who knows if the birth mother even knew about the obscure law?

A year or two ago perhaps, on the anniversary of my date of injury, John made a startling statement to me: "You know something, Dad, the worst day of your life turned out to be one of the best days of mine. Without it, I wouldn't have you as my dad." For once, I was totally speechless.

So they have, each in their own way, apparently, come to terms with whatever feelings they may have about being adopted.

I have been fortunate to be close to both the children in childhood and since they became adults—more so really after they left home and the inevitable struggles of teenage/college years were behind us.

Anne's passion was marine animals and how they communicate. She set out to work in this field as a lowly keeper at the New York Aquarium after graduating from Barnard College. She did an acoustic research project on killer whales in the straits off of Vancouver, British Columbia. Then, moving to Connecticut, she became a trainer at Mystic Aquarium, started in a Ph.D. program at the University of

Connecticut, and began a research project on Beluga whale communication at Mystic for her dissertation.

Meanwhile, she gave birth to a bright-eyed little girl she named Nile, whom she raised as a single parent, and continued at UConn to work toward a degree. After getting her Masters, she moved into my parents' cottage in Maine and took up residence for a year or two to establish a new life. She taught several semesters at the University of Maine at Machias and eventually shared a house in the area. There disaster struck in the form of a fire—no one hurt, but the house burned to the ground. This was devastating as she lost all her clothes, possessions, treasures, books, everything—even all of her meticulous and arduously gained research data. The cottage, which had since come into my possession, again became a haven for her and her child. Phoenix-like, she struggled on, taking a low-paying, entry-level job at an elementary school as a special education teacher—no easy challenge—and became committed to building her own home. This project, after some tough ups and downs and a modicum of help from us, turned out to be a great success and a major turning point in her life.

It developed that she has a genuine gift for teaching students with special needs, and she has pursued studies in that field. She is now Director of Special Education for the local school district, a job she loves and excels at, and has brought up a fine young person in her daughter Nile, recently turned eighteen. Anne is financially independent, respected in her community, and is flourishing. In recent years, I have been glad to be a part of all this as a close counselor, mentor, and parent-as-friend. I have great respect for her courage and tenacity through a long period of turmoil, trials, and triumphs.

Her interest in marine mammals has never waned. Since she lives in a fishing village on the Atlantic in the northeastern corner of Maine, she remains actively involved whenever possible. For example, she has been for many years the northernmost officially qualified person to deal with stranded animals for that stretch of coast and has saved many a seal from certain death—and was even part of a team that dealt with a 70-foot long whale carcass that had to be disposed of. Her demanding job precludes the kind of research she formerly did, but she hopes eventually to pursue this calling.

John's path has been a lot more direct but challenging nonetheless. Just out of Middlebury College, he couldn't seem to get a grip on what he wanted to do for a career and was doing blue-collar work and living at home. We were frustrated that he wasn't getting serious, and the personal chemistry became increasingly strained around the house. This was a destructive and nearly intolerable situation for all of us. I undertook some "tough love" by telling him that he had to leave home and by giving him a deadline of a few weeks. As part of the long and emotional conversation that accompanied this, I assured him as best I could of our permanent love for him and that we would always be there for him in case of real need. He was distraught—not so much with leaving I think, but with the fact that he really didn't know what he wanted to do; and he maintained that "college didn't prepare me for anything." He was in no mood to blame his own lack of focus there for his problem. I ignored this line and put out the idea that if he couldn't decide what he wanted long-term, maybe he should take up something intermediate like commercial flying—an activity he had always been interested in and one at which he could surely earn a living until he got his career options thought through. I offered to pay the tuition for his studying at Embry Riddle, a well-respected aviation school/junior college in Florida. Once he had the licenses, he would at least be employable anywhere—maybe even be a bush pilot or something adventurous like that. I wanted him to know for sure that I would be behind him, back him up. He left abruptly the next day without saying much. We heard from him in a few days. He had gone back to the Middlebury campus where he crashed with friends and got a local job as a bartender/bouncer.

Unbeknownst to us, while there, he apparently thought long and hard about how he was going to face up to things and applied to the Navy for their Officer Candidate Pilot Training Program. After a battery of tests and interviews, he was accepted and then told us. So, nine months after he left home, he entered into one of the toughest, most competitive training regimes in the military (the first phase having been dramatized in the movie, "An Officer and a Gentleman"). This was really going to be a test for a person who hadn't taken life all that seriously up to then and whose self-esteem was pretty fragile underneath an external bravado. We cheered him on, but secretly were concerned that failure or washout would really be damaging. Navy flight training is the most demanding in the world. He called us frequently, and we had many long conversations where he would vent or recount problems and his solutions, and I would try my best to give specific counsel and to sustain him. It was indeed a rocky year and a half where he was right on the edge of washout one or two times. But he persisted with admirable grit, and gradually increasing confidence. He eventually won out in the intense competition to be selected to fly jet fighters, the top two percent of the program, and ultimately earned his Navy wings as such. He asked me to pin them on at the ceremony in Texas, and it was one of the proudest moments of my life. It had special meaning for me because he achieved what I had wanted to do, and I believe he hung in there during the toughest times for my sake as much as for his own. He was selected to fly the carrier-based F/A-18 Hornet, the service's hottest new fighter plane—and the most coveted assignment in Naval aviation. He was proudly on his way.

When he left the service some nine years later, he had had two carrier tours as a combat pilot, had served briefly in the first Iraq conflict, and was a landing signal officer (LSO)—the officer on the stern who guides the other pilots to landings and grades their performance. Finally, he had become a senior instructor in all phases of Hornet operation and been qualified as a "demonstration pilot" to do solo aerobatic exhibitions at air shows. He had become one of the Navy's most respected Hornet pilots. Meanwhile, he had gotten married and started a family. He is the father of two boys, Connor and Ian, aged thirteen and eleven. After the Navy, he was accepted by Southwest Airlines as a pilot (also very competitive) and has since become a captain.

As the Navy service indicates, John has a need for adventure—a trait he's had from childhood. He will never have a desk job. He keeps himself in shape with rigorous training and is now deeply into mountaineering with an emphasis on technical rock and ice climbing.

One topic that I haven't brought up much in connection with building a family is the role of quadriplegia and the wheelchair. Barbara and the children seemed just to accept it and live with it. Not once have they made me feel uncomfortable about it, and in fact they have been universally patient and supportive. It didn't seem to affect my role as a father, and I know I've always enjoyed their respect despite some serious clashes. However, I know it has been hard for everyone, and the children's schoolmates got to them at times, which was tough. John's elementary school class had some mean boys, and they would often taunt him about me. He bloodied a few noses and once hit a schoolmate so hard that he broke his own hand.

Considering this whole aspect of our lives—adoption, nurturing, parenthood—we now can't imagine having lived our lives without the children. Beyond the inevitable challenges and the obvious fact that no children are perfect, we are extraordinarily proud of them, as they have become fine, responsible adults, accomplished in their demanding vocations, and totally committed parents—really good people. As with every family, there are, of course, some tensions arising from very typical sources such as lifestyle differences, past problems, sibling issues, etc. But we are close to our children and they have become close to each other over the years. It's a pleasure to realize that hardly a week goes by without some contact with them both.

The tale of how we built a family ends this part of my story that I called "The Climb" because it rounds out our uphill struggle to get back to the kind of a life that could be called almost normal. That memorable 747 flight back from Africa via London in May of 1972, which I described on the opening page of this section, marked that watershed in our lives. We were 40 years old. The children were almost teens. And we had come through the early years of marriage, career, and parenthood, when it seemed that we were always going against long odds just to get into the game. And we had succeeded. We were established to the extent of my being part of a growing business; we were financially viable; we had a lot of enjoyable friends and an active social life; the children were at good schools; we lived in a nice place. Now it seemed, with Africa and what followed, that we were getting into a more interesting and expansive kind of a life. It felt good.

Part III

An Experiential Life

I once wrote an article for a magazine, and the editor said in his author's profile that I seemed destined to lead "an experiential life." I had never thought about it that way, but he was right. For better or for worse, I've done a lot of interesting things: some were not planned, others were not wise, and many were actively pursued. Plenty of my experiences brought me a lot of satisfaction, among them my trips to Africa. And there were many lesser things that happened—happenings that were curious, funny, painful, surprising, scary, or otherwise noteworthy. Since quadriplegia is such an inescapable part of everything in my life, the wheelchair played a role in all of them. I set out to build a "normal" life. That actually happened, but I also went on to have a lot of far-from-normal experiences that cause some people to just shake their heads when they hear about them.

Into Africa

My involvement in Africa started in September 1971, two years after my brother Alex and I, as partners in McGhie Associates, had taken over our father's financial public affairs consulting firm when he retired.

One of my clients, St. Regis Corporation, wanted to use its 1971 annual report, which I was preparing, to feature its newly expanded overseas business. When reviewing the structure of the report with George Kneeland, the chairman, I checked off the various operations that should be included. When I came to their business in South Africa, he balked on the grounds that it was too controversial due to the international furor over apartheid—the abhorrent racial policy there. He thought that the board of directors would veto it because they wouldn't want picketing by student radicals or any other form of bad publicity. "But George," I said, "your investment in South Africa is too big to leave out of any discussion of your global business. It would be misleading to investors and to the financial community.

It's the company's biggest overseas investment in terms of cost." He still disagreed with the idea of including it but said he would think about the matter.

The next day, he called to say that, upon reflection, he was persuaded that we couldn't leave it out, but that he would have to get the board to agree. To that end, he said, "Why don't you go to South Africa, visit our operations to find out how they deal with apartheid and give me a recommendation as to how you would handle it in the annual report. Then I can make a case to the board, and we'll see how they react."

Although pleased to be asked, I was taken aback at the whole idea of such a trip for me. I thought, "How could I possibly handle such a trip in a wheelchair?" I had, by that time, traveled quite a lot in the U.S., but this would be very different. It would involve a six or seven hour flight to London, then a ten-to-twelve hour flight to Johannesburg. The biggest problem, other than fatigue, was that I would have to stay put in the seat the entire time during the flights with no access to bathrooms. This gave me real pause because if anything went wrong, it would be an insufferable situation for me and the other passengers. Furthermore, I had no idea what to expect in terms of wheelchair accessibility in Africa, or even in Europe for that matter. Also, very few people in wheelchairs flew internationally (or anywhere in fact) unaccompanied by an aide, and I would be alone.

It took a few days to decide. Alex, who would be going in my place if I did not, was emphatic that I should go. He said things like, "It's a once-in-a-lifetime opportunity. You'd be crazy not to take an all-expense paid trip to Africa. You can handle it. Go for it." Barbara knew the real pitfalls and also what it would mean as an accomplishment. She acted as a sounding board, and we bounced the subject back and forth. I thought long and hard. First, I worked out a way to deal with the bathroom problem by doubling the capacity of my "on-board relief system," the UCD, and ran a successful test. I knew that there would be other problems, some not altogether predictable. But in my travels up to then, I had always found ways around whatever obstacles turned up. I probably could do the same on this trip as well. This was daunting but a great opportunity. I concluded that it was worth the risks and anxieties.

The journey started with three days in England to deal with St. Regis' operations there, then a couple of days in Morocco, then a trip back to Portugal where I could get a good flight to South Africa. The operations I visited were all packaging businesses, in which St. Regis had a controlling interest or which they owned outright. The company I was visiting in South Africa was the largest packaging group on the continent with plants in that country as well as in Zimbabwe, Zambia, Botswana, and Namibia.

The long, 11-hour flight to Johannesburg on South African Airlines was a testament to how hated the country was in black Africa: virtually the entire flight had to be flown out over water off the western coasts of the countries along the way. Angola, then a Portuguese colony, was the only state on the continent that would permit SAA to fly in its airspace.

I dozed on and off during the flight until I finally fell asleep quite deeply for three or four hours toward morning. But as the passengers and cabin crew began to stir in the early light of dawn, I awoke already feeling that this trip was different from any I had taken before. We had been flying for more than nine hours and were only just then crossing the west coast of Namibia, about four-fifths of the way down the continent. Africa's sheer size struck home. From north to south, it was about twice the distance between New York and Los Angeles. The sun now was streaming into the left side of the cabin from the east, and I could see the last light of the morning star fade in the blue-black western sky out my window on the right side.

I was traveling international first class, and breakfast with all the fixings was soon being put before me. As I sat there regarding the steaming sausage and eggs, hot sweet buns, and coffee on my tray, I was awed by a compelling thought. Here we were in a serene flight cabin enjoying the luxury of gourmet food, while seven or eight miles below our glistening engines, dawn was breaking on the Kalahari Desert. There, in that harsh place, small, naked Bushmen and their families would be hunting for their morning meal with poison-tipped arrows, and chewing the moisture out of dug-up roots for water. The juxtaposition was startling. It left no doubt in my mind that I was headed for an experience completely foreign to anything I had ever dreamed of.

I had read extensively about South Africa and how the Dutch-speaking whites known as Afrikaners, who had gained political control in the late 1940s, had promulgated the draconian system of white domination and segregation known as apartheid. When I got off the plane and encountered the armed and unsmiling customs and immigration officials, then saw how they treated the black African luggage porters who were scurrying around the airport like worker ants, I felt for the first time the crushing power of this form of repression. It was sickening.

My client had a controlling interest in the large packaging company I was visiting. However, it operated autonomously under the direction of its founder, Oscar Fruman, who, as a young Jewish immigrant from Europe, had started the business in a shack with one black employee. My plan was to meet with Mr. Fruman to get his views on apartheid and then to visit the operations in and around Johannesburg to see for myself what was going on. But this did not prove to be easy. The two executives who met me at the airport acted coolly and said that he would not be available to see me at all due to his busy schedule and that they could answer any of my questions on apartheid. Meanwhile, since it was Friday, they had arranged for me to be taken on safari to the famous Kruger National Park (a day's drive away), and they would see me when I got back the following Tuesday or Wednesday.

Clearly, I was getting the VIP brush-off. They probably thought that this consultant from New York was going to lecture them all on racial tolerance. After I checked into the hotel and they escorted me to my room, I balked and told them, "I am not going on safari or anywhere else until I meet with Mr. Fruman. My instructions from the chairman of St. Regis are to see Fruman and the operations. If I'm not permitted to do so, I'll call my client and tell him." One of the men went down to the lobby to call Fruman for instructions. He was soon back, saying that the "boss" would see me, but that it would happen right away in my room at the hotel, and that he was being driven over.

Oscar Fruman was quite a character—a gruff and gravelly-voiced man of sixty or so with a thick middle-European accent. He ordered tea, biscuits, and sodas to be brought up and asked me what this was all about. I explained and started by asking about his business, how it started, and so forth. He began talking, warmed to the topic, and we got into a very interesting, lively discussion that lasted for more than two hours. We discussed apartheid, the packaging business in southern Africa, how he built the business, why he sold a majority interest to my client, an American company, the prospects for social upheavals, etc., etc. When he got up to leave he said something like, "Ven you get back from ze game reserve next veek, you come to a meeting I have viss my p.r. company. OK? They show me ideas for my annual report. You are big expert from New York. You advise me."

I was really drained by that time. An all-night flight, a seven-hour time change, a confrontation, a no-holds-barred discourse with a tough, self-made millionaire in a very different country, and the accumulated stress of wheelchair travel all had taken their toll. I postponed my trip to Kruger Park for a day.

Nothing could have prepared me for the jolting impressions that swept over me the next few days. Johannesburg was a surprisingly modern city with clean streets, and I was staying at the best hotel—well-appointed and well-staffed. But outside my window all night were the sounds of the central switching yard for the non-white commuter railroad just below, the small steam engines puffing and sounding their whistles. The sulphurous smell of soft coal smoke was everywhere, as it was the main industrial fuel and also the cooking fuel of the vast segregated black "townships" spread around outside the city. As a reminder of the city's gold mining past, great multistory piles of yellow deposits known as mine dumps were everywhere. They were the leavings of long-dead mines, some a quarter-mile across and many with rusting elevator towers still in place, often with the high-plains wind blowing a fine yellow dust off their tops.

The streets were teeming—mostly with blacks going about their jobs (the only reason for them to be permitted there). It was safe. Everyone was courteous to me. But blacks yielded way to whites on the sidewalks; blacks did all the menial work in the hotels, restaurants, shops, and homes; blacks rode in the backs of trucks while the white drivers rode up front; and blacks were often gruffly or abusively spoken to.

After my day of rest, I left for a three-day visit to Kruger National Park. The countryside was no less arresting. On our seven-hour drive to the game reserve we passed through a fascinating landscape. The roads were excellent, and electric power lines stretched in all directions. First, we traversed the wide-open high grassy plain dotted with mining towns and agricultural development; then we descended through dramatic, rocky, valley country; and finally we came into the lush sub-tropical rolling hills and flatlands of the eastern-most reaches of the country. There were white-owned farms in the countryside and tidy houses and stores in all the spotless towns. We saw many blacks, but they were walking or riding bicycles along the side of the road, working in fields, hanging out laundry in other people's back yards. Here and there you could glimpse crude shacks, often in small clusters, where they lived. As in the city, they were only there to work and had to have permission from the government to be there. Officially, every black belonged to a tribe that had its own "homeland." These segregated areas were deep in the country and away from the best agricultural areas. Only there were they permitted to own property. Mainly, the homelands were large, dusty, and squalid settlements in rural settings with little or no infrastructure. Apartheid was pervasive, inescapable, tragic.

Kruger is one of the world's great game reserves. Situated in the sub-tropical eastern edge of the country, the park is a vast, wild area about the size of Massachusetts. It is a protected natural habitat for all the great African animals: lions, cheetahs, leopards, elephants, water buffalos, rhinoceros, hippopotamus, giraffes, zebras, wild boars, crocodiles, wild hunting dogs, hyenas, jackals, numerous species of antelope, an extraordinary variety of monkeys, baboons, birds, small mammals, insects, and not a few dangerous reptiles.

This was an awesome and thrilling place to be: the world's first national park. It was run mostly by Afrikaner park rangers—white Dutch-descended men—who were by-and-large competent, dour, and not given to flexibility. However, their sound conservation science, incorruptibility, and dedication are still reflected in the quality of the stewardship there. Kruger has a balanced mix of great fauna and flora with few if any equals in all of Africa, yet it was open then to the public in quite a different way than what one would find in East African countries such as Kenya or Tanzania.

You were permitted into the park for a very affordable fee by reservation and stayed at one of a dozen simple and pleasant government-run camps. Each well-laid-out camp of 100 to 200 acres, full of shade trees, was surrounded by an elephant-proof ten-foot high wire fence, whose posts were lengths of old mining rail tracks driven deep into the ground. It could accommodate several hundred visitors, who stayed in small, round, thatched-roof huts that each had cots, a sink, a shower and a flush toilet. You could cook your own food on grills or have modest meals in a central dining hall. The camps, separated by some 40 to 60 miles, were in the remote savannas and bush plains that bordered on neighboring black-ruled Mozambique.

The park included expansive areas that were open and wild but also had a good road system, mostly dirt with main arteries of well-maintained asphalt. The park was committed to maintaining the natural environment. The only communication between camps was by short-wave radio, and no overflights were permitted by civilian or commercial aircraft (no contrails, which are so visually intrusive over our own national parks, could be seen). The air was pure, and the atmosphere so clear that at night the stars came right down to the horizon. The only sounds at night were the natural calls, cries, chirps, and wails of the creatures of the savanna, sometimes punctuated by the laugh of a hyena or roar of a lion.

What made the visit to Kruger more exciting than the guided safaris one experiences in books, movies, and TV documentaries was that it was up to the individual to find the game. The more common species were seen frequently, but the big cats, elephants, rhinoceros and lesser-known species were much more elusive. So spotting game was the challenge—and not an easy one because there were a lot more trees and undergrowth than on the wide plains of East Africa. It was a great feeling to be able to come back to camp at sunset having seen something rare, and better yet, having captured it on film.

My escorts were a white, middle-aged, English-speaking couple (the husband an employee of Mr. Fruman) who were addicted to the park and spent all their vacations and long weekends there. They knew it thoroughly and were expert game spotters. We didn't see any big cats, elephants, or rhinos, which were the most sought-after game, but we did see something very special: wild hunting dogs.

There are only a few hundred in this huge game reserve, and they tend to roam far from the roads and camps. These are not feral dogs. They have always been wild predators, who hunt in fierce packs of five or six, mainly for hoofed grazing animals. In the 20 years that my escorts had been to the park, they had never seen any, nor had anyone they knew. Remarkably, just after dawn one day when we had driven out of camp, we came upon a pack of these creatures asleep within 20 feet of the road. Our car woke them, but they took their time stretching and taking the measure of the day. Then they disappeared nonchalantly into the bush—but not before I got an excellent close-up photograph of one.

The night before we left for Johannesburg, I sat out listening to the nocturnal sounds of the bush, wondering at my good fortune. Here I was, halfway around the world in a fascinating, mysterious, beautiful, and surprising place, doing things I never dreamed of.

Back in the city I had work to do. My mission was to report firsthand on the apartheid issue and how it affected my client's major investment in South Africa. Mr. Fruman had given me a free hand to visit his plants and see things for myself. This I did, and what I saw caused me to draw mixed conclusions. This self-made man was a tough businessman, but his origins had given him a feeling for what it was like at the bottom, which was the status of most of his non-white employees. So there was a sense of decency in the way they were treated that I was sure was not typical in other South African manufacturing settings. You wouldn't call it enlightened, but it was better than most. This was part of the message I took back to the chairman of St. Regis Paper.

My last act before leaving Johannesburg was to honor the demand of Mr. Fruman, now "Oscar" to me, that I attend the meeting at which he was to be presented with the concept for his own annual report. I told him beforehand that it would be unprofessional for me to evaluate their work on his behalf, but that I would be glad to offer whatever constructive comments were appropriate. Group Editors, the public relations firm, showed up with its chairman leading a team of four or five staffers. It was all very promotional, more like an advertising presentation you might expect in the early days of Madison Avenue. What they had in mind was pretty garish and overdone. I made some suggestions that I thought would tone it down to be more in keeping with good financial public relations and left it at that. After the meeting, the head of the PR firm took me aside and asked, "Just what does your consultancy do? I've never even heard the term 'financial public relations' before." I spent ten minutes or so describing our firm to him and then had to leave hastily for the airport for my trip back to New York via London.

Settled in my comfortable seat a few hours later as the plane climbed to altitude, I stared out the window at the landscape fading in the twilight—Johannesburg, its comfortable suburbs, and the sprawling ghetto townships dimly visible at the perimeter through the pungent haze of a million small cooking stoves. I was glad to be headed home after my demanding three-week trip.

This was the first moment I had had to contemplate the whole experience, particularly those intense days in South Africa. I was stunned to find that tears were welling up in my eyes as a wave of sadness swept over me, completely unbidden—a deep feeling of sorrow for this country.

It was really beautiful, much of what I had seen. The nation was rich in resources. So many of the people were enterprising, energetic, attractive, tough. There was an exhilarating frontier-town atmosphere. It was a place abounding in natural beauty and opportunity. But its crude social and racial dysfunctions were exquisitely painful to behold. It wasn't just whites vs. non-whites in those days, as most Americans thought—although that was the most damaging element. Abject hatred existed between many within the white subgroups and also between the non-white categories of Asians, "Coloureds," and pure black Africans. And violent hostility was constantly just under the surface in relations between some of the thirteen distinct black African tribal groups. This highly complex interplay of status and animosity presented a daunting obstacle to the attainment of a just society. With apartheid, it was impossible. I was deeply moved. I had read Alan Paton's famous book about South Africa called *Cry the Beloved Country*. Now I knew literally what the title meant. Even today, in a free society, these animosities are a heavy burden. But they have not stood in the way over the last 25 years of what can only be described as a miracle: the peaceful transition in South Africa from the Nazi-like domination of the white minority to a genuine democracy—still with problems, but making solid progress.

The flight to London took about twelve hours, including a refueling stop. After a four hour layover, it was on to New York for another six or seven hour leg. Only when the wheels touched down at JFK airport did I let myself rejoice in the success of the journey. Yes, the business was accomplished. And it was true that my horizons had been greatly widened by what I had experienced. But the real joy was in the fact that I, as a quadriplegic, had gone to Europe and Africa and back entirely on my own. I was proud.

As for St. Regis' concern about discussing their South African business in the annual report, I recommended that proper disclosure mandated their including South African operations in the annual report, apartheid or not. I also told them that in the context of everything else in their global operations, we could deal with Africa in a way that wouldn't be controversial. The board ultimately agreed, and we included South Africa. I was right. There was not one protesting letter, not one telephone call, not one picket, nothing. Mission accomplished.

Encore in Africa

To my great surprise, my trip for St. Regis was by no means the end of my African experience. Three months later, a call came in out of the blue to my office from Johannesburg. I had no idea who it could be. Certainly not Oscar Fruman. That St. Regis chapter was closed. I was surprised, though, to find on the line the head of the public relations firm whose annual report presentation I had witnessed in Oscar's boardroom.

His name was Aubrey Sussens, and he had a proposition. He said he was "intrigued by the specialty of financial public affairs" and thought there was a market for it in South Africa. There were many sizable publicly traded companies, particularly in mining, agriculture, consumer products, and tourism. Johannesburg had an important stock market, which was of particular foreign interest because of the gold and other metals mining shares traded there. "They consistently botch their financial reports," he said.

Investor relations and communications there were indeed

woefully inadequate (as I had seen from his own presentation a few months earlier). He was sure that his firm could be a leader in boosting the quality of disclosure, that companies would jump at the chance to do it better, and that I was the man to help him "launch" a new division to render those kinds of services in South Africa. He proposed that if I agreed, his firm and the prestigious *Financial Mail* magazine would sponsor a day-long seminar given by me in Johannesburg, which would describe the best practices in the field and promote his fledgling division. He was sure the session would attract at least a hundred top executives from all the big companies. Then I would stay on for a week or two to help set up the operation and line up clients. For this, I would receive an up-front fee and royalties on any subsequent business, plus all expenses for the trip.

Aubrey obviously was not shy. He had the whole thing all worked out, and here it was—bang—just like that.

I was, of course, totally taken by surprise by the audacity of his idea and by his point-blank proposition. I had given some talks before groups and knew my subject, but a full-day seminar? And was there really a market there? This would need some thought. Was I up to it physically? Probably. I had just been to South Africa. He proposed a date in May three months hence. I allowed that it was all very interesting, thanked him for the compliment of his asking, but told him I would need time to consider it. No problem for him. He was coming to the U.S. the following week on other business, and we could go into it in more depth.

We had several meetings dealing with what our contractual arrangements might be, what my obligations were, what my seminar would cover. The travel and the seminar were my main worry. To lecture for eight hours on this complex subject would require extensive preparation, and I didn't have anything "on the shelf" that I could use and I also didn't have much time to get ready given my busy schedule at that time of year. Ultimately, after serious soul-searching and a lot of discussion with Barbara and Alex, I decided it was simply too exciting a chance to turn down, misgivings or not.

An important factor was that I liked and respected Aubrey Sussens, who was not your typical public relations type or a typical white South African. As a former prize-winning editor at a leading Johannesburg newspaper, he had studied at Harvard on a prestigious Nieman Fellowship. When we first sat down to discuss his idea over lunch after he arrived in New York, my first question was, "What are your views on apartheid?" I would not be comfortable at the thought of working with a South African company that didn't have an enlightened view on the topic. It turned out that he had long been an anti-apartheid advocate in his newspaper work. In addition, he was a great, likable, bear of a man, very smart, generous, and stimulating to be with. We hit it off, and I became convinced that I could work with him.

I was anxious that Barbara be part of all this so that she could see Africa and, for the first time in our marriage, we could go off together on an overseas trip. It would be first class all-expense paid for me, and I would pick up all costs for her. I actually didn't have the cash, but we were long overdue to get away on a trip, and I sold off some investments in our modest nest egg to finance it. I would go out first to give the seminar and meet the business commitments. Then Barbara would join me for a few days on safari at Kruger Park and then on to Portugal for four days and London for three.

When I arrived in Johannesburg in early May ten or twelve weeks later, I was very nervous about the seminar—mainly about whether what I had prepared was comprehensive enough. It got worse when I discovered that the arrangements for the actual presentation I had to give in a few days were far from complete. There were no supporting audio-visuals, no ideas for a panel discussion, no plan for the physical setup of the meeting room, etc. These were supposed to have been in place on my arrival. So it was a stressful week getting it all together with people I had never worked with before. Everyone was a little edgy.

The day finally came. Attendance was good, consisting of well over a hundred managers and senior people of well-known companies, and the seminar went well. The subject of professionalizing and upgrading corporate financial disclosure seemed to be of interest, judging by the quality of the questions and discussion. Timed to coincide with my presentation were a series of lunches with executives of large companies as well as articles in the *Financial Mail* and the business sections of the leading newspapers. Aubrey's company put out a special issue of its public affairs magazine with me on the cover. There was even a TV interview. Seeing my picture in the press and reading the coverage of my visit was a novel experience to say the least—another incredulous moment for me. I never in my wildest dreams could have anticipated this kind of thing.

But the particular significance to me was that Aubrey Sussens, a successful businessman whom I had only briefly met once in a meeting, had concluded that he wanted me to join him in an important joint venture despite the fact that I was a seriously disabled person in a wheelchair. Then he had spent a considerable amount of time and money to bring it about. Apparently, the disability had given him no pause. This was a real validation for me in terms of confidence and self-esteem. It also said loud and clear that if you are perceived by others to have something of value to contribute, your disability need not stand in the way. From then on, I applied this lesson to everything I did professionally and in other leadership roles. And it worked.

I met Barbara at the airport the following morning, tremendously relieved to have the seminar behind me. She was wide-eyed at being in South Africa for the first time—experiencing her own version of the shock that I had felt at first. Aubrey had lent me his driver Firos Malanga and a Mercedes, so we were moving about in comfort. On the way into the city, I showed her the several articles in the press about the seminar. We looked at each other and shook our heads in wonder at all of this.

We had a very interesting week in Johannesburg. I worked long hours with Aubrey to set up our joint-venture consultancy as part of his company and also to explain our new service to many potential clients. One important item was a contract we signed after some difficult negotiations, which settled on royalties and happily called for me to come to South Africa once a year to assist him and to promote this new business. Meanwhile, Barbara was able to shop and explore a little, and we were graciously wined and dined by Aubrey or members of his staff practically every night.

Then we were off to Kruger Park for a few days. Barbara, like me, was quite awed by the safari experience, saying, "You know, you described all of this to me in detail and showed me pictures. But this isn't at all what I thought it would be—so different from anything I've ever experienced. I don't think it can be described." Next we visited Capetown some 1,700 miles away for two days—a beautiful city in a totally different climate 40 miles north of the Cape of Good Hope. Finally, we went on to Portugal for a few days and ended up in London before heading home. For two people who didn't think they were going to make it overseas until their fifties or sixties, it was quite a trip.

A special part of my African experience was the friendship I formed with Firos, my driver. During my several trips to South Africa, we spent many long days together, just the two of us. True, he was a black servant and those were the days of apartheid, but I had learned that his spirit and inner being was in no fundamental way diminished by his position in this wretched society. His regular job was as a chauffeur, chief office/house boy, and general factotum for my colleague, Aubrey Sussens, chairman of the company I was working with.

When I came back to Africa to help Aubrey with his investor relations division and returned every year to Johannesburg for a week or two as advisor, Firos (pronounced fire-roas) was assigned to be my driver and to help me get around. He took very seriously the charge from Aubrey: "You stick with Mr. McGhie wherever he goes as long as he is here and see that he's properly taken care of." So Firos was my constant companion because being in a wheelchair on this continent in the 1970s was extraordinarily difficult. There were steps everywhere and general ignorance of the needs of the handicapped. He drove me around in Aubrey's top-line Mercedes from my hotel to meetings, both business and social, during my hectic stays.

What he lacked in formal education, having grown up in the dust-poor homeland of the Venda tribe in the north of the Transvaal province, Firos made up for in intelligence, a cheerfully disarming guile, wit, and bright-eyed intensity. He spoke slightly fractured English with the hint of a British accent, softened by the lilting, expressive meter of his native language. Physically he was small, perhaps five-foot-five, but quick, wiry, and strong. He had an easy, warm smile and a natural dignity not unusual for the higher-born males in a pure African tribe. I noticed that other Africans, even strangers, treated him with deference. Earnest and reliable, he was both street-smart and people-smart in Johannesburg and in the hinterlands. He was an invaluable escort and an intriguing companion as he provided a window into the life and mind of a black African. He was also a character and could be unpredictable. Because of his nature and his job as my indispensable aide, he played a central role in all my memorable experiences, as well as those of my family.

One thing I was determined to do was to get every member of my family to Africa at one time or another—an experience I was sure that they would never forget. Barbara was the first and was able to come three times. My two children came out separately at age fourteen each. I got this idea from a respected friend, a father of four, who told me that one of the best things he ever did was to take each of his kids as a teen on a one-on-one fun vacation trip for a week. He said the rapport and bonds he established then were unique and lasting. I thought it was a great idea and that Africa would be perfect for such a trip since they would see Europe as well—and also go on a safari and have bragging rights to an experience unlike any had by their peers. Everyone in the family was crazy about Firos, which didn't surprise me because I liked him myself. To this day, they can recount tales about him and what he was like. He and I had our best times in the bush. This came about because at the end of each year's business commitment, I would take a few days off and head out on safari to Kruger National Park, where I had gone for a few days on my first visit for St. Regis. Sussens insisted that I take his Mercedes, with Firos as my driver. My interest was in wildlife photography, and I had equipped myself with state-of-the-art cameras, lenses, and other gear, realizing that this was a rare opportunity.

Fortunately, in contrast to the East African style safari, in Kruger you were allowed to drive your own vehicle at will throughout the reserve, adhering to a network of mostly dirt roads. But there were strict rules, strictly enforced. You were under no circumstances permitted to get out of the vehicle except in designated rest areas, which sometimes were many miles apart. Most important, you had to be either out of the park or inside the gates of one of the dozen or so government-run camps between sunset and sunrise. The gates were shut promptly by the rangers; and should you not make it back, the consequences were severe—always a steep fine, and if you were far from camp, you experienced a lonely and scary night in your vehicle, expulsion from the game reserve when found, and no welcome back, ever.

On one of our stays in the park, we found ourselves in a situation that not only could have caused problems with the authorities but also could have been very dangerous. We had been driving all day looking for game in the central region of the reserve. It was late afternoon, warm (in the high eighties), and we were about 20 miles from camp. We hadn't seen a lot of interesting wildlife and were exploring for the first time a little-traveled narrow dirt track some five miles from the more popular roads, working our way back towards camp to be in by sunset.

I was sitting in the back seat positioned in the center and leaning forward on the backs of the front bucket seats. There, I had a good high view for spotting game and photographing it through the open windows. I had two Nikon cameras and an array of binoculars, lenses, film, and gear spread out around me, all covered with towels to keep the dust out. Suddenly, as we headed down a gentle slope to follow the track across a dry streambed, the car lurched half sideways to an abrupt stop, all my camera gear tumbling to the floor.

"Hey, Firos, what happened?" No answer at first. He was furiously spinning the wheels forward and back, with the engine roaring and then saying, "It is all soft! It is all soft!" We were going nowhere. After a few minutes, he could see it was futile and shut off the ignition, eyes wide, staring straight ahead, beads of sweat running down his face. We were stuck fast.

Nothing was said for several long moments as the seriousness of our situation sunk in: we were stranded on a deserted road with not much time to extricate ourselves and get back to camp before curfew. We had no means of communication to the camp or rangers. Our location was remote, rarely patrolled, and in the midst of potentially dangerous free-roaming animals and reptiles, many of them nocturnal. Darkness was only a few hours away. The reassuring purr of the Mercedes diesel had been replaced by a silence only gently interrupted by the metallic sounds of locusts in the warm afternoon and an occasional bird call. Of course, with my disability I was no help, and there was no way that Firos could propel me anywhere in my wheelchair in these surroundings. The bush was thick around us with tall trees overhead and we were stuck in deep, soft sand.

Firos looked over to me for instructions. I said, "You'll have to push to get us out," to which he quickly replied, "Oh no, there are snakes, and the rangers say we must not get out of the car. We will be fined." His eyes were wide open, frightened, almost panicked. I suppose he was also upset that some grave misfortune might befall us and that he would be held accountable for not taking care of me. I, too, was concerned, and an edge must have been in my voice when I insisted he get out of the car, saying that it was our only chance. This he haltingly did, leaving the door open and pushing the heavy Mercedes with all his might. The car did not budge.

Looking out the open door, I could see we were in deep, light sand up to the axles. This stream bank must have washed out in the spring rains, and the road crew had just dumped in sand for fill instead of gravel.

"Firos, we need sticks and stones under the rear wheels to get traction." Again, he was reluctant to get out, and I had to be very firm to get him to move. He scurried around and found some debris for the wheel holes. When these were packed in, he restarted the car and tried it in low gear. We advanced a fraction of an inch and settled back. I urged him on to more gathering and stuffing. Trying again, we barely moved. What we should do was rock the car, I thought; so we tried it, with Firos sitting at the wheel, flipping back and forth between drive and reverse. There was no meaningful progress, just the smell of smoking tires and our own sweat.

As time ticked on, our situation was getting more worrisome. Being late at the gate was one thing. But spending the night out in the bush with no food, emergency gear, or protection was a very grim prospect indeed. Firos was out of the car again scrounging for more stones when it occurred to me that perhaps our only chance was to rock the car and push at the same time. But how? I was stuck in the back seat, and if he pushed, I couldn't use the gas pedal in any event to supply the power.

I was sitting as usual in the middle of the rear seat and frustrated to find myself completely useless in this crisis. Then I spotted my camera tripod. It was light aluminum but a very strong professional piece of gear. Quickly, while Firos was out foraging, I extended and locked one of the legs, which had a rubber and steel tipped end. Then, with both elbows supporting myself on the backs of the front seats, I grasped the upper works of the tripod with one hand and the automatic gearshift lever on the console with the other. The extended tripod point could reach both the gas and brake pedals. With the engine off, I experimented with putting the gear shift into drive, pressing on the accelerator with the tripod leg, easing off the gas, jamming it into reverse gear, hitting the gas again, and trying to coordinate this repetitive sequence. Then I practiced quick moves of the tripod point from gas to brake, just in case we needed a quick braking. We had to try this. There were no other ideas.

When Firos got back, I showed him the concept. But he was skeptical and nervous. He said, "No! It is bad. If the car goes, you can't steer, and you drive off and crash in trees!" I had to convince him. Persuading him to start the car, I told him to stay in his seat where he would be safe. Then I demonstrated my idea by actually doing it, manipulating the pedals with the tripod, moving the gear lever, and racing the engine in forward, then reverse. He began to show interest as my coordination improved. "Now," I said, "you open the door, get out, leave the door open and stay close as you push the car. Then if it starts to move, you can jump right in and steer and take over the pedals." He finally agreed.

He repacked the sticks and stones as tightly as possible around the rear wheels, and we started our rocking action. There was no movement at first. I think we were both so full of adrenaline that our collective actions were jerky and not in sync. I stopped everything, and we just sat there for a few minutes to regroup. When we resumed, it was better, smoother. He was straining so hard, the veins were standing out on his forehead and neck, and he was sweating profusely. Meanwhile, I was intensely concentrating on the tricky pedal-gearshift sequence, which was quite awkward in my position. Ominously, the engine temperature gauge was fast creeping up. After a few minutes, I began to feel a very slight forward movement. He felt it too, and we kept at it with everything we had, yelling encouragement to each other as the engine roared. Gradually, we began to edge forward more perceptibly—miraculously, it seemed—and then soon began to inch slowly down the slope toward the streambed, where the regular track would be firm.

Suddenly, we broke free of the sand, Firos jumped in, took over, and we roared across the dry bed, fishtailing up the opposite bank, his foot jammed on the gas. He was so carried away that I had to hit him hard on the shoulder to stun him out of it. He locked up the brakes, and we skidded to a stop in a choking cloud of dust. Spontaneously, we started to laugh and couldn't stop for several minutes. Finally, calming down, he closed his still-open door and we headed back to camp with him talking nonstop and excitedly about our success. We arrived at Lower Sabie Camp about 20 minutes before sunset and the dreaded closing of the gates.

We shared a triumphal beer in my hut before supper, full of ourselves for having extricated our two-man "safari" from near disaster. Later, in the small mess hall, I was eating alone (under apartheid, black Africans had to eat in a separate room. Having a beer together was illegal, too). I could hear Firos's voice in the kitchen, loud and animated, regaling the other servants. "...and then the boss, very clever, he take the camera tripod, he lean over the seat, he push the pedals, shift the gears, and I push the car, then pull, and we rock the car forward and back, and...and... and..." He went on and on to their "Oohs" and "Ahs," with his infectious laughter punctuating the story, which was getting better by the minute.

Finally we left, and he pushed me in the chair slowly back to my hut in silence, most of the others in the camp having retired. Before turning in, we sat for quite a while at the outer perimeter fence near the Sabie River in the brilliant moonlight, the air so clear that the stars resembled tiny diamonds on black velvet. He was in his typical squatting position by my side. At peace, we just listened for some time to the extraordinary sounds of the wild African riverine bushveld—whistles of the nightjar birds, occasional screams of hyenas, and the potent rustle of large unseen mammals moving through the tall reeds by the river—elephants or perhaps hippos. Our adventures of the day eventually got us talking about childhood escapades and close calls—his in the parched and impoverished Venda homeland in the northern Transvaal province near Zimbabwe and mine on a dairy farm in Connecticut. Here we were, a white businessman from America and a tribal African with hardly any education (he didn't even know where America was). We had virtually nothing in common. Yet we talked deep into the night, as close as brothers.

One of the revelations of my time in Africa was the discovery with Firos that it was possible to have a different kind of close friendship with a black African man than any I'd had with white male friends I'd known well. The unspoken bond seemed in some ways easier and more open. There was an unselfconscious level of mutuality and warmth. No competitive bantering. It may be that I have a built-in Anglo-Saxon reserve and this was the first time I was comfortable without it. But I suspect that it is a deep cultural difference that the Africans possess, which I had the good fortune to stumble on. Often, I observed black men walking arm-in-arm, even hand–in-hand, on the street. When I suggested to Firos once that they might be homosexual, he was very surprised. I had to explain what that meant. "No, no, no!" he scolded. "They are just good friends." I believed him.

Firos was very much a part of another dicey experience in Africa. When my daughter Anne was there in 1974, age 14, I wanted her to be aware of the good and the bad of South Africa, not just to have a sanitized experience. To educate her, and also myself, on some of the effects of apartheid, I hoped to get into the "township" of Soweto outside of Johannesburg to see what it was really like. All the non-whites working in and around the city were restricted to live in townships unless they were live-in domestics. Soweto was largely a slum and by far the largest and most infamous township for its over-crowding, poverty, and crime. Its population far exceeded that of Johannesburg itself.

The problem was that access was severely restricted by the government. There were limited-route bus tours permitted with government guides but no free-lance drive-throughs. Since I was in a wheelchair, I thought it might be possible to get special dispensation for a driving visit.

Firos had a house in Soweto and knew his way around. I asked him about getting permission. After a few moments of thought, he said "Oh, we go to police, and I get permit, no problem." At that moment, we were driving through one of the upscale suburbs, and within five minutes he had pulled into the nearest police station and went in while Anne and I sat in the car. After what seemed like a long while—perhaps 20 minutes—Firos emerged, smiling, and said "It's OK" and then slipped behind the wheel. I asked him about the permit. "The permit? Ah yes," he replied. "The police here say that we can get permit from police station inside the township. No problem."

As we headed southwest towards Soweto, we passed through a number of neighborhoods that seemed to get seedier as we went.

I assumed they were the houses of white workingmen by the children in the yards and the abundant laundry flapping in the ever-present wind of the high plain. The road's condition also seemed to be getting worse the closer we got to the township. It was heavily trafficked by black Africans, walking or riding bicycles, and the occasional VW Minibus.

Soon we rounded a bend to the sight of Soweto ahead. As far as the eye could see, neat rows of small cottages covered the undulating low hills in every direction. To be frank, from afar, it looked surprisingly picturesque and colorful in the clean, bright sunshine. We didn't enter by any guarded gate as I had expected. The road we were on just blended into a road that was part of the township, and we found ourselves on a two-lane unpaved thoroughfare with houses on both sides.

Then the reality of Soweto came on us with a punishing clarity. The "picturesque" cottages were hardly more than our backyard sheds—perhaps 12 feet by 20 feet in size, some brick but mostly concrete block, two or three windows, two doors and a tin roof. There were no utilities—water, sewage, or electricity—in most of Soweto. Most appalling was that these squalid two-room buildings housed at least eight or twelve people, sometimes two families and a lodger. Government-built and owned (blacks could not own any real property outside of their distant homelands), the houses were rented to the million plus people who lived there by special permit only, as workers in the Johannesburg area. Even so, there was a shortage of housing and long waiting lists, sometimes years, for these miserable dwellings.

Every day, the people commuted to work and back by railroad —powerful electric engines pulling 30 or more cars, crowded to overflowing, with nothing to sit on except wooden benches. By daily passenger volume, it was the largest railroad in the world. As for the nights, too much alcohol, along with roving gangs of youths out for trouble, caused them to be filled with noise, mayhem, and often deadly violence.

The road, dusty and monotonous, was intersected every 150 feet or so with cross streets lined with houses about 15 feet apart. There were small front and back yards filled with drying laundry, rusting bicycles, barrels, bedsteads, and all manner of household possessions or discards. Some yards were wide open; others had low cement block walls. Often they were chain-link-fenced, and more than a few were fortified with razor wire. A number of houses were cleanly painted, yards picked up, and some even with flower boxes in the windows or showing other signs of pride and care. But most, sadly, were little more than bare, unkempt shelters. Trash of various description was everywhere, and, like tumbleweed, many bits and pieces were rolling along the dusty streets with the perpetual breeze.

We were there on a weekday afternoon, so the many people we did see were a tiny portion of the population. But they were everywhere, walking and riding bicycles. Virtually everyone was carrying something, often beautifully balanced on their heads. Small barefoot children were also pervasive and lively; although there was the occasional pensive or sad face, most children were playing with innocent exuberance, seemingly unfazed by their surroundings.

Caught up with the sights and impressions, I was deeply absorbed. But I suddenly realized that we had been driving around Soweto, off-limits to tourists without government-accredited guides or special permits, for some 45 minutes. "Firos, we were supposed to go to the police station for our permit. This is risky. We could be arrested."

"Just now we come to a police station."

Within a few minutes, we pulled into the razor-wired yard of a police station, and Firos went inside for the permit. Parked like that, I was suddenly much more conscious of our car and our situation. It was a new bright red Mercedes sedan with white leather seats, and there we were in the back seat, a white man and his blond teenage daughter, both blue-eyed and light complexioned, as well as being well dressed. Our discomfiture rose as the car was quickly surrounded by children, with adults standing behind them, all staring in the windows with unabashed curiosity. They didn't seem hostile or threatening, but time was ticking by with Firos delayed inside, and we were becoming increasingly nervous. The crowd seemed to grow. I couldn't recall any experience like it in my life—fear and self-consciousness mixed with a sense of embarrassment to be thrusting ourselves and Aubrey's ostentatious car into this community of deprived black Africans. Later, Firos was to tell me that many young children in Soweto had never seen a white person, which might account for the intense curiosity. To our great relief, he finally emerged from the station, shooed the people and children away, and drove off in a cloud of dust.

It was silent for a while, but I was getting concerned and asked to see the permit. Without taking his eyes off the road, Firos said, "It is very bad mistake the police in Johannesburg make. They say, 'Get permit in Soweto.' Here the police say that all permits must come from outside."

"So we don't have a permit?"

"It is true."

"Firos, get us out of here now! No more sightseeing. We must leave now, shortest way."

He made a U-turn, and we drove in silence to the nearest outlet. I thought to myself: What a clever trick our Firos had pulled off. No doubt, permits can't be at any police station either in or out of Soweto, and he knew it. Yet he carried off the ruse with a totally convincing confidence and demeanor. Heaven knows what he did or said inside the police stations. The reason he did it was, of course, for my benefit. We were friends, which had nothing to do with his role as a servant, and he liked Anne. I told him of my strong desire to take her to see Soweto and also that I wanted to see it for myself. I also think that, as a black African, he wanted white Americans to see what Soweto was really like, despite the government restrictions of entry. He obviously knew that individual permits were impossible to acquire and just took it upon himself to make it happen by deceiving all sides. There was a considerable risk because he could have gotten into very serious trouble with the police. I loved this guy! I never took him to task for the deception. And he never said a word about it to me afterwards.

Many years later, I asked Anne for her most vivid recollection of Soweto. It was this: At one point in our hour-and-a-half drive-through, she reminded me that we had come to a vista with stunning symbolism. Across the undulating hills of teeming squalor, stood a great pile of gold mine waste looming on the horizon in the bright sunshine, which reflected off its yellow dust. The shape of a large urban landfill and several hundred feet high, it must have been a quarter-mile long—massive and imposing. To her it seemed a permanent monument to the white wealth, dominance, and exploitation that characterized apartheid, and this loomed ironically over the very homes of those most oppressed by the system.

It has been an ongoing source of interest to me how people react to the wheelchair—and to me in it. After years of people's reactions, I thought I had pretty much experienced everything—until the period when I was going to South Africa, when I was totally surprised by a very unusual idea of what a wheelchair could be used for.

In the late 1970s, the South African situation was becoming increasingly tense as the African National Congress (ANC) stepped up civil unrest and violence. This brought accelerating brutal repression on the part of the government, which was led by the right-wing Nationalist Party dominated by the Dutch-descended Afrikaners.

The tension was palpable among the whites with whom I had contact on my visits to the country, and there was much debate among them about whether there would be a blood bath and mass confiscation of white property and assets, whether some peaceful solution would be reached, or whether the status quo would persist.

Not surprisingly, when home in New York I would find myself in a lot of discussions about this crisis, which had become internationally controversial with calls for divestment, sanctions, and the like. One evening, Barbara and I were at a party that included a number of successful New Yorkers—professionals, financial and business people, and a couple of well-known people in public service, who were friends of the host, including a man who was to become Secretary of State.

At one point, a person I had not met, introduced himself and said he had just been told of my African trips and was keen to discuss the situation there. He was well-informed, and we talked about it for a while. Then, lowering his voice, he said he could pass on an offer to me that I might want to consider: He had a South African friend who was quite wealthy and was becoming more and more fearful that the situation there would deteriorate into political and economic chaos. This individual was anxious to get "assets" out of the country, and as I well knew, there were tight government restrictions on any financial outflows. Would I be willing to "liberate" some assets for his friend on my next trip? He said that it would be easy and safe for me to do as a person in a wheelchair. Then he said it would be very much worth my trouble because his friend was willing to give the courier thirty-five percent of the value of whatever was gotten out of the country.

I thought, "What he must mean but hasn't said is that I would be asked to smuggle diamonds out of the country in my wheelchair." But my response was non-committal. I said I would think about it. He gave me his card and suggested I call him if I had any doubts or questions. Then we moved on to general topics, and our conversation ended a few minutes later.

Later after we got home, I told Barbara about it, and she was fully as incredulous as I was. Obviously, I had no intention of doing it for all manner of reasons, and my intention was simply to ignore the offer. But it was so intriguing. What a clever idea we thought. A large fortune in cut diamonds could easily be concealed in the hollow tubes of my wheelchair. In those days, travelers were almost never searched, particularly the disabled. Furthermore, in all my travels, no official had ever examined my chair.

I would have forgotten about it except that it happened again about a year later. It also was at a social occasion, but no one there had been at the other party, so there was no connection with the first offer. It was essentially the same thing. I did not know the person, and it was just a quiet conversation on the fringe of the party. The exact method was not suggested, but using the wheelchair as the smuggling tool was the obvious reason. South African upheaval was even worse by then, and Rhodesia (now Zimbabwe) was locked in a bloody guerrilla war. So it was not surprising that the percentage offered to the messenger was higher—a surprising fifty percent of the value of "assets" brought out. Again, I begged off politely and never heard from the person.

I can truthfully say that I had always thought of the wheelchair as a liability. Now I found out that I could make a small fortune using it to smuggle diamonds with very little risk. I concluded that no matter what one perceives something to be, in this case the wheelchair, others might see it differently—very differently.

It was a sad feeling to leave Africa at the end of my last trip in 1983. Although all my trips had been on business, the real pull for me was far deeper. There I had the sense that I had tapped into a more universal reality than existed in our Anglo-European-American way of life. Africa is on one level more primitive than western society, but in other ways far more complex, with its many overlays of cultural, tribal, historical, religious, and spiritual traditions—not to mention the colonial impacts. Beyond all that is its geographical size and ecological diversity, its exquisite physical beauty, and its historical contribution to art, science, and human thought. One tries to take it all in and process it. But even the serious observer finds that a certain mystery shrouds the continent, only allowing hints and glimpses of its soul. Such writers as Joseph Conrad, Ernest Hemingway, Doris Lessing, and many others have probed for the essence of Africa, and this unfinished quest has produced some of the best writing of the twentieth century.

I had been deeply moved by what I had experienced in South Africa. My feelings can't be compared with those of Isak Dinesen, who spent much of her life in East Africa. But I found that something she said in her book, *Out of Africa*, struck a chord. It was about leaving her farm in Kenya for the last time. "When in the end, the day came on which I was going away, I learned the strange learning that things can happen which we ourselves cannot possibly imagine, either beforehand, or at the time when they are taking place, or afterwards when we look back on them."

Feeding the Rat

Two or three years after my son ended his service in the Navy as a carrier-based fighter pilot and became an airline pilot, he told me of his plans to climb Mt. Rainier. I also learned that he had been serious for some time about mountaineering and ice climbing. So I asked the obvious question: "Now that you're not risking your life doing night landings on aircraft carriers in F/A-18s anymore, why do you want to take up such a dangerous sport?" His answer: "Because I've got to feed the rat."

What he meant, it seems, was that he has an inner drive to do physically and psychologically challenging things. Sooner or later, that need has to be met—the rat has to be fed. He followed up by saying something like, "You, of all people, ought to know what I'm talking about." Gotcha! It was too true, and my risk-taking tendency has been a liability and an asset all my life. As a boy, I took chances climbing trees and barn roofs and did downhill ski racing as a teen—and had some nasty falls. It no doubt contributed to my accident in the Air Force. But without the general willingness to take risks, I would never have applied to Harvard or called Barbara when she was NCAA golf champion to ask her out for a blind date golf game (we've now been married fifty years). After my injury, for that matter, had I not been willing to take risks, I would never have been able to become physically independent, to compete in the real world, to travel to Africa alone, and indeed to become an adoptive parent. Flying gliders fits the same pattern but should no doubt be described as "pushing the envelope."

This characteristic has shown up in different ways. Sometimes I would simply get involved in adventurous things out of sheer boredom or frustration. Case in point: aerial photographs of Monterey Peninsula. Several times in the 1980s and early 1990s, we visited some friends who lived in Pebble Beach—an area known not only for its great golf but also for its spectacular Pacific coastline. Our hosts were members of Cypress Point, a golf club that had an ocean-side course equally beautiful and no less challenging than the better-known Pebble Beach course. For Barbara, being a champion golfer, playing Cypress Point was as good as it gets, and she had a great time. I, however, was always somewhat at loose ends. One year, I drove every day (in a rented hand-control-equipped car) to a glider operation about two hours away at the southern tip of San Francisco Bay, where I would take glider rides as a passenger (there being no hand-controls on their gliders).

Another time, to keep busy, I undertook a project with my camera to capture the power of the surf and the sea by driving around and finding dramatic vistas and views from my rental car. However, by the second or third day, I had exhausted the supply of locations reachable in a wheelchair. Feeling frustrated, I took a picnic lunch and a book out to Point Lobos, one of the dramatic spots I had already worked over, to spend the afternoon. This wasn't very exciting, time was going by slowly, and I couldn't seem to concentrate on my book. Staring out to sea, I got an idea: why not get some aerial shots of the coast?

Returning to our host's house, I looked in the Yellow Pages and found a helicopter charter service at the Monterey Airport, a few miles away. They were booked that day but had an opening the next morning, which I signed up for, telling them of my aerial photography plan—and also of the fact that I was in a wheelchair, which didn't seem to faze them. This kind of thing was expensive, so I only booked 30 minutes.

Arriving at the flight line, I was pleased to find that their helicopter was a Bell Jet Ranger, a four-seater that is widely used as a camera platform by TV news shows, police, and professional photographers. It has a cruise speed of 120 mph, which was good for me because I wanted to cover as much of the shoreline as possible in the short time. I opted for the left front seat to give the widest range of view, and the pilot and line technician lifted me into place. Strapping myself in with the five-point harness (including a strap between the thighs), I asked the pilot if he would remove the door to give me wider camera aiming range. I didn't expect he would do it, particularly because I was disabled, but he said it was OK, and off it came. I think he had assumed by my abundant camera gear that I was a professional and did this kind of thing regularly. Realizing that at over 100 mph and with the rotor wash, there would be strong wind gusts in the cockpit, I asked them to tie down my feet, which they did with extra web strapping. I didn't want my feet banging around loosely. I had taken charter rides in helicopters around Manhattan Island, but this was the first ride with the door removed.

Part of my objective was to see if I could see Barbara and her hosts out on the course and get a shot of them; so I asked the pilot to stay in close to shore. We took off and headed west over Monterey, climbing as we passed the Cannery Row waterfront made famous by John Steinbeck and out over Pacific Grove before heading south toward Cypress Point. I had one 36-exposure roll in the camera and two extras in my vest pocket. It was a dramatic vista—the long Pacific swells piling into the rugged, high cliffs, which were often populated with sea lions. We swept down the coast at good speed with me firing away, sometimes several frames a second. I could shoot down almost vertically from my seat position at the open door. What a rush. I never saw Barbara and her partner but got excellent shots of the Cypress Point course, the Pebble Beach course, the village of Carmel, and Point Lobos. Changing film rolls with my less-than-perfect hands was a challenge in the blasts of wind. The half hour went by in what seemed like five minutes, and we were shortly landing back at the airport. As we descended to the tarmac, I thought, "This wasn't cheap, but it sure beats picnicking in the parking lot at Point Lobos."

At other times, I found myself unwittingly in precarious situations because I didn't want the wheelchair to prevent me from doing normal things. One of the craziest of these started out innocently enough. When John was about twelve, the father of one of his classmates, a boy named Hunt, had an idea: Why don't the dads of the class spend a day with their sons as a group going fishing out on Long Island Sound on one of those excursion boats for hire down on the waterfront in Sheepshead Bay? Hunt's dad, John (a real organizer and a popular parent) proclaimed, "It'll be a great father and son day! We'll have a ball." John and I were invited, but I had some misgivings about getting into the boat in the wheelchair and how I was going to handle the motion of the boat on the water while handling the rod, not having proper balance.

But I hated to disappoint my son and told him to sign us up. Big mistake. It all started out well enough on a Saturday in March. John and three strong fathers got me safely into the boat, and we were well stocked with hearty sandwiches and cold sodas from Barbara. However, the weather was not that good—damp and cloudy, temperature in the fifties with a stiff easterly wind.

The idea on these popular boats was to head out into the Sound at about 10:00 a.m. for about five hours with a party of paying guests, equip them with simple fishing tackle, find schools of blue-fish, stripers or flounders, and let the "fishermen" go at it. The actual fishing was pretty mindless once a school was found. You just put your rod over the side and dangled the bare hook where you were told. The fish were so hungry that they just attacked your hook. When you got a strike, you reeled the fish in, and one of the crewmen would, if necessary, net it and take it off the hook. Meanwhile, over a set of loudspeakers, the captain kept up a running patter of instructions, well-worn jokes, and exhortations—all in a perfect Archie Bunker style Brooklyn accent—trying to see to it that everyone was having a good time.

Everything was fine until we headed out around the protective breakwater into the open water. The wind was a lot stronger with a real chill in it, and the sea was choppy with waves of three feet or so as the tide, current, and wind were working at cross purposes—there was no even movement of the boat but sharp and unpredictable lurches of pitch and roll. This was bad for me and my wheelchair because I was sliding this way and that and a sharp movement could tip me over or dump me out of the chair. So, with John's help, I got close to one of the posts holding up the deckhouse and wrapped my arm around it steadying my other hand on the gunwale. I held on as we motored out for twenty minutes or so through the chop, to the fishing grounds. When we got there, the tackle was handed out to us all, and it became clear that with both hands occupied I wasn't going to be doing any fishing. This is going be a long day, I thought.

I expected the boat's sharp movements to ease off once we got to the fish and drifted with the engine idling. If anything, it got worse, since we weren't penetrating the waves but just bobbing like a cork on top of them. It was then that the trouble began. I noticed that several of the fishing party were looking a little queasy. Then one or two went below, followed before long by others. In less than an hour, more than half of the fathers and sons had gotten seasick. One problem was that the fish weren't biting, which would have helped distract them. Another problem was that if one of the sons got sick, the dad would go below to comfort him only to get sick himself once he was out of the bracing sea air.

My post was near the hatchway below, and I could hear the retching and moaning of those who had been stricken, not to mention the fetid smell emanating from the opening. As more joined those below, conditions worsened with some lying on the floor, which was by now filthy, some of the boys sobbing in their misery. My son and his friend Hunt were fine, as was his dad, the organizer. I too felt no sign of illness. The boys were having a great time trying to catch the elusive fish. There were two or three other adults and kids who were all right but didn't seem very happy, the fishing being so bad. I was holding on for dear life to the post and gunwale, my arms aching and my body getting colder by the minute in the chill wind. I even had a hard time eating my sandwich at noon, one-handed and shivering at that.

Time was going very slowly. We weren't due to head back until about 2:30, and I was wondering if I could hang on that long. The smart thing to do would have been to head back. Clearly, this was no "great father and son day" as promised, and the fishing was virtually non-existent. But John, our irrepressible leader, persisted in seeing it through to the end—trying his best to sustain some enthusiasm among the troops.

The scene was truly ludicrous. Here we were, freezing out in this choppy sea, being constantly harangued by the captain: "OK, we're coming up on a school of blues—real beauties. Get those ever-loving lines over the side, men. Looks like they're biting (they weren't). Bob your lines up and down. Those babies like to see something move, and they'll go for it every time. Oh! This kid just got a bite—but it got away. When they bite, son, jerk hard on the line to set the hook. It's a great day, isn't it? Hey they're moving under the boat now. Get to the other side! Watch those hooks. You don't want to catch one of your pals. Ha! Ha! OK, lines over the side…" and on and on non-stop.

Meanwhile, in bizarre contrast, below deck six or eight miserable souls were wallowing around in their own vomit just wanting to die, they felt so sick. Dads were feeling sorry for their kids and the kids themselves were perhaps seeing their dads for the first time reduced to pitifully sick versions of their usual adult selves.

I don't know how I lasted, but I did, for the full five plus hours—arms by that time numb with fatigue and body shivering from the cold. Never was I happier to feel smooth water under the keel of a boat as when we came into the shelter of the breakwater. The group debarked—a sad looking and pale fishing party, their clothes reeking, their dignity lost, the day a complete disaster. John, our leader, should never have let the agony last so long, but he was unfazed and still upbeat. "Hey, we had some bad luck with the weather and the fishing, but next time, we'll pick a better day," he shouted at the backs of the staggering group as they dispersed to their cars. There never was another father and son outing. I climbed into my car, turned up the heater full blast and headed home. Shortly after arriving, I was fast asleep under a heavy blanket. Later, over a quiet dinner, feeling quite normal at last, I vowed never to put myself in a position where I had to endure as much and be at risk when I had no control over the circumstances.

It doesn't seem like much, but my life was never quite the same once I learned to do a "wheelie." This simple stunt of balancing on the back wheels only, made famous by Evel Knievel, became popular with sport motorcyclists and children on low-slung stunt bicycles—and also became a trick for athletically inclined paraplegics. It really is an eye-catcher when you see a wheelchair being balanced on its back wheels. When I was going through rehab at the VA, I was awestruck when I first saw it done by the more adventurous paras, but never gave it another thought at the time. Surely, I could never do that.

Perhaps ten years later, though, I was more physically self-assured and a lot stronger. One weekend when visiting good friends in New Jersey, we were having Sunday brunch and for some reason now forgotten, I decided to try to do a wheelie (perhaps the Bloody Mary had something to do with it). I asked our host if he would be a safety backup for the attempt.

We moved out into the vestibule, and he stood close behind my chair, hands just under but not touching the push handles. I grabbed the rims and at the count of three gave the chair a sharp forward push. The wheels just barely got off the ground, perhaps three inches. Another time, same result. There must be some trick to this I thought. And then it came to me: pull the chair back crisply first, then go sharply forward. It worked! I got up on the rear wheels but I could only hold the balance for a split second. Then I tried again and several more times soon sustaining it for several seconds. I'm not sure he ever had to catch me from tipping over backwards. Wow! I did a wheelie. I'm sure Barbara was not as keen on the stunt as I was and was thinking something like, "When will this guy ever grow up?" Children of both families were summoned down from their activities upstairs to bear witness to this trick and greeted it with high accolades. I practiced at home with John as backup and one day when alone tried it solo. It was kind of like trying your first back dive without the instructor holding you—a bit scary.

As I said, it doesn't seem like much, but for a quadriplegic to do a wheelie was very unusual (but only possible because my injury level was lower than most). It gave me a great feeling because it meant that I had gotten to an advanced point in using this chair I was spending my life in. There was also the very practical advantage of being able jump up curbs of up to four inches without assistance —a major help in getting around in New York. And later when I began to spend a lot of time around small airports, I could push through quite high grass using forward-moving wheelies to keep the small front casters from getting snarled. Finally, it was a good way to rest the skin on my backside by temporarily changing weight distribution.

There was a real fun side to it too as I learned—kids. Often, let's say in a supermarket, I would see a couple of children staring at me just wondering what the chair was all about, sometimes with worried looks on their faces. I would smile, "pop a wheelie," and hold it, which would invariably produce wide grins and sometimes exclamations, "Mom, that man can do a wheelie—that's cool!"

I got pretty good at it over the years and could hold it for extended times. I think that John once bet me his allowance that I couldn't stay balanced for fifteen minutes. I won and furthermore managed to do a 360-degree turn while staying balanced during the period. John also had learned how to do it in my spare chair, and we had a good time around the house with the chairs. But it got out of hand when we started racing from dining room to kitchen through the pantry to front hall to living room. Barbara did not see the fun in it at all, particularly when we nicked the coffee table upon which one of her best Steuben glass golf trophies sat. We were unceremoniously busted by a justifiably angry lady and never did it again.

Obviously, one of the most frustrating things about a wheelchair is that you are confined to mostly level, smooth surfaces. As a person who had really enjoyed out-of-doors action—skiing, golfing, canoeing, etc.—I missed the freedom to partake of it except for sitting on the sidelines and reading, whittling, drawing, and observing nature from a distance.

In the mid-1960s, I discovered a product that made a huge difference in my life—an unusual all-terrain vehicle. About the size of a golf cart and having a small but powerful engine, this type of ATV was different in that it was a six-wheel drive amphibious machine with soft fat tires that could go practically anywhere in the forest, across streams, through heavy brush, and up steep slopes. Its original market was for duck hunters and other sportsmen who wanted to get into the back country—kind of a snow-less snowmobile —and was also used by power and timber companies. I owned three all-terrain vehicles over the years, each one a step up in ruggedness and reliability—the last being serious "industrial strength." I trailered them around behind my car when headed into the country, and these machines turned a lot of heads on the highway, particularly those of young boys. My ATVs were a ticket to undreamed of freedom and got me involved in a lot of adventures, most of them just good fun—exploring the woods and beaches, flying kites with my kids, and getting places I couldn't possibly get to in the wheelchair. Occasionally, though, I got into scrapes.

One afternoon after we had moved to Connecticut from New York, I decided to go out to the back meadow of our place to see how a man I had hired was doing on a brush-clearing project. I hopped into my ATV and drove the 200 yards through a wooded trail to the work area only to find that he had left for the day. So I looked around at the work in progress and as I was driving along not thinking, my machine got hung up on a stump hidden in the grass and came to a dead stop. Several of the wheels were off the ground, and the ones touching did not have enough traction to dislodge the vehicle. I tried rocking it and everything I could think of. It wouldn't budge. Of course if I wasn't paralyzed, it would have been easy: I would have just hopped out and pushed the machine off the stump.

Well, I was paralyzed, and I quickly realized that I had gotten into serious trouble. Although the afternoon was nice and warm, it was already 4:00 p.m. on a day in May and only a few hours before sunset. The night would be cool—down into the 50s or 40s, I would guess—and all I had on was a cotton flannel shirt. Barbara was in New York for the night, so there was no one around to know I was missing, to shout for, or to expect to come out to look for me. The cleaning lady wasn't coming until the next morning. Since there was no place to carry it on the ATV, my wheelchair was at the house.

It didn't take more than a few seconds for me to conclude that I only had one option—a very unpleasant one—and that was to let myself down onto the grass and try to crawl to the house. This I had never done. I wasn't even sure it could be done. But whatever the odds, they were better than staying overnight in the vehicle. And I should waste no time getting started.

So I very carefully lowered myself over the side of the vehicle, being sure my legs were not twisted. I turned over on my stomach and tried to crawl in the usual way. No dice. There was no way I could drag the dead weight of my whole body through the grass merely with my arms. I sat up to try another technique. I turned my back to face the direction I wanted to go, put my fists in the grass, lifted up my butt an inch or two (I weighed 150 pounds), and hiked myself back maybe four or five inches. It worked, but creeping along five inches at a time to cover two hundred yards was going to be quite a challenge—maybe an impossible one.

I set out and ran into problems right away. First, I was only wearing loafers on my feet, which pulled off immediately as my heels dragged backwards. So I took them off and put them in my lap. They kept falling off. Then I discovered that, after about a dozen of these five-inch lift and backward hikes, my arms would tire and start to ache. To make the whole distance, I would have to pace myself and not try to rush it. I grabbed my loose shoes and threw them behind me six feet or so in the direction I was headed. When I got to them after a dozen or so "hikes," I would rest for two minutes, then repeat the process. I felt like the crippled figure in the meadow in Andrew Wyeth's painting *Christina's World*.

My route would include about a hundred yards of field, part of it up a small hill, then a dirt path downhill through the woods, and a final sixty yards over the lawn to the house. When and if I got there, I had no idea how I would lift myself back up into my chair. At least I could get to a phone. No point in worrying about that now, I thought.

The routine seemed to work, but it was extremely slow. After an hour, I had made it 50 yards to the upgrade. This was progress that I could begin to see. Then another problem emerged in the form of brambles. There were small thorny shoots in this part of the meadow, and as I ascended the hill, my knuckles were getting scratched. By the time I got to the top of the incline an hour later, my knuckles were bloody and painful, and it was about 6:00. Now I could see the house at least. I was halfway there and I thought, "There is no way you are going to quit now. You're tired and a mess. But you can make it. You will make it." But my arms and shoulders were aching. I lay back in the grass to take a 15-minute break.

Just then, I heard something, looked up, and there was a young man on a mountain bike with a fishing pole across the handlebars headed my direction on the rough path that crossed the meadow. I could hardly believe my eyes, and I felt a great surge of relief. He was apparently coming from the stream, which was in my woods nearby. He didn't see me at first.

"Hi." I called, "I'm over here." He finally saw me lying in the grass and came over. He was kind of slack jawed with surprise at what he saw: a seemingly normal looking guy in his stocking feet prostrate in the field with bloody hands. I won't forget the look on his face.

"Hey, am I glad to see you! I'm in a jam and could really use some help."

"Sure," he said. "What do you need?" First I explained that I was paralyzed and what had happened. If he could go over to the stalled ATV, push it off the stump, and drive it up to where I was, we could solve this thing. This he did with ease and picked me up nice as you please and dropped me into the driver's seat. It was all but over. Whew!

He was a clean-cut young man about my son's age. Turns out he was doing some summer vacation work for my neighbor, who thought I wouldn't mind his fishing in the stream at the end of the day.

"No problem about the fishing" I told him, "But listen, you just saved me from deep trouble. How about coming down to the house and having a beer?" He accepted, and after I had got to the house, into the wheelchair, and washed and bandaged my hands, we sat around the kitchen, he with a bottle of Heineken and I with a healthy jolt of vodka. Turned out he was a really likable and intelligent guy of college age, and we had a good talk.

After he left, I thought, "This is bizarre. I've never seen a fisherman go to that stream. I've never seen a mountain biker on my property. And I've only once before seen a stranger up in the back meadow. And to have him come along at that exact time. Amazing! Either I was plain gut-lucky or the Lord was giving me another chance in the hopes that I would stay out of trouble." I tend to believe it was the latter.

I ordered my first cellular phone the next day.

Several other times before this (and the cell phone), I had found myself stranded and had to be rescued. Twice it was a mechanical failure and not my fault. But sometimes my good judgment would be eclipsed by the temptation to get to difficult locations, resulting in two occasions when I got hung up in the rocks or tree trunks. Barbara was involved in all of these episodes. She pulled the machine clear of one tie-up, she and my daughter, Anne, got me out of another. But she had to get reinforcements the other times. To say the least, she was unhappy with all these episodes: being anxious when I didn't return, trying to find me in the woods, hiking back to the house to call for help, and wasting a couple of hours better spent on other things. But she was used to my ways, and I must give her credit for her patience. She would mainly roll her eyes and just shake her head. I got more conservative in time, bought more reliable vehicles, and with the advent of cell phones, there were no further incidents.

For all the hassle, my ATVs were a great escape for me. In Maine, with 16-year-old John doing the bush-whacking along a half-mile trail, I got out to a dramatic cliff-top ledge, which was a good 100 feet above the Atlantic surf. The last 50 feet of steep incline through the woods down to the top of the cliff was handled by backing down with a safety line hooked around the axles and fed out inches at a time by John, who had a sturdy rope cinched around a tree trunk up in the woods. To have gotten my severely disabled self out to this spectacular outcropping with John's help was a real rush (and we did it more than once). Sitting out there, me with a cold beer and John with a soda, eating sandwiches and enjoying the spectacular view, was pretty special. We were partners in crime.

Boredom figured in another escapade with John that probably should not have taken place. Once when on vacation in Florida, John, then thirteen or so, and I found ourselves with nothing to do and discovered an unusual way to spend a few hours. We were on Sanibel Island, where a good friend had lent the family his condo for the spring break. Barbara and Anne had gone off to walk the beach and look for shells, leaving John and me to our own devices. Since the rental car we had did not have hand controls, we were stuck at the apartment. It was right on the water, and we watched the pelicans fishing in the bay for some time, then tuned in a movie on TV. It wasn't long before we got restless.

What I really wanted to do was to get up to the northwestern part of the island, where there was an outstanding bird sanctuary and nature trail. If only I could figure out a way to drive the car without hand controls, we could do it. Then I noticed a tennis racket in the closet and got an idea. If John could operate the gas pedal, I could steer with one hand and use the racket with the other to operate the brake and thereby control the main safety function. I broached the idea with him along these lines: "I'll get in the driver's side. Then you put the wheelchair in the trunk and get positioned next to me on the front seat so that you can reach the gas pedal with your left foot. I will steer with my left hand and with my right hand hold the tennis racket by one end while resting the other end against the brake pedal. You'll have to accelerate very gently and respond instantly to my instructions, particularly when I tell you to ease off on the gas. I'll also operate the automatic shift lever." Always game for adventure, he thought it was a great idea. I had confidence in John in all this because he kept his cool, was coordinated, and followed instructions well.

First, though, we needed to see if it could be done with acceptable safety by trying some very slow and cautious runs around the parking area. This we did for a half hour or so and, with practice, got good enough in our coordination that I felt we could bring it off without endangering ourselves or others. An important factor was that traffic was very light on this small island, which was only about twelve miles long, and the speed limits were low and well enforced.

Before starting out, I told John that we must keep a sharp eye out for the police and went through what to do if we were stopped. I would bring the car to a gradual stop while he slid across the seat fully to the right side. After stopping, the tennis racket would be placed on the seat between us. Since my chair would be in the trunk and I looked like a perfectly normal person sitting in the driver's side, we would seem like any other father and son out for a drive. Obviously, to avoid problems, we would drive well within the speed limit and come to full stops at lights and stop signs, easily yielding right-of-way to other vehicles at all times.

We set out extremely carefully into the traffic, being alert to any possible activity ahead (such as someone backing out of a parking space) that might require braking. We wanted no surprises. After a half-mile or so, we were out of the village heading west on the main two-lane road with hardly any traffic to contend with. So far, so good. When we got to the wildlife sanctuary, it was tricky at the gate to look and act normal as I paid for our pass. But all went well, and we made the loop through the picturesque wildlife reservation, where we saw a lot of interesting birds and two or three alligators. The return trip went off without a hitch. I turned the ignition key off in our parking space, and we shared big grins and a high five for having succeeded in this adventure. We went inside, ate the sandwiches Barbara had made, and I enjoyed a cold beer out on the lawn while we resumed our observation of the graceful pelicans at play.

In retrospect, it really wasn't good judgment to attempt the lark. It could have gone badly wrong, and I'm not proud of it. I chalk it up to accumulated frustration with the restrictions imposed by my disability. Sometimes it simply got to me, as it did that day, and I felt a compulsion to fight back. It was a small but satisfying victory, with a lot of fun thrown into the bargain—despite the guilty afterthoughts. When I told Barbara about it that evening, she just shook her head yet again in resignation.

Another time, by simply being a quadriplegic, I got into an uncomfortable situation that tested my nerves and endurance—but ultimately led to a surprising outcome.

During the 1970s in New York, we had a cleaning lady named Islin, who came regularly to our apartment. A black woman of Caribbean origin, she had a warm smile and a personality to match, and she was liked by everyone in the family. One Christmas, she surprised me by giving me a $25 ticket to an evangelical-style "healing ministry" to take place in Harlem. "Mr. McGhie, it is so sad for you to be in the wheelchair. The preacher will call on God to heal you," she said. This was much too generous a gift from a person living below the poverty line to a man who obviously was prosperous. I didn't want to do it for several reasons. I was deeply suspicious of itinerant preacher-healer types, and the neighborhood around the venue was very dangerous in those days, particularly for a white person. But I couldn't bring myself to refuse and hurt her feelings. I felt I had to take whatever risk was involved, but I dreaded it.

So, at one o'clock one bitterly cold Saturday afternoon in February, I met Islin and her boyfriend, who were in their Sunday best, outside the Audubon Ballroom at 166th Street and Broadway. An old and rundown building, it was nevertheless well known for having been a great jazz hall in the early 1900s, a meeting hall for all sorts of organizations, including early city labor unions, and most famously as the place where Malcolm X was assassinated. Islin's friend and three of his cohorts, big strong men, picked me up, chair and all, and levitated me up a very long stairwell to the second floor, the Ballroom itself. I found myself in a large, low-ceilinged room, which was way overcrowded with what seemed to be a thousand people of color, all restlessly waiting for things to start, with standees lining the wall. My group insisted I be right near the stage where my ticket entitled me to be and fought their way there as a phalanx with me in the middle.

I looked at the crowd. I was the only white person in the room. That is until the preacher's entourage came on stage: three or four whites with several black assistants. First, there was a "warm-up" period, during which the white preachers one after the other gave emotionally charged harangues to get people charged up "for Jesus." In between were gospel songs accompanied by a jazz-style piano player. He had an irresistible beat and had everyone singing, clapping, and stamping in no time. I felt the floor beginning to shake, and for the first time, I felt a twinge of real fear—an overcrowded hall (well past the Fire Department limits), poorly ventilated, and with a lot of people getting very worked up. I had thoughts of a collapsing floor or being trapped in a fire.

After an hour of this, the main preacher, also white, took the stage, to an ovation. I think he called himself Pastor Peace, and his following was built on a radio ministry. I was close to the stage, and a slicker article I've never seen—shiny blue suit, silver tie, short in stature with greased-back dark hair and shifty eyes—a midway barker, used-car salesman type. The healing part was supposed to be the climax at the end. But before that, he led a two-hour session exhorting the crowd in demagogic, emotional urgency to "love Jesus and make sacrificial cash gifts to the Lord. Hallelujah!" There were four or five rounds. First it was a $5 offering "from every God-loving soul in the room," which the black assistants went around collecting, then $10, then $20, and finally $50 for those who wanted a special anointing for healing and a prayer scarf. At least 300 lined up for the last and came forward, money in hand. I was amazed to see that so much money was being given that the assistants were now collecting it in cardboard shipping boxes overflowing with cash—by this time, many thousands of dollars by my rough calculation. Now, after almost four hours of this, the air in the room with a thousand-plus bodies was very warm and stuffy, the windows all steamed up, and I was feeling almost sick. But I couldn't leave out of obligation to Islin's generous gift, and I wouldn't have been able to get through the dense crowd anyway.

Then came the "healing" part: Each of the dozen or so people on canes and in chairs in the front of the room, including myself, had to come forward one at a time and reveal our malady to the preacher. We were prayed for individually in loud quavering tones and exhorted to expel the devil in our bodies, choose the Lord, and rise up to new lives, etc., etc.—the congregation adding their "Amens." One woman, trying to struggle out of her wheelchair, fell on the floor with her immobile, atrophied body and had to be lifted back into her chair, sobbing. All the while, the crowd was being whipped up further to pray out loud for us while the collectors and their boxes made the rounds yet again "to gather thank offerings for the healing that God was bringing to these poor souls." I was so incensed that when my turn came and Pastor Peace or whatever he called himself started incanting over me, I fixed my eyes on his in a cold stare full of anger and disgust. I could see he felt it, and he only said a few words over me before I wheeled away, feeling nothing.

This whole meeting was a bold-faced exploitation and fraud. Yet, it was being taken in wholly by these good people. Their faces were open and moved, often tearful, as they chanted, prayed, shouted "Amen," and stomped their feet. They weren't crazed; they were joyful. It seemed that, in fact, something very special was going on in the room. I felt it. They had transcended their exploiters, and their faith was giving them a direct inner response. It was in the air. As we finally left, the mood was upbeat and everyone was friendly as they smilingly parted way for my wheelchair and the other "poor souls." Some patted my shoulder and gave thumbs up signs. I said a grateful goodbye to Islin and her friends on the sidewalk, who also were all smiles, got in my car, and headed watchfully home, exhausted by the anxiety, the noise, the air, and the anger I had felt in that room. The charlatan preachers were probably driving away in their vans by now counting the bills. I thought: they'll pay somehow for what they were doing.

I got back to our apartment at 7:30 or so, bleary-eyed and with my neck still aching from the tension. I have often thought of that experience. It had been the right thing for me to do, hard as it was. And I realized upon reflection later that I had in fact borne witness to a deeply moving demonstration of a spiritual presence in that crowd of faithful people. They had accepted and prayed for me and the other disabled folks and were so moved and uplifted by the whole experience that they weren't even aware of the preachers' cynical manipulation, which appeared to be completely subsumed by their faith. Was I healed? Not physically to be sure; but spiritually I had had something of a revelation in being the subject of such a true outpouring of prayerful compassion from Islin, her friends, and the congregation. It was a generous act. I felt it deeply and I'll never forget it.

Another religious setting, the Notre Dame Cathedral in Paris, was the scene of a remarkable experience quite unlike the one in the Audubon Ballroom.

When I took Anne, then age 14, to Africa, I planned to return home by way of Paris, where we spent the better part of a week. I wanted her to experience this beautiful city that is such an extraordinary cultural jewel. I knew she would never forget it. It was in May, a pleasant time of year for Paris. I knew we couldn't get to all the tourist-popular sites because getting around by taxi was not easy in a wheelchair. So what we did was to take advantage of the central location of our hotel on the Place de la Concorde to travel on foot (and wheel) to all the interesting sites within a mile or two—a very rich collection, including the Louvre, the Tuilleries Garden, the Vieux Carré, the banks of the Seine, Ile de la Cité, and of course Notre Dame. Anne was wide-eyed and eager, soaking up the atmosphere of Paris street life, missing nothing– the book stalls along the river, the fascinating shops, the architecture, and the diverse assortment of people and characters one encounters (for all her diminutive appearance, Anne was strong and energetic, pushing the wheelchair with ease for hours as we moved around with surprising speed).

It was decided that on Sunday morning we would try to observe the principal mass at Notre Dame—but not as participants because, although baptized Christians, we were not Catholics. It is one thing to "sightsee" a cathedral, but quite another to be present in such a great edifice as it served its main function as a place of worship. We arrived after the service had begun, and those who were seated in the nave were surrounded by rows of standees. This is just a guess, but it seemed to me that there must have been well over 1,000 people there. We were disappointed because there was no way we could see what was going on. Just as we were about to turn away, one of the standees spotted us and asked, "Blessé de la Guerre?" (literally meaning, "war wounded?"). The French have a deep compassion for disabled veterans because so many men with broken bodies returned from the carnage of WWI and were seen everywhere in the years that followed. For example, special seats are set aside for them in the subway labeled "Blessé de la Guerre."

I nodded "yes" since I was indeed a disabled veteran. He immediately turned around and proclaimed to those in front of him, "Blessé de la Guerre!" They in turn looked at us and moved aside for us to come through, passing on the words to the people around them. It was a chain reaction, and as the magic words were said over and over again, the crowd parted like the waters of the Red Sea for Moses and the Israelites. In what seemed like no time, we were not only able to see the service, but also found ourselves swept to the very front row at the steps of the altar, a few feet from the ornately robed clergy of various ranks conducting the service. Someone perceived that we were English speaking, and a translation of the mass was put in our hands.

To be in the center of Notre Dame, to look up at the soaring Gothic arches, with the sun's rays highlighting the smoke of the incense drifting up to the vaulted ceiling, to hear the blessed murmur of the mass, and to receive the bread of the Eucharist in that place was profoundly moving. And the way that we were received by the large crowd with such spontaneous compassion and then thrust forward for the sacrament made it all seem like some sort of miracle.

I have described many instances in these pages where being in a wheelchair made for serious, sometimes daunting obstacles to be overcome. Here, the wheelchair made the obstacles disappear.

Some people are drawn to new and different experiences—doing things they have never tried before—whether in their careers, relationships, avocations, or any manner of life situations. Although I didn't set out consciously to be one of those, I certainly have led an unusually eventful life. Often the new experience has involved a risk of failure, humiliation, setback, or physical danger. Things can go badly wrong, as I learned from my Air Force training accident. Since many people are very comfortable in quieter, more predictable lifestyles, I've thought about why certain individuals take more risks than others. Surely, psychologists have explanations—a need for attention, a hidden "death wish," an addiction to adrenaline, burning ambition, or maybe just lack of common sense. Perhaps it's genetic. A lot of my ancestors and relatives have had a tendency toward such lives. In any event, I have always been stuck with a strong desire to do adventurous things and never got over it, wheelchair or not. There is more to come.

Part IV

Airborne

Imagine being in a sleek, aerodynamic craft without an engine, thousands of feet high in the cold blue sky, warmed by the radiant sun shining through the canopy—the silence broken only by the gentle sound of the passing airstream. This is soaring. Using your skill and wits, you can harness the awesome power of nature for your pleasure for hours without harming it in the slightest way. And being there, at one with the natural elements, you can witness such things as the birth of a cloud, a hawk flying at the glider's wing tip, snow being wind-dusted off the top of a mountain, and other unspeakably beautiful visions of sky and landscape. Mankind has fulfilled a yearning to fly in many ways. Soaring was the way I chose to do it. It was a long time in coming, challenging on many levels, and deeply satisfying.

To Fly

Alone for the first time in the two-seater glider trainer cockpit after many hours of dual instruction, I stared nervously at the tow rope to which my plane was attached on the ground in front of me as its loose-lying curves were pulled straight by the tow plane getting into position up ahead. Was I really ready for this? I wasn't as sure as I had been a few minutes before. "You could get killed doing this kind of thing," I said to myself. But I put this rebellious thought out of my mind and focused on the tow plane. After the pilot's "ready" signal, a final cockpit check of my own, and a glance at the windsock to gauge the crosswind, I signaled for the wing to be raised and waggled the rudder to give the "go" sign to the tow pilot for takeoff. Then we were rolling as he gave it full throttle.

I stayed straight and low in the crosswind and somewhat tensely corrected for the moderate gusts through the first few hundred feet of climb. The tow went well, and I released from the tow plane normally at 2,500 feet. With increasing exhilaration I made a few

199

turns in the calmer air aloft, all the while feeling more relaxed and confident. I bled off altitude to about 1,000 feet and headed into the pattern, readying myself for a crosswind landing. There was a little wind shear on the final approach. I made a quick correction and flared out to a smooth landing but a less-than-perfect rollout. I opened the canopy. Don Vosseller, my instructor, was clapping me on the back. What a feeling! All pilots know it. The classic moment of first solo.

But this one was different. I was flying entirely with my hands. It was May 1980, and after two years of going against serious odds, I had just become the first spinal cord-injured person in the world to solo a glider. It was a sweet victory! Then, four months later, I passed a rigorous flight test to obtain a pilot's license from the FAA, the first one ever issued for hand-controlled glider flight. All this was 25 years after my disabling injury in Air Force Flight School, where I had ignominiously cheated myself out of being a pilot— something I had wanted since childhood. Now, at age 48, in a kind of unheralded victory, I was a pilot at last. "Victory" is the right word. It had been a long, sometimes seemingly impossible battle. That night after my first solo, I was treated to the time-honored ritual of having my shirttail cut off and had a couple of celebratory drinks with my instructor and the other pilots on the field at Wurtsboro in the foothills of the Catskill Mountains in New York. Driving home to the city later in the dark, I remember playing the inspirational "Chariots of Fire" movie theme loud on the cassette stereo, banging my fist on the steering wheel, and shouting to no one in particular, "Yes! Yes!"

All this was a very long time in coming. After my injury in 1955, I had become totally immersed in the very basic tasks of survival, rehabilitation, adjustment, and the building of a new life with Barbara. To say the least, I led a life on the run what with long work hours, travel, and a lively family life with all the joys and jolts that go with it. There wasn't much time for recreation, or much spare money, for that matter.

Flying was never forgotten, however. I learned that a group of paraplegics on the West Coast, mostly ex-military pilots, had rigged up small single-engine airplanes with hand controls that moved the rudder pedals. After they had an extensive go-around with the FAA, the controls were certified sometime in the 1950s, and a number of these paras got new, restricted pilot's licenses. There were articles from time to time on these and other hand-controlled flying activities, and I dropped them in a file folder in the back of my desk drawer. Someday that might be for me—maybe.

It wasn't until 1968 that I became intrigued with gliding instead of powered flight as a result of an article I read in *National Geographic* magazine. What it portrayed looked like a way to fly that had both recreational and aesthetic appeal, not just motoring from one place to another. But it took me two years to find the time to get a demonstration ride at the Schweizer Soaring Center in Elmira, New York, which had been featured in the article. There, it was an immediate turn-on for me as the college-age instructor took me up for a 45-minute ride over the beautiful sun-drenched farmland. But the experience was both enticing and disappointing. I learned that no hand controls had ever been successfully made for a glider. The problem was simple but tough: the right hand would need to be on the standard joystick for elevator and aileron control; and another stick for the left hand would need to be devised to operate the rudder. This was doable. But, in the landing sequence, a type of wing flaps called "spoilers" have to be deployed with a separate left-hand lever; and they have to be constantly adjusted to control the rate of descent to an accurate and safe touchdown. No big deal for the normal person: right hand on the stick, feet on the rudder pedals, and left hand on the spoiler handle during landing. But it was a big problem for a quadriplegic. He would need three hands.

How to develop controls to do this? As I learned later, the FAA had already stipulated that, should there be such controls, the pilot's left hand would have to be holding that spoiler control lever throughout the entire landing pattern for safety purposes. This meant that for the disabled pilot, the right hand alone would have to be able to control the elevator, ailerons, and rudder. This had never been done in a glider. Part of the difficulty is that a primary-type glider requires a lot more force on the controls than a power plane to do the same things in the air. It is flying slower and has no engine to pull the airframe through its maneuvers. So, to put the three basic functions on one control for the right hand would require real power in the right hand, wrist, and arm—something I did not then have. Fortunately, I did not know all this at the time. I just knew that there were serious obstacles that no one had yet overcome—or even had tried to, for that matter. Another issue was FAA approval. Any device added to an aircraft already certified by the agency would have to undergo a rigorous testing and certification process—a bureaucratic nightmare. Nothing is simple in aviation, as I was to learn.

In my late 30s then, I just didn't have the time or resources to tackle this kind of challenge. My family and business life seemed to get even more demanding as my brother and I took over McGhie Associates in 1969. Our consulting practice grew, and I started going to Africa. Eventually, eight years later, still intrigued with the idea of soaring, I took my teenage children to Wurtsboro to have another demonstration flight. Again, I was excited by the experience and talked at length with the instructor who took me up, Don Vosseller. I told him I wanted to fly.

"The trouble is," I said, "no one has ever flown a glider with hand controls. There are none. They've got to be developed and approved by the FAA. You know what a hassle that is. I would have to start from scratch. Then, who knows whether the FAA would give me a license?"

"I know it would be tough, a real challenge," he replied. "But, you should go for it. You've got the stuff. Come back again. I'll work with you for as long as it takes." He suggested I get help from the airport owner and chief pilot, Tony Barone, to tackle the hand-control situation.

A week later on a rainy Saturday, I came back to meet with this man. I wheeled down a muddy uneven walk to the office at the corner of the hangar, wrestled open the wheelchair-unfriendly door, and went in, soaked and windblown. The room was like a movie set of a 1920s aeroplane "B" movie—dusty, walls covered with pictures of old flying machines, a WWII B-17 crew in front of their plane, several antique wooden propellers, out-of-date air charts, and so on. Underneath the messy roll-top desk was a big cardboard carton with a rusty nose wheel assembly shoved into it. There were two or three men in the small lounge area hanging around and not talking much, mostly just staring out at the rainy tarmac and thumbing through months-old aviation magazines—pilots grounded by the weather, I assumed. A sixty-ish couple was behind the counter. The man was Barone.

I told him of my interest in gliders and that I wanted to rig hand controls with the objective of becoming a licensed pilot. I mentioned that I had driven a car with controls for more than twenty-five years. I asked for his help with setting up removable controls—for which of course I was willing to pay. He looked incredulous. "You mean you want fly solo with your hands only? I don't think it can be done. Someone in your condition? It would be too dangerous. I've never heard of it."

"I think it can be made safe," I said. "It would take some engineering, metal bending, and other work. But more complicated things have been done."

He didn't roll his eyes, but almost. "Listen, I can't help you, and that's it. Look around. This is a small operation, and we're too busy for any project like this. If you want to fly gliders, you can rent here and fly with an instructor. Same thing."

He still seemed unbelieving, almost scornful. He did not use the word "cripple," but it was in his eyes and tone of voice. It was also unspoken but clearly implied that he was leery of the potential liability. What he had said had been delivered in a gruff, ex-staff-sergeant manner with everybody listening.

I was taken aback at first and felt humiliated in this room full of strangers, as if I was begging for something inappropriate. His reaction was a blow, given that he was something of a legend in the soaring community, having built up one of the best-known soaring sites in the country. But a cold anger welled up in my gut to replace my embarrassment.

Making eye contact, I slowly said, "I want to learn to fly gliders —solo. I don't know how I'm going to do it. But obviously this is not the place to begin." I started to leave. I was angry. At this point, his tone changed a little, and he told me that if I really had my mind set on it, I should talk to Paul Schweizer, the president of Schweizer Aircraft. "Maybe he would help. You should use my name." This company was the maker of the only primary trainer in the U.S. and its plant in Elmira, N.Y., was where I had had my first flight. I wrote it down without comment and left.

This was a low point. I had driven for hours in the pouring rain from the Jersey shore, where we were spending the weekend with friends, to have this ten-minute exchange. Now, I had the dismal drive back. I sat in the parking lot, soaking wet again from getting back out and into the car. I had seemingly gotten nowhere. But what really bothered me was Barone's attitude. Dammit, I thought, just because you're in a wheelchair doesn't mean you shouldn't take risks or do anything adventurous—and therefore be consigned to the sidelines the rest of your life. I was mad, and I thought of Douglas Bader, the legless air ace—how he had been sloughed off when he had tried to get back into flying fighters. Looking back on the bitter three-hour return drive, I realize that it was at that point that I truly set my jaw to the task. The following week, I called Paul Schweizer, the elderly CEO of the aircraft company, himself even more of a legend than Barone. He was cordial but also unwilling to commit any engineering time, paid for or not, to my project. However, he knew of a double amputee named Terry Frazier in North Carolina who was working on the problem and was highly motivated. This turned out to be an understatement. A Vietnam veteran and double amputee, Terry had obtained a doctorate degree on the GI Bill and had become a professor of English at the University of North Carolina. After a glider ride in Aspen similar to mine in Elmira, he became hooked on the idea of soaring. Stymied as I was at the unavailability of hand controls, he had set out to devise a system, seeking advice from pilots and engineers. Eventually, he pooled his knowledge with an engineering professor at UNC, Bill Smith, and using a jointly bought Schweizer 2-33A trainer, they devised and produced a working hand control by mid-1978 (making it a senior class project).

Under their concept, the regular joystick was replaced with another having a pistol-grip handle that could be rotated about 75 degrees either way in a vertical plane to activate the rudder right or left. The other functions and movements of the stick remained the same. With this device, the pilot should be able to control all aerial maneuvers with the right hand, leaving the left free to deploy the spoilers in the pattern, as required by the FAA. It was not a simple piece of gear. The rotating grip was connected to the rudder pedals by means of nine rods, seven gears, four universal joints, and a torque tube—in all, a combination of heavy-duty and sophisticated materials, the whole apparatus weighing fifteen to twenty pounds.

Terry and Bill went through the full FAA certification process—submission of detailed engineering drawings, static tests, a failed flight test, refabrication, and a retest. All this involved a blizzard of paperwork and long bureaucratic delays. Frustrated, Terry took another route and was finally licensed in a different type of glider using artificial leg-to-rudder attachments. However, the hand-control FAA certification finally came through in the fall of 1978, restricted, though, to his one particular 2-33 aircraft.

I had gotten in touch with him, thanks to Mr. Schweizer, in the middle of this testing process with the idea of adapting Terry's approach to a set of my own controls. Eventually though, after correspondence and two trips to North Carolina, I took the plunge and offered to buy both the controls and his sailplane for $12,000. After all, as I pointed out, he had found another way. He accepted my offer, and I took delivery in December 1978 in Wurtsboro—something of surprise no doubt to the skeptical Tony Barone, who suddenly found a hand-controlled glider tied down at his field.

Although hopeful, I had some misgivings. The controls were designed for a person with normal hand strength. For me to turn the stick handle for full rudder was difficult and tiring, given my limitations, particularly when there were strong gusts or turbulence. Nevertheless, as soon as spring weather permitted, my instructor, Don, and I began a long process that was punctuated with frustrations and occasional triumphs—and a good many laughs, for these were no ordinary flying lessons. I had to be lifted in and out of the glider. My hand limitations posed problems that must have tried Don's patience, although he never showed it. People on the field and pilots who regularly flew there seemed to take no notice of my activities. I wondered what they thought. I think that many shared Tony Barone's attitude, but I didn't really care.

The first question to be answered was basic: given these controls and my physical situation, was it possible at all? It didn't seem so for the first few months. Although I made good progress in learning the basics of aerial maneuvers, takeoffs, and landings, the stiffness of the rudder control handle was a real problem. Rudders are easy when using your feet and the power of your legs on the pedals. However, I had to be able to move the rudder one-handed quickly and with authority to deal with constant adjustments, and I just didn't have the strength to manage it in the stressful, gusty conditions that often occur during the take-off tow and final approach. Here are excerpts from my personal log: *August 4—Clear. Hot. Gusty. Lost it on tow. Too much effort required. Hand tired quickly*…and then, *August 9—Perfect conditions. WNW wind. Again, problems with tow gusts. Needed help to recover. Fatigue, over correcting*…

Flying as much as I could on weekends, we went through the summer into the fall—37 dual flights before I had to quit for the season. Don and I reluctantly agreed that solo would only be possible if I could somehow get better command of the rudder function in the turbulent conditions of the tow and final approach. There were other problems as well. One of them is described in my last log entry of that first season in 1979: *October 21—Clear. Warm. Wind SSW. No lift. Four flights. Unassisted except for severe negative 'G' drop on tow in wind shear, leaving my loose right foot stuck under the torque tube (jamming the stick back). Don took over while I sorted out my foot. Dangerous! I must rig stirrups to secure my feet.* I solved this by installing racing bicycle toe clips on the floor next to the rudder pedals so that I could strap down my feet.

All this was discouraging—and all the more so because I had clearly demonstrated that I had learned the basic flying skills. But there might be ways, I thought, for me to get better mechanical advantage. I approached the problem three ways. First, the control ergonomics; I thought I could do better with a modified pistol-grip handle, the original being a pretty crude right-angle job. Over the winter, I designed a "Y" shaped handle, which I later learned was not unlike the joystick on the British Spitfire. It had more surfaces for gripping, was angled back more to the natural position of the hand, and the "Y" top provided a place for my left hand to grab the upper flanges in assisting my right hand if need be in a severe gust.

The steel-handled frame was refabricated to my specifications, and I had contoured wooden grips custom carved that were a much better fit to my hands. Second, I reconfigured the cockpit—raising the seat, angling it back, and thickening the cushion—all to get closer and higher in relation to the controls. Third, I needed more strength. So in the fall, I started lifting weights to build up my grip, arms, and shoulders. Overdoing it at first, I strained my right arm and developed a"tennis elbow,"a pretty ludicrous situation. On a less rigorous schedule during the ensuing months, I was ready to fly in the spring of 1980—in excellent upper-body shape and anxious to test my modifications.

The moment of truth was the first flight. My log reads: *April 11—Clear. Pleasant. WSW wind. Good lift. Two flights of 0:50 and 1:15. I was unassisted except for the first 50 feet of tow altitude when I got too high in a crosswind gust. New controls make a tremendous difference! Definite capability to control and much less fatigue. The new yoke is the answer.* Two flights later, I had my student pilot's certificate, the first official step toward a license. Following several weeks of intensive practice with the new control setup, I soloed on May 12th after a total of 53 flights—over a year after my first instructional flight. I was 48 years old.

The next hurdle was the FAA, which is not known for its adventurous attitude. They had never issued a pilot's license for glider flying with hand controls, and there was no precedent in any other country as far as anyone knew. Two things were in my favor: the hand controls were already FAA-certified, and my instructor, Don, was highly respected by the agency. In fact, he had gotten them in early on this project on an informal basis, advising them on progress and getting their guidance on proper qualifications and paperwork. They were taking it seriously, and the head of the regional office in Albany,

Chuck O'Neill, was handling the matter. He in turn was in consultation with FAA headquarters in Oklahoma City.

One thing Don and I were concerned about was the "precedent" that my licensing (if achieved) would establish. The FAA tends to be cautious, and Don and I wanted my certificate to be general enough so as not to be restrictive to other disabled people wanting to fly gliders with hand controls. Quite often, the agency would in this kind of situation limit the pilot to a specific aircraft with a specific set of controls. The sole restriction we wanted was "hand controls only." The idea was that if I could successfully demonstrate safe, competent flying—meeting FAA standards—the performance criteria I met should be applicable to any other disabled person attempting to do the same.

A busy summer ensued. There were two important obligations to fulfill: I had to pass the FAA written exam with a score of 80 or better, and I had to prove to Don that I was really ready for the FAA flight exam. The instructor must "sign-off" a student pilot as fully prepared, and in my case, the stakes were higher than usual in terms of his reputation, given what I was trying to do. Don had stuck his neck out on this venture. But if he was concerned, he never showed it, and we proceeded with our air work, some solo and some dual. Somewhere along the line, I also had to log at least 20 solo glider flights, accumulating a minimum of seven hours of solo time. At this point, my problem was finding the time to study for the written exam with all my business and family commitments, including client travel and summer vacation with two teenagers. The "written" is a three-hour test on all aspects of soaring—similar to the power pilot exam but focused on the very different complexities of soaring flight. I took it in September and got a 92. Meanwhile, I completed the air time requirements without incident. Don signed me off for the flight exam in late September.

Because of the precedent involved, the FAA regional chief, Chuck O'Neill, decided to conduct the test himself. This made me nervous, but Don assured me that he was professional, fair, and had no preconceived notions. All I had to do was to pass the oral exam, execute the aerial maneuvers we had practiced so many times, demonstrate good handling in the difficult tow phase, and make a safe and precise landing and rollout. I was still nervous when the day came and even more so as the time dragged on during which he was giving another test at the field. My turn finally arrived late in the afternoon—a good thing because the air was calmer. He was thorough during the oral phase, but I managed stumblingly to satisfy him on my knowledge of the subject. When I finally got set in the cockpit for the flight phase and he was strapped into the jump seat, I was surprised to find that my anxiety had completely gone and I felt calm and confident. We took off on the tow. The flight went very well as I handled all aspects as well as or better than in practice. But the landing pattern was a little high, and I had to use a lot of spoilers to end up on the proper spot on the runway—not smooth. Then he had us go up for another flight. I knew things were going well when he said, "I can't see the controls from where I sit behind you, and there is no way I can tell that you aren't flying this aircraft in the normal manner." My landing was better. He climbed out of the back as I opened my canopy and shook my hand. I had passed. I was a licensed pilot, at last.

There are few moments in my life that have equaled the joy and deep satisfaction I felt that afternoon. The FAA Examiner had cut me no slack in the testing. Later he reassured a reporter on this point, saying, "I wouldn't give my mother a license if I wasn't sure she was a safe pilot." Furthermore, Don and I were pleased that the license limitation was very general: "Valid only in aircraft equipped with hand controls." This set a broad precedent for other disabled would-be pilots, who might be using different glider types with other yet-to-be-developed controls. I was proud, with the help of Terry's controls, to open up this special avenue of aviation to the handicapped.

Since then, perhaps several dozen or more other spinal cord-injured people in the world have become licensed glider pilots. I understand that in Great Britain, where gliding is a major recreational activity, all soaring sites are now required to have a hand-controlled glider for giving lessons.

It was also great personally to have an aviation "first"—nothing special, but a real breakthrough nonetheless. And I admit to the very distinct pleasure of proving the skeptics and hand-wringers wrong—especially that hard-nosed airport owner who had turned me away a year and a half earlier at the same location. Finally, it was a form of redemption for me to get my license some 25 years after my accident had spoiled my chance to be an Air Force pilot. Somehow, I had the sense that I had regained my manhood after that long past accident had put me in the "half-a-man" category. Now I was a pilot.

Barbara always supported me in my desire to fly. She knew of my passionate interest in anything having to do with the sky—going into Air Force pilot training in the first place; then, after my injury, my enthusiasm for model airplanes, commercial flying, kite flying with the children (John and I once flew a kite literally out of sight to 3,000 feet). I suppose she just knew it was only a matter of time before I found a way to fly my own plane. She was well aware of the risks involved, but more importantly, knew my sense of entrapment being stuck in a wheelchair. She also knew it was in my nature to be a risk-taker and even once said lightly that, "If you are going to do yourself in, you may as well be doing something that you love to do." Furthermore, she was keenly aware of how hard I had worked for the 25 years since my injury and was pleased to see me escaping the pressure and being happy—and perhaps even proud to see that I was able to get past the many obstacles to finally gain the freedom of flight.

Hangar Stories

For pilots, "there exists a kind of guild, without charter and without by-laws. It demands no requirements for inclusion save an understanding of the wind, the compass, and fair fellowship." So said Beryl Markham, the celebrated African bush pilot, the first person to fly solo east to west across the Atlantic, and the author of an acclaimed book about her adventures and the mystical call of the sky called *West with the Night*. Under her heading of "fair fellowship" is the sharing of flying experiences with other pilots, listening to their stories, and recounting your own tales—usually in the pilots' lounge in the hangar. This special aviation lore goes under the heading of "hangar stories." As does every other pilot, I have a few such stories to tell.

I have often been asked why I wanted to fly. Like many a child, I dreamed of being Superman and of soaring "over tall buildings" with help of my cape, made model airplanes, and jumped off barns into hay piles with umbrellas as parachutes. I grew up during WWII fascinated with flight and able to accurately identify any tiny speck in the sky by its name and military designation—I was thrilled by the Battle of Britain, strategic bombers, and the glory of fighter-pilot aces. I suppose that I was even then on the fateful road to my Air Force misfortune. I never lost interest after my accident either.

I was intrigued by everything about aviation and vicariously enjoyed it even when on commercial flights. When I finally was able to pursue this urge to fly, I chose gliding because I wanted recreation rather than a means of travel and I found the idea of using the natural forces very appealing. My handicap put me at a serious disadvantage, but the challenge made it even more interesting. There was another appeal as well—call it controlled risk. I found that soaring can be an inspiring experience, but you are in a situation that does not countenance much laxity in skill, good judgment, presence of mind, and resourcefulness. Your life is in your hands, absolutely, from the time you start your takeoff roll until you have braked the aircraft to a full stop after landing. This of course is also true for power flying. Soaring is statistically a very safe sport. But there is always some sense of risk. I know of no pilot who has not been in a situation when a safe outcome was in some doubt. This ever-present edge, while not the main factor, adds to the lure of flight for certain types of people. For others, the experience simply isn't worth it, or even engenders sheer terror.

It is one thing to fly a hang glider or ultralight—types of sport flying that take place mostly in unregulated airspace. These people do amazing things, achieving very high skill levels, and all I have said above can apply to these adventurous aviators. But being a licensed pilot adds another dimension: you have to measure up to specific Federal standards of skill, safety, and competence and prove it through objective written and flight examinations, which though comprehensive are not intimidating. They involve intimate knowledge of your aircraft and its aeronautics and systems, as well as the basics of navigation, weather, radio communications, and a lot more. Passing these tests permits you to fly legally in the national airspace system —a far more trafficked and complex environment than most people realize. I never felt I was a "true" pilot until I had the imprimatur of an FAA license.

Soaring in fixed-wing gliders is different from power plane flying because the pilot has no engine to muscle the plane through the air to stay aloft. Your challenge is to keep flying by using the natural upward air currents we call "lift." You must move the glider smoothly through the sky with as much finesse as you can and with minimum friction or "drag" while you seek out lift, i.e., air that is rising at a faster rate than the inherent descending glide of the aircraft. Without lift, you must land within minutes because gravity is obviously causing the glider to be going down steadily in relation to the immediately surrounding air.

So you're constantly looking for lift, and when you get in it, trying to stay in it so that you can climb. This is where the skill comes in. The most common type is thermal lift, which is found in rising columns or bubbles of warm air that you circle in like a hawk. With experience and study, you develop an intuitive feel for what is going on in the surrounding air—as you focus your senses to visualize and make the best use of its ever-changing mix.

Success is measured in different ways such as time spent aloft, altitude gained, and distance covered. As I write this, my logbook shows close to 1,300 total hours of flying time. My average time aloft in recent years has been between two and three hours. The most distance covered in a day is 200 miles. The longest I have stayed aloft is more than five hours, and the highest altitude I have achieved is close to 15,000 feet. I have also done basic solo aerobatics. I hold a Silver "C" Badge from the FAI or Federation Aeronautique International, the world body that keeps the records on flying achievements, from modest ones like mine to major efforts like solo flights around the world. A Silver "C" means that I was at the intermediate-to-expert level.

For each pilot, there are certain things that make flying compelling. For me, being able to soar like a bird in the sky for hours without an engine is challenging and absorbing. There is the rush of surging up to a higher altitude at better than 1,000 feet a minute, tightly circling in a powerful thermal or riding a mountain wave—borne aloft by the raw power of nature. And there are nature's surprises. One day, I overtook a migrating great blue heron a mile high and got within 20 feet of him before he peeled off. Then, there are moments of coasting on course serenely over the earthly panorama with just the gentle sound of air passing over the canopy.

I have flown in calm air toward the end of the day over the desert mountains in Arizona when I could balance the controls so that my hands were resting on my knees in a cockpit no wider than the stern of a canoe. I could look out on the long purple shadows of the ranges below me, accented by the golden-rich reds of the late sunlight on the western sides of the harsh, rocky peaks. In the desert distance might be a quarter-mile plume of back-lighted dust behind a rancher's pickup heading home or the restless, hardly perceptible movements of wild horses in the dark sagebrush below. Everything seemed to be in exquisite balance when I was willingly suspended like this, alone and full of keen wonder, between unforgiving reality and dreamlike tranquility.

I loved to be able to exist this way in three dimensions, to have done such things that are in harmony with nature and inherently graceful—yet at times mentally or physically stressful. Best of all, it has been just being by myself in the sky at altitude with the earth far below.

Aloft I would think, "I am solitude, I am peace, I am freedom."

But it wasn't always like that. Early in my flying days, I very nearly had a fatal accident. It was on a great soaring day at what was then my home airport 20 or so miles to the south of the Catskill Mountains in southern New York. This was during my first full summer as a novice licensed pilot when I only had about 85 hours total time. But I was learning fast and had begun to be quite successful in catching and staying in strong thermal lift, having made several flights where I stayed up longer than two hours.

Now on this day, I was happy to have quickly worked my way up to 6,000 feet where I was circling just below a cloud near the airport. I was probably 25 minutes into the flight when, without warning, my rudder failed. Obviously, I survived. But it was a near thing.

The rudder hand control let go in the middle of a thermaling turn. Suddenly, it was completely loose in my hand. Instinctively, I leveled the wings. My first split-second thoughts were: "You're a dead man, Bruce. There's no way you can get this plane to a safe landing without the rudder working." You always need to use rudder in gliders (unlike most power pilots, who need to use it mainly in crosswind landings).

Then I thought: "Was it a mid-air collision? No, there was no sound of impact. What about the rest of the controls?" I gently moved the stick and found both elevator and ailerons to be normal. "Thank God! Now Bruce, just fly the airplane straight and level for a few seconds and think." My mind began to settle down after the initial shock and chilling fear. Everything seemed to slow down and become more deliberate like a slow-motion movie.

More thoughts: "I've lost a key function. The question is just what maneuvers can be done? Above all, I must watch my airspeed and keep alert for other aircraft while experimenting." I applied about half left aileron. It banked but did not turn at all, just slipped sideways in a useless maneuver.

"Got to try something else. My altitude is down to 5,000 in the sinking air, and I can't thermal because I can't turn." I began again by moving the joystick ever so gently left only an inch or two, getting about a three-degree bank. (The stick moved the ailerons, the wing tip flaps, to make this happen—kind of like dragging an oar in a boat.) After a few seconds, the nose began tracking the horizon very slowly to the left without the sideways slipping. "OK, I can get a non-slip turn with a modest bank, but the radius of my turns would be very wide—maybe more than a quarter of a mile. But at least I can change direction and get near the field. Progress."

As I headed toward the field, I now began to face the problem of pattern and landing in a crosswind. How to get lined up for final approach at a proper altitude was the first issue. The second was dealing with a crosswind with no rudder (you need a rudder so that you can crab into the wind and not get pushed off your flight path to the runway). If I didn't get these issues dealt with, I thought, this literally would be my "final approach." These kinds of morbid thoughts kept bubbling up, and they were distracting. "Fear is the enemy. Forget it," I would tell myself.

As I got closer over the field, my mind was totally concentrated on the problems, and I got an idea: Why not make my wide turns into big circles as I descended, and convert the last (or lowest) circle into a landing pattern of sorts, making a very long final approach—all the while keeping a close watch on the traffic in the air and on the field. I had no answer to the life-threatening crosswind issue at that point.

It seemed to take me forever to get down. I did some serious praying during the descent, having accepted by that time that a safe landing was probably impossible. My mantra became, "Just stay focused and give it your best shot. That's all you can do."

I made five or six big circles to get into my wide landing pattern. I elected to come in "hot" with extra airspeed to add directional momentum. Normal landing speed for me was about 60 mph. I pushed it up to 75 mph.

I finally got around to the final approach just where I wanted to be, perhaps a half mile from the runway threshold with about 700 feet of altitude, then leveled the wings to line up with the runway. I faced a right crosswind with considerable turbulence caused by the wind as it tumbled over a ridge line near the field. Shortly, this mixed up air began to drift the sailplane to the left toward a cornfield next to the runway in the distance—exactly what I feared. I had to try something. "I'll drop the right wing hard into the crosswind," I thought. "Maybe that will slip me back to the right." All this may sound like deliberate, careful thinking. It wasn't. The thoughts were intuitive, the decisions instantaneous. I had to try something, anything.

First, the nose angled to the left, but when bank was established, it blessedly began to move right. I let it track past the runway center line quite a bit to overcompensate, then leveled the wings to resume a normal descent rate.

Now a quarter mile to go. Altitude is OK. I kept saying out loud, "Watch your airspeed. Airspeed. Maintain the airspeed." (Stalling because of inadequate airspeed is what causes most small-plane fatalities in the landing pattern.) I was drifting left again. I dipped the right wing hard with the same course-correcting results. Now I was over the perimeter of the field at maybe 150 feet of altitude. No more surrounding trees to contend with, at least. I had to make another wing-dip course correction. Here comes the runway threshold —50 feet altitude—and now I was holding the right wing steadily down into the crosswind, and I was in quite a slip. I leveled the wings just before coming down hard on the runway with a bang and a blessed screech of the landing gear on the pavement.

The problem now was my high speed and lack of directional control with no rudder. My slip had put me down aiming a little left, which was aggravated by a gust that picked up my right wing, veering me sharply off the runway toward the nearby cornfield at maybe 65 mph. I slammed the right wing into the ground and held it down, hoping the friction caused by the wing tip skid would pull me around. It did and helped slow me as well. Now I crossed over the runway, going to the right, wings level and rolling out toward flight operations at moderate speed. I braked and came to a stop safely past the other aircraft.

I sat there struck dumb and amazed to be still alive, not to mention having no injuries or damage. One of the pilots came over and asked, "What are you doing on the ground? It's a great day, there are strong thermals everywhere." I couldn't speak and simply showed him the loose hand control for the rudder. Then it was his turn to be dumfounded because he knew I was an inexperienced pilot. "You mean you landed this in the crosswind with no rudder control? That's quite a piece of flying. You're very lucky to be alive." Amen, I thought as I sat there sweating, my hands still shaking.

Why did the control fail? He quickly saw that one of the pins holding a linkage connection together had worked its way out, severing the direct tie between the hand controls and the rudder pedals to which they were attached. There were eight of those pins, and with his help, we had them all safety wired within the hour. They would never get loose again.

I went home that night feeling a bit shaky but mostly just glad for the safe outcome—even a little proud that I had brought it off. With the safety fix having been made, I felt no qualms about going up the next day and got in a good flight.

Later, I thought a lot about the experience and asked myself: "What are the basic lessons here, leaving aside the hand-control issue?" They were simple, some quite obvious. (I have since come across several of them in writings about stress management in flying.)

These are the points I came up with: First and foremost, keep flying the airplane and watch the basics of airspeed, coordination, traffic. Many accidents happen when pilots get distracted from simply controlling the aircraft while they are trying to solve an emergency problem. As for the psychological factors: do not panic or you are dead; do not give up no matter how impossible it seems; do not try to solve the whole problem all at once; play the odds; and rely on intuition if it isn't clear what to do.

Although I never again got into an emergency this serious, I did have some very dicey situations in the air in later years where these lessons helped me to end up with safe outcomes.

In the mid-1980s, I was flying in Connecticut and was able to replace my trainer-type glider with a more advanced, German-made sailplane. A fiberglass two-seater with much higher performance characteristics, it was a Grob 103 Acro. The "glide ratio" was 36 to 1, compared with 24 to 1 in the trainer. That meant that as it glided through calm air, it would descend one foot for every 36 straight feet of flight, a gain of 50 percent over the trainer. The increased efficiency enabled flights of wider range and greater duration.

It was trickier to fly because the sleeker design made it harder to control airspeed, which is critical in any kind of airplane but more so in gliders. Furthermore, the manufacturer's hand controls called for switching back and forth with my left hand between the rudder lever and spoiler handle during the landing sequence. This required very quick and deft moves on final approach and landing, particularly in crosswinds. The right hand of course was fully occupied with the joystick. So for me, the transition to the higher-performance craft took longer than a normal pilot. I wasn't really comfortable with the landings for over a year, and I made some bad ones along the way— no damage except to my pride.

Once I got my technique refined, I loved flying this plane. I sat in the ergonomically designed front cockpit with great visibility and the instrument panel right between my knees. I put in over 700 hours in that plane. I became very proficient in "working" the thermals, and was secretly pleased once in a while to find that I was the only glider still able to stay aloft in the fading lift as the sun sank lower in the sky.

In the early 1990s, I realized a long cherished dream to fly in the West. I had had a client in Phoenix, Arizona, where we also had friends. On my many trips, I checked around in my spare time and found that the area would be favorable for me to soar at certain times of the year and I found a suitable site, about 25 miles south of the city. I decided to bring out my own sailplane. This meant towing it behind my van in its 35-foot enclosed trailer—a 5,500 mile round trip with five motel overnights each way.

I would depart in February, leaving the winter behind, and spend five weeks flying over the desert and mountains. I towed it out four times, once with Barbara. Then I did the other trips alone because, with her back problems at the time, the rough ride hauling a trailer was too uncomfortable. In a lot of ways, these trips were arduous undertakings for a lone quadriplegic in a wheelchair, dealing with the trailer, my luggage, and a different motel room every night. But there were aspects of the experience that I really enjoyed, particularly seeing parts of the country that were new to me and ticking off the miles on the open road—the quintessential American experience so celebrated in literature and song. My route took me down through the Appalachians, Kentucky, Tennessee, and Arkansas. Then, I would cross Texas in a day-and-a-half. Once I got into west Texas and then into New Mexico, I was in a part of the great open Southwest that I came to love—long, dramatic vistas, bare land punctuated by the occasional mesa or mountain, and sometimes only a few other vehicles to be seen for hundreds of miles. I had my radio and tapes as company, playing a steady mixture of country and western tunes that told the tales of loves gained and lost, hard lives and happy endings, regrets and rebirths. I felt loosened from my tightly woven life in the Northeast—eagerly anticipating the unstructured days I would soon be spending at the small desert airport and soaring in the warm sun. Barbara would join me by commercial air, and we would stay in a rented apartment. She would play golf and together we would enjoy our friends.

In 1994, I bought another glider in Connecticut and then transplanted the 103 Acro glider permanently to Phoenix along with an old van that I had retired. Thereafter, I too commuted by air, which was a lot easier.

Estrella Sailport near Phoenix, where I flew, is one of the best soaring sites in the country. They were willing to provide the extra help I needed on the ground due to the wheelchair. Among their rental fleet were three gliders exactly like my Acro, in which they gave rides, regular flight instruction, and taught aerobatics. These planes were designed for the extra centrifugal-force stresses of aerobatics and could safely stand 6.5 positive Gs and 4.0 negative.

The unit "G" is used when measuring the forces experienced in fast-moving vehicles such as aircraft, racecars, or roller coasters. One G equals the force felt by the pull of earth's gravity. So if, for example, you pull up sharply at high speed and experience five positive Gs, the aircraft and pilot are five times heavier during the maneuver than normal weight. It puts extra stress on both. The two 27-foot wings flex as much as three or four feet, and the pilot is pressed into the seat, organs are compressed, and blood tends to drain down within the body. It can be quite uncomfortable if you are not used to it. Negative Gs are even more uncomfortable. On a roller coaster or when a commercial airliner experiences strong turbulence, you will feel both positive and negative G forces. That's why they include the sick bags.

I watched the aerobatic flying wishing I could try it. It looked like a lot of fun. My glider was stressed for it, but I didn't know whether I could manage it with hand controls and also whether, with my poor circulation, blood would drain down excessively, causing me to black out easily. I finally approached the owner of the operation, a good friend, to get his frank opinion. He thought I might be able do it in a limited way, but the only way to know would be to try it out. I agreed, he got us some parachutes (required for aerobatics by the FAA), got me strapped in really tight, and we went for a demonstration flight in my plane.

I admit to having a few butterflies as we were towed to 5,000 feet, released, and he began to "wring it out," as they say. We did loops, inverted flight, aileron rolls, split Ss, wingovers, and a few other maneuvers. We didn't exceed 4.0 Gs, and while uncomfortable, I had no blackout or fadeout problem (I learned later, experimenting with another pilot, that I would start to blackout at 5.5 Gs). The one obstacle was that, not having full body musculature, I couldn't stabilize myself in the cockpit when pulling negative Gs. But my friend thought I would have no problem with the positive G maneuvers and agreed to give me instruction.

We worked on some specific moves for a couple of days, and then he declared me safe to do them solo. Now it's one thing to do these things with an expert in the rear cockpit, but a very different thing solo. Things can get out of hand very quickly if execution isn't precise and coordinated.

Talk about butterflies—now, I was really nervous. Up I went solo to 5,000 feet to do loops and wingovers. I gritted my teeth and started my first loop. You have to nose over and aim for the ground at 45 degrees until you reach a speed of about 110 mph before pulling back hard on the stick to bring up the nose; you monitor the G-meter until you are pulling 4 Gs, then you ease off on the stick pressure until you find yourself floating over the top inverted at zero or one G and slowed to about 60; then as you start down again, speed rapidly builds again and at 110 you pull back again on the stick to pull 4 Gs as you come fully through, regaining as much altitude as possible.

My first loop went off without a hitch. Then I did two more for good measure before doing some wingovers and setting up for landing. Now that was a rush I'll never forget. With more practice, I got so accustomed to pulling the Gs that I hardly noticed them.

These were simple, basic aerobatics, but I had great fun doing them—particularly when I would arrive back over the field after a two or three hour flight and still had extra altitude. Doing some aerobatics was the perfect way to burn off altitude quickly and celebrate a good day of soaring with a little adrenaline rush before gliding in for a gentle landing with the sun low in the sky. It did occasionally spook bystanders at the field. They would see the empty wheelchair over by the hangar and wonder where the occupant was. "Oh, that's him up there," one of the line crew would say, pointing to my plane as I was inverted in a loop over the field.

Often I took interested friends or others for rides in my gliders, but no flight, though, was quite like my airborne radio interview by Faith Middleton, the award-winning host of the Connecticut Public Radio show, "Open Air New England."

Barbara, on her own volition, had written to the show suggesting me as a subject since I was the only spinal cord-injured person in the world licensed to fly gliders at the time. I wasn't that enthusiastic, not being fully comfortable as yet in my second glider, having flown it only a limited number of hours. This higher performance plane was a good deal trickier to fly with hand controls than my first. Actually, I never thought the interview would happen, but sure enough, the producer called me, and a few weeks later, Middleton met me at the airport with tape recorder in hand. I had told her that if she had a history of motion sickness, she should take some medication because good soaring always involves turbulent air.

At first, we sat by the glider with a tape recorder, and she asked me questions about my injury, how I got into flying gliders, and glider flight itself—what it was like, what to expect. It was immediately clear why her talk show was a success. She was a quick study, highly articulate, and she asked penetrating, sensitive questions. One example: she asked something like, "You told me that your injury in the Air Force had washed you out of pilot training. Wasn't your becoming a glider pilot your way of redeeming that loss?" Surprised at her candor, I gulped. She was dead on, and I simply said a quiet "yes."

All this was to set the background for the flight itself where Faith, her listeners, and I would experience it for real in a half-hour ride in my glider.

As we talked and I gave the glider its preflight inspection, I noticed that the weather conditions were turning out to be ideal: a clear blue sky with occasional small puffy clouds, steady light wind and bright warm sunshine. All this meant that heat would build up quickly over the more reflective surfaces such as rooftops, road pavements, plowed fields, and parking lots, creating strong thermals—just what we needed to climb to good altitudes and have an interesting flight.

Faith was curious about everything going on the field and described it all into the tape recorder or asked me to explain things. She loved the sleek look of the more advanced planes such as mine and was amazed at how many instruments the cockpit had as well as the knowledge required of air mass dynamics. Obviously, she had thought glider flying was a lot simpler.

Ultimately, we got out to the flight line or takeoff area seated in our tandem cockpit seats, securely buckled in, and a microphone clipped to my collar. The tow plane arrived, and we were hooked onto a 250-foot rope. After a quick final run-through of my checklist, we closed our canopies, and I gave the signal for takeoff. We climbed rapidly as the powerful tow plane, a former crop duster, took us to altitude. The air was choppy, indicating strong thermals very conducive to good soaring. At 2,500 feet above the ground, I released us from the tow plane. Faith asked me to explain all this to the listeners, so I had been doing most of the talking.

Almost immediately, I found a very strong thermal updraft and banked sharply in a right turn to stay within this rising column of air. I heard her exclaim, "Oh-h-h-h" as we felt the powerful surge of the uplift. The strong lift was just what I had hoped for because I would now be able to demonstrate what it's really like to soar without a motor and stay airborne if desired for hours at a time. We had gained 200 to 300 feet in less than 30 seconds and were climbing fast.

At first, it was all quiet in the rear cockpit. Then she asked in a worried voice, "Are you going to keep turning like this?" This wasn't good.

"How are you feeling?" I asked, realizing that the rough air and steeply banked turns had made her queasy. No answer. "I'm headed back to the field," I said. "We'll be on the ground in less than five minutes."

She said, "Just tell them what you are doing." These were her last words of the flight. I reminded her of the location of the airsick bag, put out the airbrakes, and we made a rapid descent toward the airport. All the while, I was rhapsodizing into the microphone about the view and what a great experience it was to soar, as well as describing exactly what I was doing to make the landing. Soon we were safely on the ground and I braked the glider to a full stop near a shady area away from the runway. She turned off the tape recorder, opened her canopy, stumbled over under a tree, and collapsed. There she lay, feeling miserable, for a good half-hour. She did not get sick, but as anyone who has had motion sickness knows, she probably just wanted to die—it's such a rotten feeling.

Finally, she felt well enough to talk a little, and I asked her whether she had taken anything before the flight. "No," she replied, "I'm doing a live show this afternoon, and if I use a patch, it makes me too jumpy. Plus, I didn't realize it would be like that." I had to tell her that turbulent days are usually the "best" days. I doubt she ever went gliding again, but I give her great credit for having the courage to try it. As a journalist, she knew that the interview would be much more interesting if it was conducted during an actual flight, and despite being prone to seasickness, she gamely took the chance.

It was broadcast two days later. After the tape was edited, the listener would never know she had been so affected. The show turned out well, and was rebroadcast on her Saturday feature replaying the "best of the week." A year or so later, I was a telephone panel guest on her show, and she made a joking reference to the experience.

The next year, I took a photographer from the *Hartford Courant* newspaper aloft to get some pictures for an article they were doing on me. He too got ill, and we had another very short flight.

Soaring isn't for everyone.

On another occasion, I took a teenager up for a ride—the daughter of the fiancée of a pilot friend. Nothing unusual except for the way it came about and her surprising reactions. My friend and I were aloft, each in our own gliders. At one point, I lost the updrafts and headed back to the field for a landing so that I could get another tow and try again. Meanwhile, my friend was in good rising air and having a decent flight.

Apparently, he, at one time, had told the teenager that if she ever wanted to take a glider ride, she should stop by the field and he would take her up. Well, this was the day and the moment that she showed up unannounced for her ride. She inquired at the office and they informed him on the radio. He was flying his single-seater, which meant that he'd have to land and try to rent one of the two-seat trainers, if available, to take her up. He realized that at best it was going to be awkward to give her the flight he'd promised. But he noticed that I was landing and, guessing correctly that I was going to take another flight, he had a brainstorm: "Bruce can take her up if he's willing and it would be a much better flight for her in his sleek new two-seater." He called me on the radio and asked me if I would take her up. "No problem," I answered, so he called the office back with the plan and she was directed to meet me at the launch point at the end of the field.

It was just then that I landed, and a ground crew of two came over to my plane with a four-wheeler to tow me back to the flight line—one driving and the other keeping the wing tip from dragging. Since it was a hot day and I was getting uncomfortably warm as the sun beat into the cockpit, I got out a golf umbrella I always stowed in my cockpit and put it up as we rolled down the field toward the launching area (normally, pilots get out and hold up their own wing tip during the short pull to the flight line).

There, I was met by a cheerful and wholesome-looking, 17-year old who introduced herself as Amy Dews. Later I learned that, seeing me not bothering to get out of my plane to help and just staying cool lazily under my big red umbrella, she thought, "This must be some really important guy, getting all that help and all and not lifting a finger. Wow!"

I gave her the usual briefing for a first glider ride: what it would be like, how thermals work, what the instruments mean, what to expect, emergency procedures, etc. Then, with the help of the line crew, she got into the rear cockpit and was strapped in. Soon we were airborne, got to soaring altitude, and I released from the tow plane. The conditions had improved, and we had a nice flight of 45 minutes or so. She seemed to be having a good time, asking questions, listening to my explanations, and enjoying the view—a pleasure to have as a passenger.

When we landed, I rolled my glider to a stop near my tiedown spot at the side of the field. Amy got out right away while I waited as one of the line crew or a nearby pilot pushed my wheelchair up to the side of the cockpit for me to get out, which I did in the usual deliberate way. She thanked me for the ride, and we had a pleasant talk while waiting for my friend to land.

Later, I learned that she had had no idea that her substitute pilot was going to be a severely disabled guy who gets around in a wheelchair. No one had thought to tell her, including me. She later told her family, "He was paralyzed and flies a glider! I never would have known. And now I see why he didn't get out of the plane and everyone was doing stuff for him. I thought he was some kind of big shot." I am told it was a sort of an epiphany for her—a lesson in life—to see first-hand that it's possible for handicapped people to do such things as fly sailplanes.

As for myself, I took it as a compliment that my friend entrusted me with this fine young person without giving it a second thought.

In the early 1990s, the commercial gliding operation where I flew in Waterbury, Connecticut, appeared destined to close for lack of business. I concluded that if I was to continue flying in Connecticut, I needed to explore alternate approaches before it closed and I found myself grounded.

It was during that time that I learned that the manufacturer of my present glider was introducing a motorized version of the same model, a so-called "self-launching sailplane." It had a retractable 2-cycle engine and propeller, which allowed you to take off on your own without the help of a tow plane and climb to your chosen altitude. There you could shut off the engine, fold it into the fuselage behind the cockpit, and become a pure glider. In addition, if you found yourself getting too low, you could extend the engine, start it, climb to a safer altitude, and stash the engine away again for more gliding.

Made in Germany, the glider with its 60-foot wingspan was a beautiful airplane to look at and fly. Its engine system was very cleverly engineered. Nevertheless, it was still a complex airplane to fly when you were switching into or out of powered flight, and you had to master the sequence and "switchology" to achieve quick and smooth results—and to deal with emergencies should they occur.

If the air-start sequence was properly done, you could extend the engine and get a cold start within thirty seconds.

It was expensive, but I had been doing well with the part-time consultancy I had been running after my retirement. Then, I rationalized further that if I flew the motorglider in Connecticut and left my other glider in Phoenix, where I flew in the winters, I would avoid having to trailer that plane 2,700 miles out and back every year—a tedious chore.

I assumed that since the design of the new plane was very close to my older one, that a similar hand control system could be installed. So I approached Grob's U.S. operation in Ohio to express an interest. I knew the manager, Mike Shade, well, and was quite surprised when he seemed skeptical about my being able to fly the motorized version. He didn't think I could deal with all the cockpit functions plus fly the plane, all with hands only—just too much to do, particularly in an emergency. Plus, he pointed out, I had some hand weakness as well. True enough. I didn't disagree, but I proposed that the only way to get a better idea was for me to sit in the cockpit as he looked over my shoulder and talked me through all the sequential functions of engine management and emergencies to see if I could reach everything and operate it adequately. He wasn't enthusiastic but would do it if I was willing to drive the 1,400-mile round trip to give it a try.

A few weeks later, I sat in their hangar in their demo ship and did just that. We spent an exhaustive hour or two with me sitting at the controls going over all the possible system scenarios. He was surprised because it didn't seem overwhelming to me. We determined that if the throttle and trim levers were lengthened to provide more mechanical advantage, it might well be doable. Of course we would also need hand controls for the rudder and spoilers. He agreed to place the order with the plant in Germany, and I wrote a hefty deposit check. I drove back dreaming of being able, in a new plane, to be practically independent at the airport and be safer flying cross-country.

Two weeks later, he called to tell me that the company wouldn't accept the order. He said that the engineering and production people had balked because they were so overloaded with other work they couldn't get into engineering new hand controls for the 103C self-launcher. I was dumfounded. Here was a willing customer, who already owned one of their planes and flown it safely for years and was ready to pay a hefty price for one their new products. And I was being turned away just because of some extra engineering, for which I was prepared to pay. It didn't make sense, and I thought, "Here I go again. It's almost like being turned down 13 years earlier at Wurtsboro Airport." I suspected that the real reason was that they didn't want the product liability given that the pilot would be a handicapped person.

I asked if the decision was final. He said probably yes. But he added, "You can always write 'The Old Man' (meaning the chairman, Dr. Burkhardt Grob, the celebrated inventor and founder of the company). It would be a long shot, though." After thinking this over for a few days and cooling down, I told Mike I would write to Dr. Grob and give it one more chance. I then asked if the chairman knew English. Apparently, he did but was of course much more comfortable in German. What kind of German? "High German," said Mike, "the kind all the college professors, scientists, and diplomats use."

After a few calls, I found a woman in Connecticut, German by birth and university educated, who had been a secretary to a German executive. She was totally at home in "hochdeutsch," the high version of the language, and would be glad to translate a letter for a fee.

So I set about composing a letter that ended up being two full pages, single-spaced. Among the many points elaborated on was the fact that I had logged over 500 hours without incident in my

Financial Mail June 16 1972

Holding shareholders' trust

Setting reporting objectives and implementing them

can help foil the takeover artists

Ask the unfortunate *FM* staffers who have to decide the annual report awards. South African corporate reporting is a lot worse than it need be.

It's not that chairmen, company secretaries, even public relations teams, don't try. The plain unvarnished truth is that so many of them don't really understand what they are trying to do.

That may sound an unnecessarily harsh criticism. But it tallies with the broad view of local reporting standards taken by Bruce McGhie, a US consultant whose speciality is shareholder relations.

In an extempore comment at the recent *Financial Mail*-Group Editors' seminar on management shareholder relations, he rated our reporting standards about 20 years behind current US practice.

That cannot be an across-the-board criticism. If the *FM*'s annual competition achieves little else, it records those companies whose boards have grasped for themselves McGhie's basic injunctions. Decide your reporting objectives. Don't hesitate to use professional expertise to execute them. And, once your programme is running, test its effectiveness by feed-back.

Bruce McGhie... we've a long way to go

This leads on to the benefit of credibility. A management that has reported frankly and responsibly for many years is more likely to be taken seriously when it speaks, and it's more likely to see a fair market price for its shares. As a

But how do you decide what standards you are going to set, and for whom? Here the suggestion of deliberately stimulating feed-back from the marketplace is one of the better ideas to have crossed the Atlantic.

Every financial journalist has had the experience of listening to a chairman elaborate on all the useful information he provides shareholders, when a little market research would reveal that it's of no real interest to anybody but those inside his corporate HQ.

As McGhie rightly suggests, management could readily establish what it should be saying through informal contacts with half-a-dozen analysts.

Using more costly market research techniques, America's General Electric has made itself into a real innovator in shareholder relations-techniques.

A second particularly useful tip is to analyse and watch the company's share registers. What kind of people are members? What proportion of them are institutions and what proportion private holders? Where do they live? Once those questions have been answered, it should be a good deal easier to decide what kind of information they really need.

Anne McGhie

Firos Malanga

TOP | On safari in Kruger National Park in 1974.

BOTTOM | Searching for game on the Oliphants River, South Africa.

Rodney Smith

John McGhie

TOP | Alex and I, partners in McGhie Associates, Inc.

BOTTOM | In my ATV on a headland over the Atlantic in Cutler, Maine.

TOP | With instructor Don Vosseller after first solo in 1980 in my Schweizer 2-33A.
MIDDLE | Soaring over Connecticut in my Grob 103A Acro in 1985.
BOTTOM | Taxiing out for a 1996 flight with John in the Grob 103C SL (self-launch).

Bruce McGhie

TOP | At the top of a loop over the desert at Estrella Sailport, Arizona.
BOTTOM | Soaring over the Teton Range at 13,300 feet in 1991, using the
rudder hand control with my left hand. Earlier that afternoon, I had flown
over the Grand Teton, upper left, at 14,700 feet.

ABOVE | A great day for soaring, 1997.

Bruce McGhie

Bruce McGhie

TOP | John and his F/A-18 Hornet, 1993.
BOTTOM | John giving a cockpit brief to a friend.

Bruce McGhie

Bruce McGhie

TOP | Anne at Christmas, 2000.
BOTTOM | Barbara in Maine, 1998.

Grob103 Acro using their hand controls. Pulling out all the stops, I ended with an appeal to his conscience and sense of social and corporate responsibility, which began: *Unsere moderne Weltschafft Zugaenglichkeitsmoeglichkeiten fuer Behinderte und akzeptiert diese Moeglichkeiten als alltaeglich…* "In today's society worldwide, accessibility for disabled persons is increasingly accepted as normal practice." For example, I wrote, "On my last business trip to South Africa, I rented a hand-operated BMW without any difficulty whatsoever. I would hope that Grob, a progressive company, would be as enlightened in its approach to such concerns as it has been in the past."

I had given it my best shot.

It worked. Two weeks later, Mike called with the good news that Dr. Grob had sent a copy of my letter down to his operating executives with a note that said, "Do it." My plane was put into the schedule.

I didn't take delivery until six months later because we had to work out a way for me to get an endorsement for powered flight before I could fly the plane solo. My pilot's license was for gliding flight only. For flying a powered glider, you need to get the equivalent of a power plane license. To do so you have to pass oral and flight tests with a designated examiner. Mike had set aside a week when I could come out, take four days of instruction from him, and end the week with the examiner's test.

A lot of this was new territory for me, so I did a good deal of advance preparation—many hours of studying the manual, including fabrication of a simulator of sorts out of cardboard consisting of an exact scale mockup of the instrument panel.

I was nervous driving out to Ohio for the test because I had invested a lot of money, time, and effort in a project that just might not succeed. I was out on a limb. Despite all the workup with Mike and the specially designed controls, we still did not know for sure whether I could deal hands-only with the complexities—and my hands weren't full strength at that. Time would tell.

You know the feeling when you take delivery on a new car. Pretty special. Well, when I saw my new plane the next day, it was many times more exciting. Glistening white carbon fiber wings, fuselage, and tail section. And the cockpit: It looked more like a fighter plane's than a glider's. The ergonomics looked perfect, and the fit and finish were what you would expect in a Porsche.

We wasted no time as I climbed into the front cockpit and we started the instruction. Spending about three hours total a day of flying and devoting the rest to studying and working up my checklists, the four days went fast. Take-offs, landings, extensions, retractions, air starts, simulated surprise emergencies, fuel problems—over and over. My advance work proved to be extremely useful. However, although my flying was safe, it was far from smooth, and I felt awkward most of the time. Mike professed to be surprised at my quick progress, which he said was a good deal faster than many of his normal new owners. He cleared me for the test on Friday.

I felt pretty good about it when the day dawned, but everything would depend on my performance under pressure. Fortunately, the examiner's approach was quiet and low key, and the wheelchair didn't seem to bother him. It started off well, and I knew I had it passed in the first ten minutes. Ultimately, we landed, there were handshakes all around, and he endorsed my logbook. Done. After lunch, I made final payment and signed all the paperwork to acquire the airplane. The flight and maintenance manuals in both English and German stacked about a foot high.

After a great night's sleep, I returned to the airport to take actual delivery. It was a special experience to drive away, pulling the 35-foot trailer with my gorgeous new motorglider. But the deeper satisfaction was having overcome serious obstacles to do something that no one like me had done before. Another first.

Several months later, there was an article about it in *Soaring* magazine.

One of my more memorable flying experiences involved this motor-glider, which by that time I had been flying for four or five years.

On one beautiful soaring day in June, I invited a friend along as a passenger for what looked to be a fine flight. His name was Burt Rhodes. The circumstances were somewhat unusual in that Burt would normally have been flying his own glider. But he was fighting a losing battle with cancer and heart problems and could no longer fly. He was a long-time soaring friend, who had been very helpful to me several times as an instructor and most recently when I ran into difficulty transitioning to my new motorglider with its added complexity and new hand-control setup. Of late, I had been asking him along to give him a break from his now restricted lifestyle, which included heavy doses of chemotherapy. That spring, I had had him out to Phoenix for four or five days of desert flying. Since my planes had dual controls, he was able to do some of the flying.

An engineer by profession, his sport had been soaring, and he spent every summer weekend either flying his own high-performance glider or giving instruction to others. He was a very experienced pilot having flown 50 missions over Europe in WWII as a B-17 commander in the 8th Air Force. In the years since, he had flown many types of small powered aircraft and gliders, accumulating over 13,000 hours overall. In gliders, he was about as advanced in skills as you can get, having received a Gold Badge and several "Diamonds" from the FAI (Federation Aeronautique International).

The day's soaring conditions were unusually strong for Connecticut. After putting the engine away at 3,000 feet, we climbed in thermals to about 7,000 feet and headed to the northwestern part of the state. We had explored a little across the Massachusetts border and were headed back into Connecticut when we came on a large area of weak or nonexistent lift, which sometimes occurs even on the best of days. Despite my best efforts to find thermal lift, we had descended to about 2,500 feet above the ground when I decided to get the engine out and power us back to an area where there was active lift. Engine extension and startup went smoothly, and we climbed steadily toward better air and in the direction of our home field.

At about 6,000 feet, I decided to retract the engine and finish the flight as a pure glider. At that point, we were within ten miles of our home base and could make it easily. After shutting off the engine and letting it cool a little, I hit the switch for retraction. The engine then moved back about five degrees and stopped, waiting there for me to brake the propeller into vertical mode so that it could fully retract. The brake failed to work, and the prop kept windmilling slowly around, creating severe drag and causing rapid loss of altitude.

I tried everything I could think of in re-sequencing the switching with no luck. Burt was also coming up with ideas, but nothing worked, and we continued to descend. It helped that he was totally calm and cool, not surprising for his long flying career. Things are a lot tougher in these situations if you have a frightened passenger. We gave up on the unsolvable engine problem. Now, it was time to think of a forced landing. At this point, we were over a mix of farm fields, the occasional house, and woods—gently rolling terrain. We saw two possible fields, one a meadow with cows grazing at one end and some patches of randomly situated small boulders the size of bowling balls, which I would prefer to avoid. The other a cornfield that appeared to have stalks one-and-a-half to two feet high, which Burt thought was too far away for us to make with our rate of descent. We were now at about 1,500 feet and the ground was coming up fast with our rapid sink rate. I thought we could make the cornfield and made the decision to go for it. We'd have to come in over some woods and a house at the end and drop down onto the field.

I turned off the engine and the master switch, telling Burt, "You've had a lot more experience in emergency landings than I have. If you think we need more or less control input on short final approach, just get onto the controls and take the lead." He reminded me that I was "pilot-in-command," which I, of course, knew. I said, "Look, Burt, get on the controls if we need it. The rules don't matter. What we want is a safe landing." We cinched down our belts and shoulder harnesses as hard as we could.

My judgment looked pretty good as we approached the edge of the cornfield with about 50 feet of clearance over the house. I was intensely focused on maintaining a safe airspeed. Just after we cleared the house, Burt increased my air brake setting from 50 to 100 percent, a good move as we dropped more steeply in over the corn, giving us more field to work with. I flared the nose up over the crop at about five feet to slow the plane to stall speed so that we could settle into the corn at minimum speed. Soon we could hear the seed pods slapping the landing gear, and we dropped into the stalks at about 40 knots. The corn was over two feet high, and it grabbed the fuselage and right wing tightly, stopping us in a wrenching half ground loop. We settled in a terrific cloud of dust and a downpour of seed pods that had exploded up in the air as we plowed through the stalks. A safe landing, thank God!

"You OK?" I quickly asked, having been concerned all through this emergency about Burt's heart and generally fragile condition. He said he was fine, and in truth, he showed no indication of stress, shortness of breath, or signs of anxiety. It was no wonder that he had gotten his B-17 and crew through one of the most dangerous combat tours in WWII with only one crew member being slightly wounded. We opened our canopies, and he climbed out to inspect the airplane and assess the damage.

Meanwhile, I took stock of our situation, which was not good. It was 3:30 in the afternoon, the sun was still high, and the temperature in the mid-80s—too hot for me for any extended period. I had not made any "Mayday" calls on the emergency radio frequency because I had been too busy coping with the malfunction and getting safely on the ground. So no one was aware of our situation. Without my wheelchair, I was stuck in the cockpit—and even with the wheelchair, I wouldn't have been able to move in the cornfield. Burt was a very sick man and physically weak despite his mental toughness. I didn't think he could walk very far for help either, stumbling through the corn, climbing stone walls, etc. We made quite a pair. What we needed was my van and chair and people to help, but they were back at the airport. Unfortunately, this late in the day, there weren't many power pilots around that could help because they do most of their flying in the morning and go home. We were in serious trouble, and it looked like our best bet was the police. I got out my cell phone, doubting that it would work in this rural location. But we were near a hilltop, and sure enough, I picked up a signal.

Surprisingly, Burt's inspection turned up no indication of damage, only green stain from the stalks striking the wings. Just then, I had another idea. I remembered that Ray Plourde, who was president of the local pilots' association at the field, often worked on his plane in the late afternoon, and he had a phone in his hangar. This was a long shot. I only had his home number but lucked out by catching his wife and got his unlisted hangar number. I tried that, and there he was on the line to my great relief.

"Frenchie," as he was known, was just the man we needed. A good guy, as well as being big, strong, and used to emergencies much tougher than ours. In Vietnam, he had been a Huey helicopter crew chief and gunner on a search and rescue team. I filled him in quickly on our landing and physical situation as I switched on my flight computer with its GPS to get a close fix on our location. Shortly, I was able to tell him that we were 8.5 miles northwest of the airport at a heading of 315 degrees. He proposed that he over-fly us in his plane and locate us relative to nearby roadways and access to the field. Then he could fly back, get my van, and come and get us out of there. Twenty minutes later, we heard an engine, and there he was at 500 feet headed right over us at the exact heading. He waggled the wings, circled the site twice, and headed back to the field. Just after our landing, once we had found ourselves safe, I was concerned about publicity. The press loves air mishaps, and ours was unusual to say the least. Now we were going to get out of this with minimum fuss—no scanner, State Police, ambulance, or TV reporters.

About an hour after his fly-over, Frenchie and one of the other pilots came striding through the corn with big smiles and greeted us with a couple of cans of ice cold Coke. Never did a can of soda taste better. Shortly, we were joined by some people from the neighboring farm, who were curious about all this action and slack-jaw surprised when Frenchie lifted me out of the cockpit and dropped me into my wheelchair—the pilot, of all people. Concerned about wanting to pay for any crop damage, I gave them my name and phone number and asked them to pass the information on to the farmer. We had to leave the plane overnight, and they assured me it would be OK.

The next morning, I had lined up a crew of three who helped hook up my 35-foot glider trailer and came with me to the airport. There, we picked up some more help and headed out to the landing site. In an hour and a half, we took the plane apart, got it carefully loaded into the trailer, and drove back to the field. After a thorough inspection and cleaning-off of corn stain and dust, we reassembled the glider and tied it down. The only damage was a two-inch tear in the molded fiberglass streamlining around the nose wheel.

One of the helpers was a friend who was an insurance claim investigator. I had him get close-up photos of a broken spring—the culprit in the forced landing—a stress-fractured tensioner that had prevented me from getting the engine put away, which in turn led to its malfunction. I later sent the pictures along with a detailed engineering analysis to the manufacturer, who later claimed to have already redesigned the entire prop-stop tensioning function with different parts. Retro kits were eventually made available worldwide to all other owners of this type of plane.

All in all, this episode turned out amazingly well—no one injured, no apparent ill effects for poor Burt, to my great relief. There was only very minor damage to the glider and no publicity. There were so many things that could have happened to make this a disaster. As we were leaving the cornfield, Burt and I had a chilling moment. About 35 yards directly in front of where the plane stopped, we discovered hidden in the corn a large rectangular boulder, about the size of a pool table and too low to be visible unless seen from directly above. We looked at it silently and rolled our eyes. If we hadn't made that tight-in final approach and had floated further down the field, we would have smashed into that boulder square on.

By far the most challenging flying I ever did was over the mountainous terrain near Jackson Hole, Wyoming. There, the Teton Mountains are one of the nation's most spectacular ranges, equaling the grandeur of the Alps. The snowy peaks rise sharply from the lush grassy plain and riverine landscape to the east. The Grand Teton itself, at 13,770 feet, is among the taller summits in the Rocky Mountains. On the other side, to the west, the mountains slope more gently some twelve miles down through dramatic canyons and foothills to the Idaho border and a broad fertile valley dotted with large ranches and a few small towns.

One of these towns is Driggs, Idaho, where my son John spent a college summer in the early 1980s on a working ranch. When he got back, he said, "Dad, you've got to soar the Tetons! There's a small glider operation in Driggs, and I'll be your ground crew." That never worked out because of his Navy fighter pilot career (F/A-18 Hornets from 1987 to 1996). However, I hadn't forgotten his challenge, and in early 1991 at age 59, I decided that if I was going to try to do some serious mountain flying, I'd better get at it. That spring, I had trailered my glider out to Phoenix, where I had flown with great enjoyment for five weeks in the desert hills and low mountains to the south of the city—the second year in what turned out to be a nine-year annual event. As part of my plan that year, I left the plane, trailer, and Jeep at the soaring site there and flew back east commercially with the idea of returning in the early summer to give the Tetons a try.

After some research, I chose early June as a good time, as the snow would be gone in the valleys. I was able to recruit my nephew, Mark McGhie, as my crew. A college student, he was just home for summer break and not having good luck so far at finding a summer job. I called him up and said, "Mark, I'm going to make you an offer you can't refuse. How about an all-expenses paid round trip to Jackson Hole, Wyoming, for a week, where you can crew for my experiment in real mountain flying?" Being an outdoor buff and an adventurous young man, he signed on immediately—great news for me because he was strong and quick, as well being very good company.

It was about a one thousand mile drive from Phoenix to Jackson Hole. The plan was for me to drive most of the way and for him to fly out to Salt Lake City, where we'd join forces. I took two days to get there, figuring that this would be the only time I would ever have an opportunity to visit the very special Bryce and Zion Canyon National Parks in southern Utah.

We met at Salt Lake City just as planned and that night were ensconced simply but comfortably in Driggs, Idaho. Looking at the mountain peaks 15 miles away in the warm light of the setting sun as we drove to dinner, I thought, "Beautiful, impressive, but intimidating nonetheless." Over dinner, we agreed on our approach: we were going to try to go for the peaks only if I am convinced that I can fly those mountains safely. So we'll get the plane rigged in the morning, set up the oxygen system, and hang out at the airport. We'll talk to instructors, pilots, whoever can give us good local knowledge. Then, I'll fly up into the range with the instructor and get his take. Then, I'll start exploring them on my own. If we ever get to the Grand—and we may well not—it will be as safe as we can make it. Obviously, the main goal was to "summit" the Grand Teton and to get above the mountains—but following our safety game plan to the letter.

At that time, I was flying my Grob 103A Acro glider, and my accumulated total time was about 600 hours, all in hand-controlled sailplanes. It was by no means a sure thing that I would want to attempt the highest peaks. I had never flown in mountains higher than 4,500 feet. At higher elevations, the flight dynamics are radically different—high winds, severe turbulence, bitter cold, much thinner, less buoyant air—and you need supplemental oxygen. The next day, by noon, we were rigged and ready and seriously pursuing the local knowledge in the airport office and hangar.

On my first flight, I took the local instructor in the rear cockpit, who briefed me on the proper altitudes that should be achieved at various waypoints for a safe ascent of some 8,000 feet from field elevation, which was at 6,000 feet above sea level, to reach the peaks 15 miles away. After two more days of exploration with Mark as passenger, I had learned the anatomy of the strong thermal lift rising from the sunny sides of the canyons, as well as how the prevailing wind carries these updrafts higher up the mountains over the ridges and glaciers—much like rivers running in reverse. Often, the peaks would be shrouded in clouds—definitely not accessible. But, gradually, I was getting us higher and higher and closer to the Grand Teton summit.

On the fourth day, I worked my way up and past every waypoint at target altitude, and the base of the clouds was 1,000 feet or so above the Grand. The lift was very strong, but it was challenging flying because the winds were violent and gusty, tossing us around in severe turbulence—sometimes knocking us into a 70-80 degree bank. Finally, after two hours with my arms beginning to ache from fighting the rough air, we topped 14,700 feet at the Grand Teton, safely more than 900 feet above it. The air smoothed out somewhat and victory was ours above the summit. The 360-degree view was breathtaking: Yellowstone National Park to the north, the Continental Divide, Jackson Hole and Teton National Park below us, the Wind River Range to the southeast, and the expansive valleys and ridges of Idaho to the west. Mark's classic comment: "This doesn't suck, Uncle Bruce."

The peaks were in clouds the next day. But the following day, I flew back up to the Grand Teton, this time alone because Mark wanted to explore the park in my Jeep. The winds were even stronger, and I had a tricky time around the high peak. One downdraft on the lee side dropped me about 1,000 feet in seemingly less than 30 seconds. However, I had allowed extra altitude above and good distance away from the pinnacle so that I wasn't in danger. It was a tense moment though. A few years later, a glider pilot who was flying too close was killed when a similar downdraft sucked his plane into the backside of the peak—like an eddy behind a boulder in a stream where the current in close actually flows upstream.

After circling the pinnacle, I flew as much as I could of the whole range—about 40 miles of some of the world's most beautiful scenery. There I was a lone figure in a silent craft—an almost invisible speck in the sky at 14,000 feet, as solitary as an eagle. My eyes were active with the view, the conditions, the instruments. My hands were constantly moving the controls in the rough air. But my breathing was easy. My ears heard only the soft hiss of the air that I was passing through. My mind was full of the peace and grandeur of the vista and the bizarre incongruity of my being there as a quadriplegic— here, now, today—impossible. Yet it was true! Very few people are fortunate enough to experience the beauty and power of nature as I was doing that afternoon. It was an unimagined triumph.

When I landed, Mark was there to greet me with a high five. We had a great time that evening at a favorite pub relishing our adventures of the week. The next day, we packed up the sailplane and headed for Salt Lake City where I flew to New York while Mark set off to trailer my glider back East. It was a week of the most challenging and exciting flying I ever experienced.

I couldn't help remembering the poem that virtually every pilot knows called *High Flight* by John Magee, a Spitfire pilot who died in WWII:

> *Up, up, the long delirious, burning blue*
> *I've topped the wind-swept heights with easy grace,*
> *where never lark or even eagle flew*
> *and, with silent lifting mind I've trod*
> *the high untrespassed sanctity of space...*

Final Approach

In the early and mid-1990s, I experienced increasing pain in my shoulders, a problem that had a serious impact on my flying. I shouldn't have been surprised, given the tremendous stress I had put on my upper body for more than 30 years—pushing a wheelchair, often aggressively, and making 10 to 20 transfers in and out of the chair every day (a 155-pound lift each time). The shoulders are not designed for this kind of hard use, and mine had gradually deteriorated. But I just kept going "through the pain," believing that it was just another problematic side effect of my disability that I had to face down and overcome.

This was unwise. The pain accelerated, and matters came to a head in April 1998. One day, I was making a high-lift transfer into my Jeep Cherokee, and an almost unbearably sharp pain shot down my right arm, taking my breath away. I barely made it home and back into the wheelchair without help. The pain persisted, although slightly diminished, and I had to cut back sharply on all activities, trying to find new ways to transfer and move around (and even eat) with less use of the right arm, hand, and shoulder. Flying was out of the question at this point, and with great reluctance, I had to ground myself right at the beginning of the season.

I sought help from rehab specialists without much success, and they advised me to get a diagnosis from an orthopedic surgeon. I went to a highly regarded shoulder specialist at Yale-New Haven Hospital, who gave me an MRI and full examination. His unwelcome conclusion was that I had, over time, irreparably torn my right shoulder rotator cuff—through long-term repetitive stress. Not mincing words, he said that surgery would be unwise and very likely unsuccessful—"heroic, bordering on stupidity."

He recommended moderating the stress by using a power wheelchair for some of the time, eliminating hard transfers, and following an exercise regime. He indicated that the flying activity, as I had been practicing it, was no doubt adding to the damage, and that I ought to start thinking about giving it up permanently. His message, tactfully put, was that the realities of aging have got to be faced sooner or later, particularly by someone like me.

After some months of cutting back on all activities, my shoulder pain settled down somewhat. But with my kind of tear, the shoulder is limited in range of motion and a lot weaker. I simply couldn't lift myself around with the same confidence, pushing the wheelchair was much more difficult, and I had constant discomfort. A wrong move and the pain was severe and lasting, further limiting my mobility. I made the decision to phase into using a power wheelchair and took delivery on one in mid-winter. Meanwhile, I passed up my usual winter-flying visits to Phoenix in October and February-March.

By the spring of 1999, it was clear that the new regime was making a significant difference. I began to think that I had a chance at least to get back to flying, perhaps at a reduced level. I wasn't going to give up flying without a fight. My aircraft had been kept in service, and I made tentative plans to recommission my powered glider in Connecticut in May so that I could give it a try. First, I consulted my orthopedist, who thought that my shoulder's response to the new regime was encouraging. While he thought the rotator cuff would never be fully functional, at least the deterioration had been slowed or stopped. I might very well be able to fly provided that I did not lift myself in and out of the aircraft and did not push around the airport in my manual chair.

In early May, I had an unofficial check ride with a flight examiner to determine whether my shoulders could safely handle the cockpit stresses. I flew the entire time, going through all the complex engine management procedures and emergencies, plus Dutch rolls, stall recovery, and other maneuvers calling for forceful use of the controls. To my surprise and relief, there was no pain. We debriefed at length on the ground, and he gave me his judgment that I was safe to go but needed serious practice to regain my normal technique. I also had to see whether I had any residual pain from the experience. But the shoulder was fine the rest of the day and OK the following morning. I was good to go!

Shortly thereafter, I began a series of practice flights to sharpen up, keeping them brief to favor the shoulder. In addition, I changed my ground activities to rely on others (friends and volunteers) to prepare the plane for flight and to clean it up after, as well as to lift me bodily into the cockpit per the doctor's admonition. After so many years of fighting to be physically independent, it bothered me to have to back off and accept this kind of help—particularly the lifting in and out. But being able to fly again solo was a powerful motivator for the new approach. Furthermore, I concluded that others didn't see it as a retreat. In fact, probably the opposite was true. My pilot friends and helpers at the field seemed very pleased that I was back on flight status, albeit with different ground rules. In my new approach, I became more conservative so as not to overdo it. I flew on the calmer days and would land after only an hour or an hour and a half. It paid off. There was no sign of shoulder pain from flying. I flew the rest of the summer.

As the soaring season began in 2000—two years after my serious shoulder episode—I was optimistic. However, I had had health problems over the winter, and I found that the process of getting things operational for the summer was difficult and raised a new set of questions about the viability and wisdom of continuing to fly. I began to have doubts.

One day in June with good soaring conditions, I went out to the airport. It was midweek, though, and there were no other pilots around to help me. I waited around for a couple of hours with no luck. This had happened before and was extremely frustrating. Sitting there in the shade of my wing unable to get airborne on this great soaring day got me pondering yet again about the whole question of my flying, and it just came to me in a flash: "Bruce, it's time to quit." I secured the glider and drove home. Not wanting to make a snap decision I might regret, I took a couple of hours that afternoon to put the entire rationale for quitting on paper (writing something out forces me to think more analytically, more comprehensively, and I had often approached other tough choices in my life with paper in hand to help the thought process in this way). Here is what I wrote:

"My not flying in Phoenix in the winter due to my shoulder problems has cut way back on my flying time. I only flew a total of 17.5 hours in 1999, compared with the usual 80 to 100. This affects proficiency. The more you fly, the sharper you are. It's not a safety issue with me. I'm flying well. Furthermore, my license is 'current' with a fresh biennial flight review last September and a check-ride two weeks ago, both by a former FAA Examiner. But flying such few hours dulls the skills, and I'm not approaching flying with the same confidence and enthusiasm. I want always to be 'ahead of the airplane.' I'm a safe pilot, but I'm not as sharp as I was.

"I've also got physical issues that affect the whole activity. The torn rotator cuff and low-grade pains that are almost always there in my shoulders don't impact my basic flying ability, but do make the ground activity much more complicated. I now need two volunteers to lift me in and out of the cockpit. Then I need one of them during preparation, preflight, taxiing—and later during tying down and securing the plane. Such help is hard to come by. It has to be arranged on short notice, the night before or on the day itself. It's next to impossible to hire people for such random and infrequent work. So I mostly use other pilots or bystanders who happen to be on the field. However, on any given day, I'm never sure that help will be available. I've scrubbed a number of flights for lack of help—after an hour's drive to get there. It gets very frustrating.

"Shoulder problems also inhibit the type of flying I can do. It doesn't make sense to subject my shoulders to the stresses of thermaling when conditions are turbulent (steep banking turns), which are always present on the best soaring days. Also, I've given up aerobatics for the same reason. So this means my flying is milder, less interesting, and not as challenging. As a result, I don't have anywhere near the same motivation to go through the hassle that goes with being a disabled pilot. And the flying I do now is simply not as much fun as before.

"I also miss the excitement of the mountain and desert flying I was doing in the West, where conditions are a lot stronger and the topography more rugged and interesting—as well as being part of a gliding operation with its camaraderie and shared experiences (plus willing and eager help). Being at a power-plane airport is OK, and the other pilots are very friendly and helpful, but we're definitely not doing the same kind of flying. There is a different ethos.

"Finally, there's the get up and go it takes to get flying on a given day what with the disability. It was never easy. Now, with the added obstacles, there is a lot more to overcome to accomplish a flight. At present, I don't bring the same extra drive that it takes to make it all happen smoothly.

"So I've decided to give up flying while I'm still 'playing within my game.' I've been able to do many things I was proud of like mountain flying, aerobatics, and staying aloft for over five hours. I was the first spinal cord-injured person in the world to solo a glider and get a license. That was in 1980. And also the first to get a power-glider rating. I've trailered my glider four times across the country alone, round-trip. While doing all this, I've made some very good friends—fine relationships that transcend the soaring experience. There's a lot I feel good about. I've flown for 20 years, and it's been an amazing and fulfilling experience. It's time to hang up the white silk scarf and goggles."

That's how I summed it up.

Within a year, I had sold my two gliders, trailers, and other gear. Looking back, I have no regrets about giving it up. Sure I think about it when I see a circling hawk or eagle gracefully working the lift in a thermal updraft. But I can say to myself, "I did that. I know what it's like. I felt that freedom."

Epilogue

Sides of the Coin

"Tails, you lose." It's a bad feeling when you lose. Face it, my injury in 1955 set me apart as one who "lost." It turns out, though, that as I have lived the reality of the loss, I have discovered that a coin has more than two sides.

There is no doubt that this kind of setback raises obstacles that are staggering. The question is: how does one react? My answer wasn't neat and tidy. After the initial despair, I settled into a mode that could best be described as licking my wounds and making the best of it day-by-day. I saw no alternative.

Yet a strange thing happened along the way. And it came as a surprise. As I began haltingly to work my way back into the normal world, things were different—but not as you might think.

Somehow, the sun seemed brighter, the sky bluer, and the ordinary rituals and experiences of life had new meaning, new purpose. People were the same, but they seemed a little different because I saw new things in them. I'm not saying life was better. Not at all. It certainly was a lot harder and still is. I just saw it differently.

The tougher the challenges, it seemed, the sweeter the victories.

Could it be that, having lost almost everything I always took for granted and then fighting to get back the elements of a decent, fulfilling life, I've gotten more out of living than the average person does?

It's a radical idea.

Getting from There to Here

So what is my life as a quadriplegic really all about? Does it have any significance, any relevance—other than being a unique story? Should anyone care? I've thought a lot about these questions as I have been writing about my adventures and misadventures. I don't have any clear-cut answers, just some observations.

When you are in a wheelchair with a permanent spinal cord injury, your ongoing life is a lot more complicated—physically, emotionally, and mentally. Consider the physical side first. As is probably clear from the experiences I have described so far, there are a lot of big challenges with which to deal, but how about the small things—the nitty-gritty of everyday life? What did I need to do differently from what the average man would have done as the day unfolded? A lot—and the devil is in the details, some not very pleasant.

Here is what a typical work day in New York was like for me in mid-winter when I was in my late forties. The alarm goes off at 6:30 and I pull myself up into a sitting position with my arms and get balanced (having no thoracic musculature). Grab shoes and socks from the seat of my chair, which is facing the head of the bed, and put them on by pulling up my feet each in turn to rest across the opposite knee where I can reach them. Socks are a problem because of weakness in my fingers, but I work them up slowly over the calf eventually followed by loafers, which are easy. Next, getting out of bed: I put one arm under my knees and, in one movement, swing my feet over the side of the bed onto the pedals, maintaining a balanced sit-up position on the edge of the bed—a 90 degree turn. Now, I lift my body up in another same-direction turning movement and drop myself onto the wheelchair seat cushion—another 90 degrees. This seat is, in fact, a complex item—a self-designed and homemade cushion about five inches deep, which is made up of five layers of glued-together pieces of temperature-sensitive foam of three different densities. I have cut and shaped it to fit the non-symmetrical hard contours of my backside—all this because I'm going to be sitting now for about 18 hours straight and must avoid undue pressure on all points due to skin vulnerability—a big concern.

I head into the bathroom, clean the bedside jug I used overnight, and rig up the daytime fluid-collection system. This is a very deliberate and careful process because failure during the day can make for an embarrassing and uncomfortable incident, followed by having to come home to do a difficult cleanup, all of which shoots a three-hour hole in the working day. It has happened maybe 30 times total over the years. I estimate that I have rigged this system some 24,000 times since 1955, so my batting average is pretty good. But let's face it, incontinency is no picnic.

After the normal routine of shaving, etc., I get dressed. I am proud of my fast and unique (as far as I know) method for getting on my slacks solo. Work the pants legs over the shoes up over the knees and under the thighs, put my heels up on a strap above the pedals to raise the thighs off the cushion, grab the back top seam of the pants, lift my body with my other arm, leaning over the armrest for stability, to get clearance under the butt, and shove the back of the pants all the way under to the rear of the cushion. Sitting down, I would then straighten everything out, getting the cuffs even and so forth. The shirt is no problem (although back in the late 1950s, when I started wearing dress shirts again, it took me a year-and-a-half to find a way to get the top button done without help). Now a tie and suit jacket and I'm ready for a quick breakfast, including a glance at the newspaper and whatever comes up with Barbara and the kids regarding school, family issues, or plans—or just plain conversation —and then off to work at 7:30. My outer garments were easy. All I ever wore were a scarf and an unlined parka.

Going for the car, I push my chair about two blocks uphill to my garage, where the attendants will have brought the vehicle down for me. The process of getting in and then loading in my chair behind the seat is laborious. It involves a number of separate moves, 20 in all, before I am ready to start the engine. One, open the door; two, toss my brief-case across the seat; three, put the right foot in; four, put the left foot in; five, lift the body up and into the seat—and on and on. It takes three or four minutes. I had long since gotten used to this routine, but I can't help remembering, now and again, how mindlessly simple it was to get in and out of a car before my injury. Then, I navigate the busy New York traffic driving with my hand controls to my office, which is in the hub of midtown. I park using a Special Permit, which is issued by the NYPD only to the seriously disabled (full-time workers or students). I try to end up very close to the curb, if such a space is available. The 20-step process with the wheelchair is then reversed. Sometimes I have to get out of the car on the street, which is more hazardous and requires finding a volunteer eventually to help me up onto the sidewalk (still no curb cuts in those days).

After opening a heavy door with some difficulty, I head into the building. Such strongly sprung doors are not designed for people in wheelchairs. You have to approach them from the side (if there is space, doors in corners are really tough), grab the handle, and pull it open to one side—enough to poke the chair pedals in. Then, you push it open wider with one arm to fit the chair's full width in and then propel yourself with the other arm through the open space into the lobby—sometimes in a strong gust of wind. Many times, with all these gymnastics and twisting, my briefcase has fallen off my lap to the floor.

Often, I will need to drive to client meetings in the city—sometimes two or three times in a day—each time following the same routine with the chair, including parking, doors, etc. Finally, there is the drive home at 6:30 or 7:00. By the time I reach home at the end of the day, I may have made as many as ten transfers in and out of the car, depending on the number of my appointments. Needless to say, when the weather is bad, it all gets a lot more difficult.

At bedtime, I have two more chores related to my disability aside from getting undressed (much easier in the evening), brushing my teeth, etc. I have to remove and thoroughly clean the fluid collection system to be ready for the next day, paying particular attention to personal hygiene. Finally, before bed, there is my daily adventure with the elimination department, which I can only describe as time-consuming, distasteful, often difficult, but effective.

As I have said before, I was not a typical quadriplegic because my spinal cord injury level was lower than most. This gave me partial, though functional, use of my hands—a decent grip—and, very critically, the upper arm strength to lift my body for transfers. In this I was a very lucky man.

This daily physical routine was one I followed with some variations for the 25 years we lived in New York (and still do, but I use a van with a lift, which is much easier, and am not as physically independent due to my shoulder injuries). Although it is obviously impossible to forget that I am in a wheelchair, I have become mostly inured to going the "extra mile," and the dogged plodding it takes to get there. It's just been built into my routine, I allow the extra time, and I focus instead on the central life elements of family, career, and avocations. I have adjusted to the fact that everything requires more ingenuity, patience, and just plain grit. It doesn't make it any easier, but I take satisfaction in knowing that I have gotten through another day.

Since the disability is so obvious, you have to assume that you are viewed by others as "different"—handicapped, disabled, challenged, a hero, a cripple, a survivor, a saint—whatever may be in their minds. Also, of course, you simply have limited physical options for dealing with any difficulty that might arise. Put these factors all together and there is a lot of potential for the unusual. This makes for a life that is full of uncharted twists and turns and many surprises, problems, and solutions.

One thing that intrigues me is how extraordinary the human body is to adjust to the catastrophic changes forced upon it by quadriplegia. Take my hands: the level of my spinal cord injury was C-7/8, which severely impaired the two branch nerves that serve the hands. This deadened about 80 percent of the muscles that work the fingers, but it's spotty. The thumbs, forefingers, and middle fingers are very weak while the last two fingers are quite strong. When you think of how many things you do with the thumb and forefinger, as well as the other finger interactions—picking up a plate, holding a pencil, turning the volume knob on the radio, opening the ketchup bottle, etc., etc.—you can see that every single thing you did before has to be rethought and retried and the weak remaining muscles have to be trained and strengthened to get the task done in a totally new way. Yet, with a lot of work, my hands ultimately became functional enough for me to be fully independent. Beyond that, most of the body, being paralyzed, has suddenly become sedentary— a reluctant couch potato. This affects everything: metabolism, circulation, organ viability, and so on. Amazingly, the systems of most spinal cord-injured people adapt very well to most of these changes provided the individual recognizes that his or her body is much more vulnerable to problems. Any abuse, such as overeating, drinking too much alcohol, not protecting the skin, is much more likely to cause problems. There are a lot of pitfalls to avoid. Early on, the VA gave me a life expectancy of 25 years. It seems I shouldn't have made it past 1980! Yet here I am 52 years after my injury, still alive.

What about the mind? I am equally interested in what causes the psyche to strive against such serious losses for some level of mental balance, physical independence, and a decent life. Obviously, I can only speak from my own experience.

Pride has been a big factor for me. Before I was injured, I had had some real academic difficulties at school and college due to an undiagnosed learning problem (a frustrating inability to absorb and retain detailed information from the printed word—ideas yes, facts no). But I pulled it out in the end to my great relief through dogged effort. After graduation, I completed my obligations for a commission in the Air Force, and, while waiting for my orders, I spent a successful several months interning at a large company that wanted me to join them after my military service. I was engaged to be married. I was out in the real world at last, and things were really shaping up. Then, to meet my Korean War obligation, I had gone off to Air Force pilot training full of high hopes and bravado.

Within weeks, however, I was reduced to a quadriplegic for life by a preventable training accident—my dreams shattered at age 22. Survival was the first priority. Then I had to get through the bitter grief. But as soon as I got far enough along to see that there were ways to regain at least some small part of what I had lost, I got dead serious about rehabilitation.

I was extremely angry—not at God or the world but at my own situation. I felt that I had lost my manhood just as I had gained it. I wanted redemption. I wanted respect. I wanted to be proud. And it didn't stop with rehabilitation. I was determined to squeeze every ounce of possibility out of my diminished body, to make something worthwhile out of the terrible mess that I had found myself in. I was highly motivated.

That determination was my biggest weapon. It was private and unyielding. A lot of the experiences I have talked about involved getting past obstacles and unfavorable odds by simply plowing ahead, regardless of whether it had been done before or whether anyone else thought it was a good idea. I kept thinking, "There must be a way; there will be a way; I'll find a way." I don't know where the hard-nosed idea of "overcoming no matter what" came from. I had not been a particularly assertive child, teenager, or student. My best guess is that my dire situation forced me to tap into pre-existing character traits that I did not know I had. Franz Kafka may have been right when he wrote, "Man cannot live without a permanent trust in something indestructible in himself." Curiously, several months after my injury, I had this vague, almost eerie feeling that somehow I had "done all this before."

I recently talked with a professor at Yale Divinity School whose specialty is the pastoral-care side of religious ministries and who has authored several books. He believes that the key attribute in transcending catastrophic disabilities can be summed up with one word: *resiliency*—"the ability of matter to spring back quickly into shape after being bent, stretched, or deformed," a definition I found in the dictionary. This has been central to my winning back a sense of self-respect and to my being accepted in the world at large.

First it had to come from within, but Barbara was by far the most important close-in source of motivation and support. We have had an extremely tight and affirmative relationship, and the journey has been a joint effort all the way. I have to grope for the proper words to do justice to her role. She stuck with me from day one. My accident was a devastating blow to her, but she was determined to at least give the relationship a chance. Here was an attractive, young Wellesley graduate in economics, a successful businesswoman in the making, and one of the top women golfers in the country—still on the rise in tournament competition with more potential to be realized. Yet, she walked away from all this, defied her adamantly objecting parents, and left home and their financial support behind to join me in the tenuous early weeks of my injury in Texas. Then, in time, when we concluded together that we might be able to rebuild some kind of a life, she made a commitment for the duration.

"Courageous" doesn't do justice to her attitude. It was hard for her then; it has never been easy and it still isn't. No matter how independent I became physically—probably close to as much as any quadriplegic ever has and more so than most paraplegics have—she has had to do more for her husband than the average wife. And then there are the inconveniences: places and events to which we can't go, things we can't do together, embarrassments when I get into awkward situations, and just being more conspicuous when we are in public. Yet, she has never once complained or made me feel guilty for causing us to have what is a far more challenging lifestyle than the average couple. I think that after my injury, she concluded that given my attitude, I was still essentially the same person she wanted to marry, but in a different body; then made her own peace with that. She has always treated me exactly as if I was a normal man. Above all, she, more than anyone, knew how tough it was for me to live life every day and to meet the ordinary obligations of family and livelihood. To give me this unspoken, unsentimental empathy, is a priceless gift. Her support has empowered me in the most basic way. It still does.

I don't want to idealize things though. Like most marriages that work, there are rough spots and uneasy periods. Always there has been my hard edge, the inner toughness that I needed to survive and to overcome the disability. It worked for that purpose, but as others have told me, "You come on a lot stronger than you realize, sometimes too strong." What they mean, I believe, is that the assertiveness necessary to deal with the disability spills over into my relationships with others, and I tend to be too "controlling" in a lot of situations. That tendency of mine has been hard for Barbara (and others) all along and has taken its toll over the years. But she is also strong-minded, and we have always managed to return to equilibrium after problems have surfaced. Overriding factors are our deeply felt mutual affection and respect, the enjoyment of each other's company, a shared sense of humor, and a willingness to move on.

Early on, a college classmate of Barbara's had gushed (as I was being carried in my chair to a party backwards up a circular stair-case), "Oh, your lives must be such an adventure!" There certainly has been much of that, but more important is that we have done something meaningful together in building lives under adversity—kind of one plus one equals three.

The story on these pages has centered on my own adventures. But individually, it isn't only I who has done interesting and demanding things beyond our marriage. I've mentioned Barbara's accomplishments in the early years—championship golf and important hospital work. But, in just the last ten years, she has visited Italy eight times on art and architectural tours and taken up the study of Italian, now both speaking and reading it. She has also become a serious music student, practicing demanding compositions on her own 780-pipe organ in the living room.

In addition, my parents were a major source of strength. My mother had always been a strong and wise person. Growing up, I had seen her go through some extended hard times, when she displayed courage and perseverance. After my accident, she was a very sustaining presence in the early weeks and supportive for the rest of her life in innumerable ways, which would surprise no one who knew her. My father was also strong in adversity. They were good role models. I respected them. And physically, my family on both sides has a long history of good health and longevity—so my genes were good.

My father's particular support came a year or so after my accident when he brought me into his fledgling business. What my father did was ease me very gently back into the mainstream without ever making any big thing out of it—no pep talk, no exhortation, just a thoughtful, quiet pursuit that unfolded over time. There was never any sense that he thought he was doing me a big favor. I think he realized that if I was going to be successful, it had to be my victory to win. Result: by doing so, I pulled myself out of the nether world of disability and into the vital, everyday work of life. It was a breakthrough.

Now where, it might be asked, does God fit into the picture? Certainly not, in my opinion, as having had anything to do with my accident, as in: "There is a reason for everything. God must have had a purpose." I never have believed that God sets out to hurt people, to test people, to tempt people. I believe that my injury was an accident, pure and simple. It happened as a result of several specific factors, none individually damaging, that came together disastrously at a single moment in time.

As for my religious beliefs, I've always had an interest in the spiritual side of life. I have been a practicing Christian since college years. My faith has deepened as I have learned more about it and as I have participated actively in church worship and lay activities for decades. It's an ongoing and growing spiritual dynamic that I draw much from—both in the "normal" side of my life and in facing the adversities of quadriplegia.

I found that the Christian message has particular relevance for someone like me. My disability causes me to suffer. I don't want to overdo this, but I obviously can't go down the road I'm on without a good measure of physical and mental pain of one sort or another.

But because I believe that the Lord knew human suffering himself and that his spirit dwells within me, I have comfort in the assurance that I am never alone with my trials, no matter how difficult they may be.

I believe in a merciful and loving God, and the Gospels are full of stories of people who were healed. But I never expected that I would be healed miraculously in body like the paralytic that Luke tells about whom Christ healed, saying, "Stand up and take your bed and go to your home." I've never prayed for that kind of healing. What I have prayed for is the strength to deal with whatever befalls me. In answering that prayer, I believe that God has provided me with a kind of inner healing and spiritual support that helps me to be a "whole" person despite what I am missing.

Although good, bad, and sometimes crazy experiences have punctuated my life, putting them all together end-to-end may well be misleading. I have not been on a wild gorilla ride swinging from vine to vine through the jungle of life. In fact, most of the time, I have been quietly doing normal things: working full-time at a desk in an office, dealing with clients, spending time with the kids, doing things with Barbara, enjoying friends, reading, flying gliders for recreation, and volunteering my time in not-for-profit activities.

For me, one of the more satisfying accomplishments is the sense that I have been able to overcome a "personal deficit," something that bothered me a lot when I was first injured. What do I mean? Well, as a severely disabled person, I was unhappy to be a "cost" to society. Simply put, I was taking out more than I was putting in. Before I was injured, I had thought, perhaps idealistically like many young people, that I had something important to contribute. I was intelligent, I could communicate, and I had leadership ability. Then, with my accident, all that seemed lost. Yet, somewhere along the line, I went from "liability" to "asset" as I got out of the hospital into the world, became a husband and parent, did work that was constructive, paid taxes, and gave my time in lay ministries, becoming

the senior lay leader of our church. I also was president of our coop-
erative apartment building corporation in New York and had a leadership role in an acclaimed therapeutic riding nonprofit in Connecticut,
as well as a being a counselor to other spinal cord-injured people.
Finally, I achieved some modest firsts in the sport of soaring.

There is another thing that bothered me early on: my veteran
status. Recently at a car wash, the young man who was toweling
down my van saw my disabled veteran plate and, refusing a tip, said,
"Thanks for serving your country." This has happened often over the
years, and I used to wince because my injury was only because of a
training accident. As a result, I could never serve as a pilot in the defense
of my country. But over time, I have come to feel no embarrassment
about it. I signed up in the depths of the Cold War during the Korean
War because I felt it was my duty, while many of my contemporaries
joined the Reserves or National Guard to avoid being drafted. Some
got exemptions for post-graduate work or scholarships and never
served. I trained in the ROTC preflight program for four years and
went through tough officer-candidate training. I made a serious
commitment, which was just getting under way when I had the
obstacle-course accident. I was injured in the line of duty and have
paid an extremely high price for my commitment to serve my
country. It's history now and I can live with it.

I'm not angry anymore. I've got respect. I've got a full life.

However, I don't sit around in a glow of self-congratulation. Far
from it. I feel that I have had many things working in my favor
beyond what I have already mentioned—compared with many
other spinal-cord injured people who have struggled with the same
challenges and pitfalls. For one, I come from a very healthy family
and my body adapted remarkably well to the radical changes of
quadriplegia (my primary care doctor told me after an annual physical
when I was about 50, "Bruce, despite your disability, you are the
healthiest middle-aged man of all my patients"). Also, as a veteran

injured in the line of duty, I received enough financial support from the government to help Barbara and me in the early years of our marriage and to help ever since with the substantial added costs of being in a wheelchair. And finally, I was blessed to have a good education and always expected to make my living with my head, not my hands. A lot of the veterans who were with me during rehab were not so fortunate and felt that they were starting out with two strikes against them—which they were indeed. A majority of these men overcame the odds with true grit, but sadly there were also many who fell by the wayside.

Although this has been an account of my experiences that gives weight to the positive side, I do not want to obscure the negative. This is no Pollyanna story out of Hollywood. The full downside of quadriplegia is never overcome. The stark reality of my paralysis and all its ramifications are with me day-in-day-out for life and can't be put aside. I am also more vulnerable now to illness in general and face an aging process that is daunting because all the usual problems are magnified by my disability. I am finding ways to deal with these inevitable new challenges, such as reduced independence and other issues, as they develop, unfortunately, with increasing frequency.

The problem of my torn rotator cuffs, for example, deprived me of my primary source of recreation, which was flying. But it did give me much more time to pursue seriously other life-long interests that had long been pushed aside. Most important was that I could get back into my creative work—photography, drawing, painting, and of course, writing. So over the last four years, I have made them central and found great pleasure in reevaluating and archiving my earlier work and stepping out in entirely new creative directions with pencil, paper, and camera.

Do I have regrets? Yes, of course I do. You cannot be deprived of so many physical abilities as well as the fundamental experiences and pleasures of a normal life without wishing it hadn't been so. I am particularly sorry that my difficulties affected the things that Barbara might have been able to do and have always made life more difficult for her. And I know that my accident caused great pain to my parents. Very occasionally, my mind wanders to what I might have accomplished in life without quadriplegia. But these thoughts fade quickly away as as I always think of the good things that have dominated my life, eclipsing, but never totally obscuring, the regrets.

Until I got into counseling the newly spinal cord-injured on how to cope with their shattered lives, I had never analyzed how I had dealt with mine. But I thought it would help them to have a check list—a sort of "Ten Commandments" to refer to—something to put up on the mirror or refrigerator. So, I tried to identify the attitudes and actions that have been behind my life and helped me through half a century of disability.

Here is the list I gave to the patients, which I called *Ten Guidelines for Survival and "Getting a Life" in a Wheelchair:*

- Never forget that you are the same person as before. It's your body that's different. Most people will accept you for the person you always were and adjust to your physical limits— so long as you do so yourself.

- Strive to be as physically independent as you can, recognizing your limits. But accept help graciously when you need it; remember that you are in charge of your body. A good balance between going it alone and accepting help maximizes your quality of life.

- It's OK to be discouraged and down at times. But never, never give up.

- *Perseverance* and *patience* are the best weapons in the fight to rebuild your life. But it won't be easy and it won't happen overnight.

- Every new thing you can learn to do for yourself, no matter how small, is a personal victory.

- Some people get recovery of motion and sensation—some more, some less. Others get none. Almost everyone ends up with some pain and/or discomfort for the rest of their lives.

- Remember, there are always others less fortunate than you.

- Each spinal cord injury is different. Everyone deals with it in his or her own way, but you learn a lot by watching others.

- Take care of your skin. Manage your fluids. Keep good personal hygiene. Watch your weight. Stay in shape. Avoid substance abuse. All of these things are much more important when you have a spinal cord injury.

- Keep your sense of humor. There are crazy, outrageous, funny things in this business just like in everything else.

I probably would have added an eleventh "commandment" if I had thought of it then. I don't know the source, but it says: "When the going gets tough, the tough get tougher."

I no longer volunteer at the hospital, but I have continued to counsel spinal cord injured people when asked. Recently, I was called by the therapeutic riding center in Connecticut about a young woman paraplegic from France, who was interning with them for the summer. She had broken her back in a fall as a steeplechase jockey and had told them that she wanted to learn to fly—clearly an adventurous sort. They suggested she talk with me, and I spent the afternoon with her, telling her about my flying experiences, giving her advice on how to go about it, and talking about dealing with the long-term challenges of a spinal cord injury in general. She was attractive, bright-eyed, and eager and seemed to be soaking it all up with keen attention, asking many questions. A few weeks later, I received an e-mail saying, "I keep a very good memory of my time I had with you. You gave me advices I will follow for my 'wheelchair life.' Different life, 'not comfortable life' (as you said); but it is a life, and the way I have seen you have 'taken' yours, I want to 'take' mine." We have kept in touch, and just recently (only 18 months later) she e-mailed me saying, " I am very happy to be able to tell you that I have flied by myself! It was really wonderful to be alone in the sky!!!!!" It was her first solo. This was accompanied by a picture of her alone in the cockpit after landing, her face radiant with a joyful smile. I remember that feeling after my own first solo as if it were yesterday. I was moved to have been able to make some difference for this exceptional girl in her late twenties, who has a severely testing life ahead of her. I know she will meet the challenge.

But what about the rest of the world? How does quadriplegia impact the other people you are dealing with every day? This, of course, is one of the most perplexing and difficult things about being severely and visibly disabled—how normal people are affected by your presence and how you deal with it. Of course, you never really know about their inner lives. Many of them can themselves have serious disabilities that are hidden—addictions such as alcoholism, diseases like diabetes or cancer, deep psychological problems, whatever. But somehow, a quadriplegic in a wheelchair is so obviously handicapped. It often makes people feel uncomfortable, perhaps guilty that they don't have to face these things. They think, "Why am I OK and he is suffering?" Or "How can this guy go through life like that?"

Or, "I couldn't cope with what he's dealing with, the poor bastard." It is very natural that they feel uncomfortable and think, "He must be wishing he was me." Sometimes an insecure person reacts almost with hostility and a sense of superiority, thinking, "What right does this cripple have to pretend he is as good as the next person?"

When I pick up any of these kinds of feelings, perhaps in a facial expression or something said, I ignore them. In the vast majority of cases, as soon as I can relate to that person or a group, they see that I'm not jealous of them, and that I'm not bitter about my situation or at the world. I'm simply going about my life in a different way because I have to. They see that they can relax around me, and they do. But if someone pushes me around in any way because of my situation (an extremely rare occurrence), I react with some back pressure, which establishes that I expect to be treated as an equal.

What I really hope will happen—and mostly does—is that people will accept me simply as I am—an individual with a disability who has it under control and seems to be at peace with it. Amazingly, many people have made statements like, "I completely forget that you are in a wheelchair." My hope is that they are left with the idea that it is possible to overcome great difficulties and come out as a full person—and that they will take it to heart in their own lives when they face the inevitable hard problems or suffering.

A few pages ago, I posed the questions: "So what is my life as a quadriplegic all about? Does it have any significance, any relevance? Should anyone care?" My response is this: yes, I think there is indeed something very important in my life, something significant—and not just in mine. There are thousands and thousands of unsung, seriously disabled people who over time have built meaningful, rewarding lives and done amazing things.

The real truth of a life is in the *doing* of it—hour-by-hour, day-by-day, year-by-year. No interpretation of theology, philosophy, or psychology can calculate the sum of a person's thoughts and acts. They make their own sum.

Here is the critical point: there is a wide gap between what life normally calls upon us to do and what we are truly capable of doing—"humanity's awe-inspiring ability, time and again, to surpass itself," according to one wise observer. We have deep, untapped reserves of tenacity, ingenuity, endurance, and courage. So, when the human body and spirit are put to severe, seemingly impossible tests, they often respond in ways that could never be predicted, but may be astounding, mysterious, even miraculous.

Acknowledgements

I am very grateful to my family for generously waiving their concerns about privacy so that I could tell a full and meaningful story, of which we all are part. Also, my wife, Barbara, and my children, Anne and John, made numerous insightful comments that added ideas and helped me sustain a balance between the raw realities and the near miracles of my life.

I am indebted as well to the many others who have played key roles in this book. To Nathan Garland, my long-time colleague and close friend, who nudged, badgered, and finally reasoned me into setting down my story and whose thoughts and advice have enriched its content and graphics. To Mark Singer, staff writer at *The New Yorker*, whose critique of an early draft was tellingly sharp and constructive. To my friend, Bill Phillips, who brought my story to the attention of David Finn, the publisher, who in turn, saw its potential and put words into action. And finally to Susan Slack, my perceptive editor, and to the many others in the Ruder Finn organization who have brought their talents and high standards to bear on the fine volume that you hold in your hands.

Bruce McGhie

A Selection of Remarkable Photographs, Drawings and Paintings

David Finn

My friend Bill Phillips, who has always been interested in the Ruder Finn publishing enterprise, called me one day to tell me about a friend of his who had written an amazing book about his unique life story. Bill subsequently introduced Bruce McGhie to us, and we were thrilled to learn about his accomplishments. When we read his amazing text, we felt it would be a privilege to publish this remarkable book.

What we didn't know at the time was that among Bruce's extraordinary achievements were his accomplishments as a photographer and an artist. Since I have been a passionate photographer and an artist most of my life and have published many books over the years, I was astonished to see the quality Bruce had achieved in his work.

His photographs deserve to be recognized as images of superb quality. We have separated selections of them into several categories, and in each we can see that he has produced remarkable prints. The selection of landscapes and street scenes are sensitive images of the forms he discovers and the people he sees through his viewfinder. His portraits somehow tell us more about his subjects than we might get from a lengthy description of their lives. His still life images show how much he cares about the delicacy of flower combinations. When we see the detail in his floral images, we can imagine him exploring different landscapes to discover extraordinary views of some of his favorite subjects. He looks at the sky the way Alfred Stieglitz used to, and he discovers forms that all of us have seen but rarely appreciated as much as he has. His photographs of animals in Africa—as well as birds on the trees—are as impressive as any I've seen taken by experts who have traveled in those remote areas. And when we realize that these are just selections from his collection of images, it's not hard to imagine how impressive it would be to have a book devoted just to the fine photographs he has taken over the years.

Bruce has created fewer drawings and paintings than photographs, but a selection of them shows that his sensitivity has enabled him to produce fine works in those media as well. We see remarkable compositions, fine details, always with evidence of a striking imagination.

Like so many gifted artists whose creative activity is different from their main occupation, Bruce is modest about his creative achievements. But we feel privileged to publish a few examples of his outstanding works to show how gifted he is in portraying the world he sees through his sensitive eyes, and how well he records his visions with his remarkable skills.

Black and White Photographs

TOP | *Laundry Day, New York City*
BOTTOM | *Chemical Plant, Florida*
RIGHT | *Old Barn, Campobello Island, Canada*

ABOVE | *Winter, Coney Island, New York*
RIGHT | *Ocean Squall, Maine*

ABOVE | *Hallway, Rio de Janeiro, Brazil*
RIGHT | *Copacabana Beach, Rio de Janeiro, Brazil*

Portraits

ABOVE | *My daughter, Anne, on Graduation Day*

TOP | *Allen Fitzhenry, Fisherman, Maine*
BOTTOM | *Douglas Maker, Lobsterman, Maine*
RIGHT | *Mary Farris, Tending the Wharf, Maine*

ABOVE | *Glenn Farris, Lobster Dealer, Maine*
RIGHT | *My Mother, Maine*

TOP | *Richard Ellery, Artist*
BOTTOM | *Maya Duesberg, Piano Teacher*

Still Lifes

ABOVE | *Old Silk Flowers*

RIGHT | *White Roses, Morning Sun*

ABOVE LEFT | *"Consider the Lillies…"*

ABOVE RIGHT | *Daffodils and Brass*

FAR RIGHT | *Lissome Iris*

Floral

ABOVE | *After a Thunderstorm*

ABOVE | *Bluets, Springtime*

ABOVE | *Siberian Iris*

Sky

ABOVE | *Sky XXIII*
RIGHT | *Sky XXXVI*

ABOVE | *Sky XXXVII*
RIGHT | *Sky I*

Africa

ABOVE | *Lion at Daybreak*

TOP | *Elephant*

BOTTOM | *Young Cheetah*

TOP | *Burchell's Zebra*
BOTTOM | *Greater Kudu*

ABOVE | *Maribou Storks at Sunset*

Drawings and Paintings

ABOVE | *Salt Marsh, Maine*
RIGHT | *My Granddaughter, Nile, in 2003*

ABOVE | *Tension*
RIGHT | *Taking Flight*

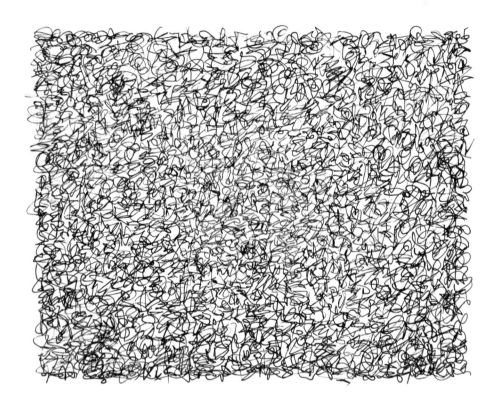

ABOVE | *Random, 2005*